Economic History and the Historian

Collected Essays

Economic History and the Historian

Collected Essays

Charles Wilson

Fellow of Jesus College, Cambridge, and Professor of Modern History in the University of Cambridge

Weidenfeld and Nicolson

5 Winsley Street London W1

Printed in Great Britain by
Cox and Wyman Ltd,
London, Fakenham and Reading

SBN 297 76498 5

Contents

Preface ix

1 Economics and Politics in the Seventeenth Century 1

2 The Decline of the Netherlands 22

3 Treasure and Trade Balances: the Mercantilist Problem 48

4 'Mercantilism': some Vicissitudes of an Idea 62

5 The Other Face of Mercantilism 73

6 Cloth Production and International Competition in the Seventeenth Century 94

7 Taxation and the Decline of Empires, an Unfashionable Theme 114

8 Canon Demant's Economic History 128

9 Government Policy and Private Interest in Modern English History 140

10 The Entrepreneur in the Industrial Revolution in Britain 156

11 Economy and Society in Late Victorian Britain 178

12 History in Special and in General 201

Index 217

Acknowledgements

The author gratefully acknowledges permission from the following to use his previously published material:

Chapter 1 is from *The Historical Journal*, V. I (1962).

Chapter 2 was adapted from 'The Economic Decline of the Netherlands', which appeared in the *Economic History Review*, first series, Vol. 9 (1939).

Chapter 3 is from the *Economic History Review*, second series, Vol. II, No. 2 (1949).

Chapter 4 is from the *Economic History Review*, second series, Vol. X, No. 2 (1957).

Chapter 5 is from the *Transactions of the Royal Historical Society*, 5th series, Vol. 9 (1959).

Chapter 6 is from the *Economic History Review*, second series, Vol. XII, No. 2 (1960).

Chapter 8 is from the *Cambridge Journal*, Vol. VI, No. 5 (1953).

Chapter 10 was adapted from a paper appearing in *History*, Vol. XLII (1957).

Chapter 11 is from the *Economic History Review*, second series, Vol. XVIII, No. 1 (1965).

Chapter 12 was published by Cambridge University Press as an Inaugural Lecture in 1964. (© 1964 Cambridge University Press.)

Author's Preface

Most of the essays included in this selection represent a kind of economic history. It is not necessarily the most important kind, but it is the kind that interests me most. It is concerned not so much with the fashionable problems of measurement (though these enter into several of the essays) as with the relationship between economic and other factors in history – political, governmental, fiscal, sociological.

The first essay, for example, deals with the relation of economics and politics during the upheavals of the seventeenth century. Was there a simple alignment of political phasing with the stages of economic change, as some eminent scholars have argued? Three essays examine the characteristics of those economic ideas and policies commonly called 'mercantilist'. It was John Maynard Keynes who first initiated a re-examination of orthodox attitudes here. Was the mercantilist concern with precious metals and the balance of payments merely 'a puerile obsession'? How far was Keynes's rationalisation of those ideas historically acceptable? Were mercantilists merely, as Tawney and others proclaimed, hardfaced advocates of low wages? Or have they some claim to have initiated important ideas of social reform?

Another essay explores the consequences of the idea, as old as the Tudors and as new as Harold Wilson, that it is the business of government to govern: to lead, not to be led. It questions the view that social and economic change results exclusively from the operation of 'lobbies' representing special private interests. Again, Keynes neatly summarized the argument: 'We have', he wrote, 'vastly exaggerated the role of vested interests' in history compared with the "gradual encroachment of ideas"' To which might be added, not only ideas but a persistent conviction that somewhere there exists a total social 'interest' that is not necessarily the same as the sum of the individual 'interests' in society. Change results from a continuing conflict between these three elements, not just from the force of one of them.

Other essays query some widely received concepts of the social, or anti-social, character of capitalism, of the dynamic factors in the Industrial Revolution, and the neglect by historians of the factor of commercial enterprise in favour of technological innovation. Was the late Victorian economy as inert, as stagnant and devoid of enterprise as we sometimes assume? Or is our assumption due to our habit of treating that economy as simply concerned with 'pig-iron and cotton stockings'? Have we neglected too long taxation as a factor in growth or retardation? This essay, on the Netherlands, should be read in conjunction with the very early one (it is nearly thirty years old) on Dutch decline, to which it is a recent appendix.

In brief, the function of most of these papers has been to question assumptions that seemed out of date or unsatisfactory in the age in which we live. You cannot go on referring students of mercantilism living in the century of Schacht, Keynes, the New Deal, the Russian or Indian plans etc., etc., to economic history written in the full faith of classical economics. The historic antecedents of economic nationalism, protection, tariffs, bounties, conscious import substitution, labour training, export drives and the like deserve to be examined seriously, if only because so many of them ended in disillusion with government intervention and the rise of the grand vision of universal harmony and progress that would be the reward for 'leaving things alone'.

I have included my Inaugural Lecture for two reasons. Several of the papers illustrate the argument I developed then on the relativism of historical judgements. They have been modified by subsequent argument and research. Nevertheless I print them as they stand (including a few repetitions of ideas) because they helped to start a useful dialogue. And when the dialogue of history dies, history itself will be dead.

Equally, if it is to continue, we must ensure that the process by which it is taught and learnt is as effective and exacting as possible. My lecture was delivered just after the Robbins Report on higher education had been officially (and in my view too uncritically) accepted by the Government. Against its criticisms of what it called 'the old-fashioned tutorial system' I remarked that our job was to attract students into 'that degree of involvement and participation' in the academic process which alone could remove the need for stick or carrot. 'Participation' is a word more familiar in 1968 than it was in 1964. It is no more and no less important than it was then; neither is the intellectual discipline that it implies.

If the study of history has a high educational value (as I believe) it is because it demands that the student should systematically re-create a past that is partly objective and partly subjective. He must try and unravel situations that once faced ruler, statesmen and ordinary men and women. The historian's models are neither mathematics nor make-believe; they are real. The present British Minister of Education (July 1968) has pronounced that it is more important to know about Viet Nam than about the Wars of the Roses. He is the victim of an elementary fallacy. It is obviously important to know about both past and present; but the character of the knowledge that it is possible to acquire in the two cases is quite different. So are the processes by which it is acquired and used. There can be no certainty that any particular interpretation of an historical problem or episode will be final. But historical problems can be viewed with a degree of detachment that cannot be achieved with contemporary issues in which we are still involved. The materials available will be a fraction of the whole but the events themselves will have been completed *in time*. Their treatment therefore demands techniques that are in part those of the scientist, in part those of the artist – narrative, analysis, selection, re-creation. Therein lies the unique value and fascination of the study of history.

I

Economics and Politics in the Seventeenth Century[1]

Unique in itself, unique in its historiography, the English Civil War has an irresistible claim on the historian. In our own day, the problem of its origins has provoked an epic debate which reflects the contemporary tendency to seek sociological explanations of historical action. The explosion of the mid-seventeenth century is seen by both parties to the debate not merely as the fight for religious and constitutional liberty that it was for Gardiner, but as a consequence of social tensions that arose out of the changing relationships between social groups. Marxists, post-Marxians and anti-Marxists have alike concentrated on the supposed period of gestation. Marxists have seen the war as the climax of a struggle for power generated by economic change. Parliamentary support came from the bourgeoisie and a minority of radical gentry. The result of the war, though a political compromise, was to accelerate enormously the growth of industrial capital – and 'to set the stage for the industrial revolution in the century that was yet to come'.[2] According to this interpretation, the war was economic in origin, its outcome was determined by economic alignment and its consequences were economic. Politics follow suit obediently and immediately. Political institutions respond to economic need. The House of Commons becomes the forum of spokesmen representing economic interests. Political action follows. Such views have in the past influenced articles, monographs and studies of special

[1] This paper was published as a review of *The Century of Revolution, 1603–1714* by Christopher Hill in *The Historical Journal*, V. I (1962), pp. 80–104.

[2] M. H. Dobb, *Studies in the Development of Capitalism* (1946), 168–76.

topics of seventeenth-century history. Recently, and for the first time, they have appeared as a powerful influence in a comprehensive study of English seventeenth-century history. The results merit the attention not only of students of the seventeenth century but of any student concerned with problems of synthesis in the present state of historical studies.

Mr Christopher Hill is one of the most stimulating of the seventeenth-century historians. His recent books – *Puritanism and Revolution* (1958) and *The Economic Problems of the Church* (1956) – combine a Marxist approach with an insight and sympathy that come from years of dedicated inquiry. Like his latest book, *The Century of Revolution*, they make it plain that the Civil War lies at the centre of his interests. Brisk, clear and readable, the latest study is likely to be widely read. One can imagine that many a student, bewildered by the complexities of older works, will turn with relief to an account that provides attractively neat explanations of the upheavals of the seventeenth century. For 'explanation' is Mr Hill's declared purpose, and he has never concealed his opinion that there is a kind of history that conspicuously fails to give the 'explanation' at which he aims. Of Miss Wedgwood's history of the Civil War he wrote that it was 'a narrative, not an explanation. It tells us all about the war except what they fought each other for – Miss Wedgwood's refusal to analyse makes it impossible to see below the surface of mere events.'[1] By contrast, Mr Hill's method is to explain – as current jargon has it – 'in depth'; to see politics and social movements as the reflection of larger economic movements of change, and economics as in turn controlled by the distribution of political power. 'Narrative' history is accordingly reduced to four rather casual pages of 'what happened'. Yet from the final analysis the Civil War and its effects emerge as central. This formed 'the turning-point in the evolution of capitalism', eliminating the 'one barrier' to the entrepreneur and a *laissez-faire* economy. Here was a victory for the 'propertied classes', followed in 1660 by a compromise between Cavaliers and Roundheads 'directed against the lower classes'. The year 1688 saw a second turning-point as the 'industrialists' defeated the monopolistic ends of the great commercial capitalists of the trading corporations. At both points political revolution deriving

[1] *Spectator*, 12 December 1958.

from fundamentally economic causes broke up the established order. Plainly Parliamentary victory in the first Civil War is crucial to Mr Hill's reading of seventeenth-century history.

In his *Puritanism and Revolution* Mr Hill took Messrs Brunton and Pennington to task for contenting themselves with an analysis of loyalties in the Long Parliament that did nothing to explain why the Civil War was fought, why large numbers of men were roused 'to heroic activity and sacrifice' about 'issues of principle' (pp. 20, 23). 'The Civil War', he then sensibly remarked, 'did after all take place . . .' (ibid. p. 24). But is there not another question? If the Civil War was so decisive economically, politically, socially, is it of no importance to establish how it was waged? Why and how did the Parliamentary forces manage to win, and the Royalists to lose, the Civil War? In the *Century of Revolution* the decisive phase of the Civil War itself – from 1642 to 1647 – is dismissed in two pages. What of any 'explanation' of the Civil War itself? 'If we want to understand the Civil War,' Mr Hill writes, 'a glance at the maps on p. 22 is far more important than the most elaborate analysis of members of Parliament.' The two small sketch-maps purport to show the geographical nature of what Mr Hill calls 'support' for the Parliament and the King on 1 May 1643 and at the end of 1645 respectively. 'Support' for Parliament came, he says, from 'the economically advanced south and east of England', support for the King from the economically backward ones of the north and west. To this he adds one or two more suggestions: that the local 'industrial areas' (as he calls them) were for Parliament, the 'agricultural' ones for the King. Thus in Yorkshire it was Bradford which 'forced a reluctant Fairfax' to lead them into action. Since Lord Fairfax does not appear in Mr Hill's index, this presumably refers to Tom Fairfax. That few of the later leaders on either side were itching to precipitate war is a commonplace that needs no further proof. But no source is quoted to substantiate this implication that the Rider of the White Horse, whose zeal, courage and military prowess are beyond doubt, needed to be prodded into action by eager capitalists. It was, in fact, the other way round. Fairfax had to strain every nerve to rouse support in an area where most of the cards were stacked against Parliament.[1] But the picture takes

[1] See C. R. Markham, *A Life of the Great Lord Fairfax* (1870).

shape. 'The ports were all for Parliament.' Were they? London, of course. Hull also, but more, it would seem because of Hotham's hatred of Strafford than because of the loyalties of the citizens, which were evenly divided.[1] At Bristol Parliamentary sympathies were uppermost but there was strong support for the King, and Bristol served the Royal cause well from its capture by Rupert early in the war to its surrender in September 1645. So did Falmouth and Chester. Exeter, with its small but useful port of Topsham, was a Royalist centre. Newcastle was the funnel through which the northern Cavaliers got valuable foreign help, which Mr Hill says they were denied. The defection of the Fleet was not the social revolt of professional 'tarpaulins': naval loyalty had been badly strained by Charles's unpopular pro-Spanish policy. The genuine popularity of Warwick and sheer confusion did the rest.[2] That the loss of London, Hull and the Fleet was a grievous blow to Charles is true, but these events do not of themselves explain his failure. Even less is it to be explained in terms of the other military factor to which Mr Hill attaches great importance: the performance of the London trained bands who were 'the most reliable Parliamentary troops in the early stages of the war'; which in turn presumably reflects his belief that Calvinism turned out 'the most effective fighters' (p. 168). Twice he credits them with 'checking the royalist advance at Turnham Green and preserving the army at Newbury'. It is no doubt attractive to think of these middle and working class regiments as playing a decisive part in the war. But did they? The battle of Turnham Green was never fought. It was not valour but numbers that frightened the impressionable Charles, who promptly retired to Hounslow.[3] The account of their valorous stand at Newbury rests mainly on Serjeant Foster's patriotic apology for his regiment in that battle. It is not altogether easy to reconcile with his earlier confessions that it was a complaining and mutinous collection that marched west – even more mutinous, it has been expertly said, than Hopton's Irish. In November 1643 the Westminster regiment refused orders and

[1] C. V. Wedgwood, *The King's War* (1958), 87; E. Warburton, *Memoirs of Prince Rupert* (1849), 1, 301–3.

[2] Warburton, 311–12 and n. 2.

[3] A. H. Burne and P. Young, *The Great Civil War* (1959), 33.

when directed to attack deserted with loud cries of Home! Home![1] It seems more than likely that at Newbury the trained bands were preserved by the efficient deployment of the Parliamentary artillery. Even Foster's account breathes gratified relief at being preserved by the Almighty, rather than pride in superior skill or valour. Perhaps a just verdict is Colonel Burne's conclusion that the prowess of the London trained bands 'seems to have been somewhat exaggerated'.[2]

The picture that emerges from Mr Hill's account is simple but unsatisfying: an England divided geographically between an advanced economic region attached to advanced political causes, producing a valorous, eager volunteer army, against a retarded region led by reluctant semi-feudal commanders. This, as far as I can judge from Mr Hill's further three pages of 'explanation', is his version of the royal defeat. Well over half a century ago, Trevelyan wrote of the Civil War that it was 'on the whole a war of North and West against South and East'. But he added a saving clause:

> . . . the North never felt that it was engaged in a death struggle with the South, nor were West and East roused to battle by conscious intention to subdue one another. In every shire there were two parties, of which the weaker only waited opportunity to join hands with an invading force from the other side of England. For in motive it was a war not of class or of districts, but of ideas. Hence there was a nobler speculative enthusiasm among the chiefs and their followers, but less readiness to fight among the masses of the population, than in other contests that have torn great nations.[3]

This still seems to me to tell us more than Mr Hill's maps: and nothing in it is contradicted by more recent research.

Nevertheless, the valour of tradesmen or mechanics apart, the theory that victory was assured to the Roundheads by superior material resources is not to be dismissed lightly. It has been accepted quite lately by the authors of what is by far the best analysis of the tactics of the Civil War yet written: *The Great Civil War*, by Col. Burne and Col. Young. On the face of it, their argument corresponds closely to Mr Hill's. But a little analysis reveals a major fallacy in the belief that the outcome

[1] *Ibid.*, 120 [2] *Ibid.*

[3] G. M. Trevelyan, *England under the Stuarts* (1904).

of the war was determined, *ab initio*, by what are called 'resources'. This is to ignore a vital period during which the whole issue of victory or defeat was in the balance. In their conclusion, the authors of this excellent book descry four strands of war (as they call them): leaders, the led, morale and resources. 'The Led', they describe as being 'fairly similar', 'all of the same blood', with a leaning towards Cavalier superiority. Under the heading of 'morale', they see the Cavaliers with an initial superiority which was slowly lost to the Parliament. But Parliament they explain, enjoyed a great preponderance in resources, and 'this fourth strand had greater effect than the other three strands combined', so that by late 1644 it made the issue of the war 'as nearly a foregone conclusion as anything in the realm of war can be'. The late date is worth noting. So too is their conclusion about leadership, for from this issues their conclusion about resources. In the matter of leadership, they see 'a glaring contrast throughout the greater part of the war. Whereas on the Royalist side, there was *unity of command, under one supreme and unquestioned head* [my italics], on the side of Parliament the war was conducted by a committee, consisting mainly of civilians who naturally were ignorant of military strategy. ... Furthermore, the Royalist commander was the sovereign, respected and implicitly obeyed.'[1] As a commander, Charles is credited with keeping 'steadily before his eyes the primary principle of war that the essential target is the enemy's main field army . . .' together with a 'resolution and determination – Charles never abandoned hope; his optimism was unquenchable, and often unjustifiable – it was also encouraged by Lord Digby who even after Rowton Heath was writing letters full of confidence and hope'.[2]

If all of this, or even part of it, were correct, we should be well on the way to agreeing that the course of the Civil War was determined primarily by the relative allocation of material resources. But on the high strategy of the war Messrs Burne and Young seem to me to have gone astray. (Their views are obviously their responsibility. They do, however, make acknowledgement to Mr Hill for his efforts to keep them 'on the rails' where the political aspect of the war is concerned.)[3]

[1] Burne and Young, *op. cit.*, 224.
[2] *Ibid.*, 228–9.
[3] *Ibid.*, preface, xiii.

That the Roundhead conduct of affairs was a fumbling business it is not necessary to question. This certainly contributed to Charles's early successes. The Cavaliers won (as Messrs Burne and Young point out) seven out of the sixteen main battles of the war, all in the earlier stages. After Edgehill, Charles sat down before Banbury in that state of continuous indecision that was his natural posture, refusing Rupert's offer to push on to London. Arrived at Turnham Green, his 'prudence' (not the valour of the London trained bands) again supervened and he lost one of the biggest chances of the war by being dilatory and indecisive. The decision to besiege Gloucester instead of marching on London was another example of the same fatal indecision mixed with obstinacy. At the first Battle of Newbury, Charles's decision to withdraw instead of inflicting a final defeat on Essex probably determined the course of the war. As Messrs Burne and Young themselves put it, 'Had he [Charles] decided to bluff it out next day, it is now by no means certain that Essex would have continued with the fight'.[1] But at Newbury as at Turnham Green it was apparent that the capacity to bluff was no part of Charles's make-up as a commander. At Cheriton the caution of the indifferent Ruthven, his chief of staff, was allowed to overtop the zeal of Hopton, one of his best commanders, and again disaster followed. Even so, in the summer and the autumn of 1643, the advantages had nearly all still rested with the King. There were risings for the King in Kent and Shropshire. At King's Lynn the Royalists held out for a month. Lynn could have proved the centre from which the Eastern Association might have been overrun if Newcastle had not been too obsessed with the disastrous siege of Hull.[2] Charles's army was well quartered, when the enemy were in want and without shelter. His forces lay between them and London. Only the fatal decision to ignore Rupert's advice to wait brought disaster. On the field of battle, Charles's claims to ability seem negligible, unless we allow his gallantry at Lostwithiel when it was probably too late to retrieve victory.

That Charles possessed courage is beyond doubt: optimism too. But in a commander-in-chief these are not the only necessities. The combination of general optimism with tactical

[1] Burne and Young, *op. cit.*, 105.
[2] C. V. Wedgwood, *The King's War* (1958), 265.

caution was fatal. Worse than anything he did or failed to do in the field of battle were Charles's faults as strategic organizer, which reduced to a shambles any chance that the Royalist cause might be led and decided (as Col. Burne thinks it was) by 'a single and unchallenged supreme commander'.[1] On the contrary, the story of the Royalist strategy is an unbroken series of decisions taken only to be countermanded, commands created only to be invalidated, intrigues that went unchecked until it was too late, dissensions fostered by weakness and delay. It was this 'fatal facility and weakness [as Warburton called it] so often and so pertinaciously misconstrued into perfidy and crime' that wrecked the Royalist hopes in the first two years of the war. Even when he was roused to some energetic action Charles invariably compromised it by half measures that nullified the effects of his decision.[2]

This personal defect in Charles was all the more disastrous because there was not until late in 1644 any acknowledged commander-in-chief. Theoretically, strategy was determined by a Council of War, with Ruthven as a kind of military chief of staff. In practice, there was perpetual chaos and dissension. Of the generals in the field – and indeed off it too – Rupert was unquestionably the greatest. Time after time, Rupert's strategic judgement proved correct. Time after time his plans were rejected, or worse still, accepted only to be changed when his back was turned. After Edgehill Rupert would have pressed on to London: would have pursued Essex after Newbury. He was not allowed to do so. The Oxford campaign in the spring of 1644 was wrecked because no sooner had he gone north to relieve Newcastle than his plan for reinforcing the west midland garrison was abandoned, and Abingdon was lost. Marston Moor was the direct result of Charles's disastrous letter commanding and conjuring Rupert to relieve York. Rupert, well aware of likely recriminations, carried the letter with him till his dying day. The decision to attack at Naseby was the work of Digby and Ashburnham, those 'two hopeful and inexperienced civilians'. as Miss Wedgwood has called them,[3] who saw yet another chance to thwart Rupert, left as always to make the best of a strategy he deplored. On the field, at the crisis of the

[1] Burne and Young, *op. cit.*, 8–9.
[2] Warburton, I, 317–31.
[3] Wedgewood, *op. cit.*, 450.

battle it was Charles's failure to throw in his cavalry reserves that lost the day.[1] And with Naseby the contest was virtually over. Throughout all these sordid and miserable episodes, Rupert had the consistent support of the best men amongst the Royalists – the gallant Hopton, Will Legge, Nicholas, the Duke of Richmond. But he faced the opposition of a group round the King and Queen, whose talents for intrigue were strictly professional, even if as soldiers they were amateurs: Digby, gay, optimistic, irresponsible, the worst of Charles's advisers, who 'promised all things and succeeded in none',[2] Wilmot, Percy, Ashburnham. Then there was the Queen, the arch intriguer and Rupert's worst enemy. No one has ever calculated what was lost by the diversion of resources to escort her on her absurd perambulations about the Kingdom. Her arrival at Oxford put an end to any hope of either peace or victory.

It may be argued in defence of Charles that his position was hopeless from the start because of the semi-independence of his semi-feudal local commanders like Newcastle, whose troops consisted to a large extent of his local tenantry and supporters: that Rupert was a foreigner, without lands or followers, too young to be made commander-in-chief. This will not hold water. In the end, when it was too late, Charles did appoint Rupert commander-in-chief. If it could be done in 1644 it could have been done earlier and there is plenty of evidence to show that with Charles's firm backing Rupert could have easily made his authority unquestioned. But this did not happen. The Royalist command was, through all the crucial stages when Parliament's own affairs were in a catastrophic muddle, divided and distracted, the very reverse of that unified command described by Messrs Burne and Young. To quote Warburton again, it was '. . . the disuniting of the army to conciliate private and petty interests . . . the want of one far-reaching, resolute and commanding mind to rouse, concentrate and direct the vast energies and powerful elements combined in the Royal Army, that was truly wanting'.[3]

Rupert was, as Messrs Burne and Young have said, much more than a dashing cavalry brigadier; indeed they have done much to explain his greatness as a field commander. He was

[1] Burne and Young, *op. cit.*, 207.
[2] Warburton, I, 306.
[3] Warburton, II, 299–300.

also a master of the siege, a pioneer of horse artillery, and there seems little doubt that he could have been a major strategist. The best tribute to him came from Charles, typically after he had abandoned Rupert's western plan in May 1644 in deference to Digby, and given Goring an independent command without telling Rupert. 'I must observe to you', he wrote to Rupert, 'that the chief hope of my resource is, under God, from you: and I believe that if you had been with me I had not been put to those straits I am now in. I confess, the best had been to have followed your advice. . . .'[1] But Charles had not followed his advice. The defects of his character had helped to lose the war, even more surely than they lost the peace.

The theory that the unequal distribution of resources and support doomed the Cavaliers to inevitable failure must be rejected. Economic resources do not, by themselves, win wars. Mr Hill's maps and analysis of 'support' explain nothing in the early decisive phases of the war. It was the failure in leadership, the dissensions and intrigues in the high command, that prevented the King from exploiting the considerable tactical victories he won, and dispersed and dissipated his resources. Only this gave the Parliamentary command time to organize itself. While the bold and brilliant Fairfax held off the enemy with one hand, Cromwell was busy organizing and training the army, though it is important to remember that he was never an army commander in the first Civil War, and that he may have been amongst those generals who (in the famous phrase) 'took to their heels' at Marston Moor.[2] But slowly the superior *potential* available to the Parliament was made actual. In the interval while that was being done, Charles lost the war: and – to avoid any misunderstanding of the purpose of this review – let it be added, a very good thing too.

The theory that 1660 represented a 'compromise' of the victorious class with their defeated 'class' adversary, directed against the lower classes (p. 308) derives from the theory that the Civil War was in origin a class struggle. Closely related to this is the theory that resources ineluctably determined the

[1] *Ibid.*, 415.

[2] Burne and Young, *op. cit.*, ch. 12. The evidence for the story is not strong. It may have come from the Scots after they were infuriated by Independent claims that the victory was theirs.

victory. Neither the parent theory nor its offspring stands up to examination. One error has merely generated another. The Marxist theory that the Civil War represented the bourgeois revolution, with parties following closely economic and social lines, has been set out succinctly by Mr Dobb.[1] Mr Hill's account follows the orthodoxy but with variations forced upon it by historical facts. The dominant economic classes, finding their path obstructed by government, broke the absolute monarchy by a bourgeois revolution. This cleared the way for a reunion of the parties divided in the Civil War; a two-class society emerged, with a *laissez-faire* economy and a new system of government in which the propertied classes determined policy by pulling all the strings. But Mr Hill knows too much history to propound, or expect others to accept, the 'class' interpretation in its primitive form. The explanatory process, therefore, is not so much devoted to explaining 'what happened' as to explaining why Mr Hill's chosen instrument of explanation – class interest and solidarity, provoking class hatreds and the class struggle – breaks down at all the crucial points: why the ruling class was divided in the 1640s, still divided in 1660, why the lower orders cheered on the Seven Bishops at the Revolution. The necessity for much of this 'explanation' derives from the assumption, which Mr Hill seems to take for granted, that class solidarity based on economic interest is the natural state of affairs in seventeenth-century England. In reality the world of seventeenth-century politics was one of multiple factions, based on personal, family and local sympathies and antipathies. These tended to polarize round a two-*party* organization, an entirely different matter from a two-*class* organization. We need only look at the social structure of a small part of the gentry (as Professor Trevor Roper has done) or at the gang structure of the City merchants (as Mr Price and Mr Letwin have done)[2] to see that the notion of class homogeneity is a myth. In rejecting political narrative in favour of history 'in depth' Mr Hill has merely substituted one type of historical oversimplification for another.

In the process, history has been chopped into pieces not only

[1] *Studies in the Development of Capitalism* (1946), 168 ff.

[2] J. M. Price, *The Tobacco Adventure to Russia* (Trans. American Philosophical Society, 1961); W. Letwin, *Sir Josiah Child, Merchant Economist* (Harvard, 1959).

by topics but by periods. Where older historians used to divide by reigns, Mr Hill divides by 'revolutions'. The attempt to correlate political, economic and social history means that dates like 1640, 1660, 1688, acquire, or have to be assigned, economic and social as well as political significance. The weakness of this is that vital underlying economic trends are obscured, vital continuities of policy suppressed, to suit a pre-determined chronology of socio-political development. Thus the crisis of the 1620s is interpreted in terms of the shortcomings of Stuart government, which was a part, but only a part, of the story. The organic and fundamental economic problems faced by government – the changing structure of England's foreign trade, the collapse of the Old Draperies, the increase of population within a still rigid economy – are mentioned. Their crucial importance is obscured in an account which concentrates upon James's picturesque and corrupt bargain with Cokayne and the tycoons. This, as Dr Supple has recently shown,[1] is only an incident in the economic fluctuations of the age, whose complexity would have taxed the resources of any government, however businesslike. Nevertheless, early Stuart government was not without some claim to pioneer work on economic policy. The Commission on Trade of 1622 was a watershed both in thought and policy. The prohibition of wool export, which aimed to keep prices low for the local manufactures, dates effectively from this period. It formed, as even its later opponents recognized, one of the two principal pillars of the regulated economy they later called the mercantile system. Nobody who has examined the petitions from trade and industry that streamed into the Privy Council and its *ad hoc* committees in these years, or the measures taken to deal with them, can suppose that government was any less 'responsive to the interests of trade' than its successors in office whom Mr Hill credits with more commercial ideas. That it was less wise or successful is a different matter.

By Cromwell's time (we are told) things had changed. Cromwell's foreign policy 'was dominated by economic considerations'. Why then did he wind up the successful Dutch War in 1654 and resist business pressure to start it again? Mr Hill's

[1] B. E. Supple, *Commercial Crisis and Change in England 1600–1642* (Cambridge, 1959).

attempt to represent the treaty of 1654 as a victory for 'trade' is unconvincing. Cromwell forced the Dutch, he says, to pay tribute for fishing in English waters – 'a matter no previous English Government had been able to secure'. But Cromwell did nothing of the kind. On the contrary, Cromwell deliberately dropped the claim in the interests of a reasonable settlement with a potential Protestant ally. The Dutch got a peace on far better terms than they might have expected after a disastrous war. As Clarendon points out, the merchant warmongers always believed that Cromwell could have 'totally subdued' the Dutch in 1654 if he had not deliberately chosen to subordinate economic to political and religious aims.

The continuity of policy and ideas on foreign trade, maintained by successive governments faced with similar problems of national responsibility, has been clearly brought out in another study which Mr Hill quotes with approval: Dr Hinton's *The Eastland Trade and the Commonwealth in the Seventeenth Century* (1959). But Dr Hinton's main conclusion does not at all bear out Mr Hill's contention that the nature of government 'response' to traders' demands altered. On the contrary, it concludes that the relationship between successive governments and the Eastland Company were based on 'ancient and conventional ideas about the common weal which the subjects abundantly shared and *which easily transcended the interests of particular groups*'[1] [my italics].

The idea of policy evolving by revolutionary jerks as successive governments responded to the demands of dominant economic classes seems to lie at the heart of Mr Hill's historical 'explanation'. But to deny to government any autonomous, or at any rate arbitrating, role in policy leaves many major problems unsolved and insoluble. How and why was a House of Commons, where trade was represented by only some ten per cent of the membership, persuaded repeatedly to pass, maintain and strengthen laws to keep down wool prices, and to maintain the land tax as by far the largest single source of income? If fiscal policy was merely a wangle by men of property, why was land taxed so heavily? If Parliament was merely a struggle decided by the weight of money-bags, how were the great trading companies eased out of their monopolies? Because,

[1] *Op. cit.*, 164.

Mr Hill argues, they were opposed by the rising power of the 'industrialists'. But where was the 'industrialist' – the title itself is anachronistic – who could outbid great merchants and financiers like Child, Heathcote and Janssen? And if the effect of the Navigation Acts was to divert capital from investment in industry generally and retard industrial development (p. 213) (a doubtful proposition to say the least of it) how had 'industrialists' suddenly become so influential? Petitioning the Privy Council was the traditional method of bringing pressure – not least from manufacturers – on government. Consideration of only one party to such transactions – industry – does nothing to explain the increased efficacy of that pressure, especially when, according to Mr Hill's argument, the industrial interest was being neglected or starved of capital.

The improvement in economic conditions later in the century owed much to improved economic conditions generally after the Peace of Westphalia. In the altered conditions, England, with an increasingly diversified economy and a strong navy, was able to enlarge her share of trade. More coherent policies helped, as Mr Hill recognizes. But the alteration of policy was not simply due to the more effective lobbying power of new economic groups, exercised through Parliament. Unless there had been a different, wider and more experienced assessment of the nation's economic needs by government and informed (not necessarily self-interested) opinion, the lobbying might well have produced mere chaos. Along with the changes in the economic and political context went a change in the relationship of the executive and its immediate advisers. In James's time, the Privy Council had often shown itself wiser but weaker than its master. Few things were more important and few have been less investigated than the influence of a succession of Crown servants of high intelligence after the Restoration – Downing, Pepys, Blathwayte, Newton, Locke, Davenant and many others. Such men were able to draw on a wealth of economic debate that was the outcome of successive economic crises, and to bring the immense inherited power and patronage of the executive to bear on economic expansion. Theirs was not merely a response to the irresistible or obvious demands of dominant economic groups. Parliamentary sovereignty should not be confused with effective government. Lobbies rarely got everything they wanted. The

Navigation Acts satisfied none of those who petitioned for action completely. Often the function of government was to resist pressure groups as much as to satisfy them. Downing defeated the bankers, whom he hated as the King's enemies. Charles, in person and through the ministers, urged war for years against the East India Directors, Child and Papillon especially, as Whigs displeasing to his person (not Tories as Mr Hill supposes). The enlarged Council of Trade, with its fringe of merchant advisers, disintegrated in 1670 because Charles came to the conclusion that its merchant members were 'a pack of knaves' incapable of giving him the disinterested advice on policy he needed.[1]

Politics and government did not operate simply as a function of bloc interests, nor can economic development be explained in terms of political arrangements that altered radically within short periods. Mr Hill recognizes that social mobility frequently brought with it an identity of interest between land and trade. But it also needs to be recognized that the merchant 'community' had no community sense. The great tycoons were always split into warring cliques, as the East India, Turkey and Atlantic traders were. On few issues did any economic class present a united front, so that, except when the government behaved with crass stupidity and aroused inter-class opposition, it could rely on its traditional prestige and immense powers of patronage to get its way. Generally, governments acted from a variety of motives that varied from a genuine concern for the national welfare to a natural desire for convenience and a quiet life. Administrative convenience was as powerful a determinant of tax policy as class interest. Excise appealed to every politician from Pym to Walpole because it was easy to collect and because there was an obvious limit to the Customs revenue, more than because it suited bourgeois interests. Against that consideration, even the concerted opposition of that powerful gang of 'industrialists' (almost the only ones to qualify plausibly for the title) – the London brewers – was impotent. To tie the revolutions of 1640–60 and of 1688 to changes in the power of economic interests is to attribute a homogeneity to them which they did not possess. The one kind of opinion no seventeenth-century government could safely ignore was religious, and many of Mr Hill's pages bear unacknowledged witness to the fact.

[1] Letwin, *op. cit.*

Mr Hill wisely enjoins his readers not to force later categories of analysis on his century of revolution. But in spite of refinements and concessions, the essentially Victorian structure repeatedly shows through his own synthesis. He remains as enchanted by the explanatory power of Marxist economics as Mr Betjeman by St Saviours, Aberdeen Park. Thus the political influence of 'property' is invariably discussed in terms that remind one of more recent Marxist assessments of the political influence of industrial capital, whereas it was in fact the vestigial remains of the medieval equating of political power with land. The key quotations that justify Mr Hill's pin-pointing of the Civil War's central economic importance come from Mr Lipson's text-book, a synthetic compendium in many respects outdated by recent research. Figures of wages and prices come from Thorold Rogers's history of 1887. Recent research that threatens to disturb the neat pattern of historical evolution dictated by the older orthodoxy gets short shrift. Thus, much is made of the importance of the transfer of land during the interregnum from the Royalists to the new property seekers. This is followed, somewhat contradictorily, by the admission that after all the bulk of the Royalist landlords stayed put. Mr Hill does not mention Miss Thirsk's important article which shows that, for the most part, the *status quo ante* was restored before 1660. Professor Jordan's study of charity as mainly a function of the social responsibility of merchants, gets a brief acknowledgement (pp. 26 and 103). But it should not be forgotten that a whole generation of historians who persisted in regarding the seventeenth-century merchants as a hard-fisted, socially irresponsible class who subordinated social welfare to ideas of economic nationalism have been put totally out of countenance by Professor Jordan's discoveries. One might have expected that the simple political deductions implied by diagrams 2 and 3 (based on Thorold Rogers's figures) would have been accompanied by some reference to Professor Jordan's total scepticism about their value as a source of information about social standards. There is none. In any case, Professor Jordan is quickly forgotten. By the later years of the century, the poor have been abandoned, and the only hope is held to be in trade unionism (p. 154). But who in 1700 were still founding schools and apprenticeships, preaching high wages?

Was it not still merchants like Child, Firmin, Cary, Nelson, Mackworth? The most detailed analysis of Professor Jordan's statistics comes in appendix C and its purpose is significantly different. Between 1601 and 1640, Mr Hill notes, the total of charitable benefactions was over £1 million. By 1660 it fell to £387,000. But for Mr Hill the interest lies in 'the significant decline (in the second period) in the relative contributions of the nobility . . . and the equally significant rise of the contributions of yeomen'. Significant? The proportionate decline of noble contributions was 2·43 per cent: the rise in yeomen contributions 1·25 per cent. Are we intended to infer that these risible fractions confirm the old thesis of a declining aristocracy and of a rising yeomanry? Why not go on to infer that the increase in the gentry's offerings by 0·77 per cent supports the theory that the gentry were in the ascendant? The treatment is nevertheless revealing. New discovery has to be trimmed, new wine put back into the old Marxist bottle. But these manipulations are not limited to modern work. The essence of late seventeenth-century economic thought is summarized on p. 272 thus: 'the poor were unproductive, the rich alone productive'. This is, of course, a caricature of a generation which first formulated the concept of labour as a factor in production. No topic occupied thinkers of the age so much as the problem of training the potential labour force represented by the poor. The insouciant handling of detailed economic problems such as this makes it difficult to take seriously the analysis (on the same page) of the alleged disequilibrium between trade and luxury and what is called 'industry'. Subsidized shipping, overseas trade, aristocratic building and luxury court expenditure (we are told) absorbed capital which might otherwise have been 'invested' in industry. But were not shipbuilding, housebuilding, with their ancillary industries, and all the industries which worked for the upper and middle class market, to say nothing of industries like sugar boiling, tobacco cutting, and a score of industries that depended on the import trade for raw materials, 'industry'? Has Mr Hill read *The Fable of the Bees*?

So back to the fundamental problem: the relationship between economic interests and policies, economic classes, political action and political and economic results. The Civil War remains crucial. The problem, Mr Hill says, is to decide how

Charles I 'got a party at all', to explain why his supporters in and out of the House of Commons increased after May 1641. The formation of a royal party was due, he suggests, to 'shifts of opinion among the propertied classes'. But why 'propertied'? Was it not that when it came to the sticking-point, men of all classes were drawn back into allegiance to the monarchy – often in spite of the person and qualities of the King himself? Neither the formation of the Royal party, nor the course of the war to 1644, nor the settlement of 1660 or 1688 can be satisfactorily explained in terms of socio-economic movements that give at most only a peripheral importance to non-economic factors, including personal loyalties and antipathies and beliefs that a later generation may (if it likes) regard as irrational or superstitious. Anglicanism emerges as a function of the interest of patrons, tithe impropriators and avaricious bishops, all with their hands deep in the till. Lancelot Andrewes comes on stage only to feature in a rather good anecdote about James I and taxation. *Paradise Lost*, by a tortuous process, becomes a reflexion of the new (?) attitude to marriage as a function of money and property. Mr Hill ends his book by commending to us the actions of the men of the seventeenth century. Yet one looks in vain for a single case where a man of action in that century is credited with a human virtue or a human capacity of decisive historic importance. Even Cromwell's claim to applause rests on his love of the arts and his open-mindedness in allowing himself to be painted warts and all. No doubt the older historians were too little conscious of the social context within which the historic individual acted. Here he is too often reduced to a mere reflection of social forces. The result is not to explain greatness but to explain it away. Significantly the one paragraph of unstinted admiration for an individual is devoted to Harrington for fathering the idea that history could provide 'laws relating to the behaviour of human beings in the mass'. Few identified members of what Mr Hill usually calls 'the propertied classes' emerge with any credit. The non-propertied naturally do better. They have the advantage that they are collective, anonymous, unidentified. They only stand and wait. Perhaps they are lucky.

The charge that the older narrative history failed to answer the questions that a present-day student wants answered is not entirely unfounded. But at its best the narrative method was rooted in a sound instinct – the sense of the essential wholeness of history, the close texture of causation in which historic event and individual, however much themselves the product of larger causes, in turn influenced the new phase of history they initiated; the perception that the anatomist has to begin by killing his subject.[1]

The felt need for a new historical synthesis transcending the conventionally circumscribed task of the narrative historian derives from several sources. The specialized inquiries of non-political historians in recent times have revealed a world of interests, tensions and conflicts often unknown to older generations of historians. At certain points these appear to have important affinities with contemporary political action. Sociological method suggests that such affinities can be multiplied as explanations of political behaviour. From Marx is derived an interpretative theory that offers a consistent and dogmatic explanation of those affinities in terms of material group interests. Thus is generated the ambition to provide not merely partial explanations of self-evidently related groups of actions, phenomena or institutions but a total explanation of every aspect of history through a synthesis of the disparate analyses of the historical specialists. Yet the synthesis remains mechanical, not dynamic. For the Marxist cannot opt out of his self-created dilemma. His own 'explanation' is ineluctably the product of its own age. Its value as an historical tool is essentially in relation to the long-term trends of economic and social development. Applied to the short-term, it positively invites contortions while the attempt to sophisticate the Marxist analysis merely produces contradiction and confusion.

We end with precisely that imposition of later categories of analysis on the material of earlier times which Mr Hill rightly deplores. The evidence adduced to correlate political behaviour, religious belief, group interests and economic development is obviously inadequate for scientific proof. This poverty of immediately relevant evidence forces the historian saddled with an *a priori* theory to adapt whatever evidence he can. Each category of evidence – economic, political, philosophic – tends to be treated not for its inherent importance but for its convenience in explaining the other categories. Ponderous and

[1] See Wedgwood, *op. cit.*, 12, for a statement of the case for the narrative method.

far-reaching generalizations about the attitudes of whole classes of men have to rest on the slenderest foundations: second-hand expressions of opinion, casual allusions, literary evidence, or pseudo-statistical evidence which has been shown to be of limited validity. Class hatreds, for example, are the 'essential background to late seventeenth-century politics'. They lie 'at the back of gentry political thinking'. But this 'deep hostility', Mr Hill adds, is 'usually unspoken' – 'rarely openly discussed'. This reticence (odd in a century which was rarely mealy-mouthed or inhibited) is apparently broken by four pronouncements (two of them anonymous) during a period of more than a quarter of a century after the Restoration. This appears to be the only warrant for a generalization crucial to Mr Hill's argument. It does not self-evidently support the claim that history 'in depth' represents a scientific advance over the methods of earlier historians.

As attention shifts from the individual to the group, the problem of explanation becomes larger and more impalpable, the historian's method more artificial and remote, not more scientific but less. As the historian shifts his focus, it becomes concentrated not on the historic act or event but on the supposed gestation or motivation of the act. The problem why men of the same material background chose differently in 1642 remains a problem. Neither maps nor graphs can resolve it. They merely substitute an illusion of concreteness for reality itself. It is as though instead of attending the play in the auditorium, we are invited to attend at the author's birthplace in a Wigan slum to discuss those maladjustments in childhood which caused him to write as he does. This seems to be the natural consequence of separating the action – 'what happened' – from its alleged cause and relegating it to a minor role, a tale fit only for children. History is thus in danger of becoming a kind of terminated pregnancy. Yet the logic of division into action and explanation is inherent in the Marxist method. The historic individual is dispensable because there is neither need nor room for him. But equally, there is no room – except in the anonymous aggregate – for those 'ordinary Englishmen and women' whose importance Mr Hill thinks underrated by historians. They can only achieve the status of people to whom things happened. Nor is there room for government as an autonomous factor. It can only reflect the interests of the dominant classes for the time being: as though alternating Chancellors in our own day were to be seen merely as the puppets respectively of the FBI and the TUC.

Mr Hill is right to stress the historian's liability 'to explain'. But the liability is not unlimited. It is bounded by the evidence available, by the rules of evidence, by a strictly finite human capacity to explain. Anyone who has tried to write contemporary history knows how convincingly the documentary evidence and rational deduction combine in a natural process of expansion, until the apparently inescapable solution presents itself. But he knows also how often the living testimony, itself checked and cross-checked, explodes this balloon of imperfect logic. For earlier periods, the historian can only remind himself continually of the limited and defective nature of most of his evidence. Otherwise he may end, like Buckle, with history that is no longer a seamless garment but a ready-made suit.[1]

[1] Mr A. Woolrych's *Battles of the English Civil War* (1961) appeared too late to be considered here. A trifle harsh on Rupert, it conveys eloquently the real *suspense* of the war: in every respect an admirable corrective to determinism.

2

The Decline of the Netherlands[1]

Posterity has come to regard the Dutch Republic as the model state of the seventeenth century, the archetype of its age. Here was the cradle of a civilization that revealed new beauties in the visual arts, new peaks of scientific achievement, disclosing novel subleties of philosophy and achieving unprecedented technological skill. Of all their accomplishments, it was the long lead established by the Dutch in the useful arts that evoked the largest volume of contemporary comment by other nations. English, French, Spanish, German and Scandinavian observers noted repeatedly that the Dutch were economically precocious and in advance of their own nations. This was illustrated by the nature of their economic functions which consisted to a large extent of performing for the rest of the European peoples tasks which they were as yet unable to perform for themselves – broadly, to fetch and carry, buy and sell, and in general act as a world entrepôt, providing incidentally the services of credit and payment for the less advanced peoples whom they served. Defoe's description of these services derives from the eighteenth century but it is equally valid for the seventeenth. The Dutch, he wrote, were '. . . the carryers of the World, the middle Persons in Trade, the Factors and Brokers of Europe . . . they *buy* to *sell* again, *take* in to *send* out; and the greatest part of their vast Commerce consists in being supply'd from all parts of the World, that they may supply all the World again.'[2] Theirs,

[1] This is a revised version of an article which appeared under the title 'The Economic Decline of the Netherlands' in the *Economic History Review*, 1st series, vol. IX (1939), pp. 111–27.

[2] Daniel Defoe, *A Plan of the English Commerce*, London (1728), p. 192. For a good general description see J. H. Kernkamp, 'De Generale Stapelmarkt in de Nederlanden', *Historia*, November 1949.

then, was a middleman's function, and it was in this capacity that they served as a model for imitation. Yet since the middleman has rarely been a popular figure, the desire on the part of others to imitate the virtues of the Dutch was accompanied by an equal determination to be rid of them from their national economies where their presence served as a permanent reminder of technical, economic and strategic inferiority. Such was to be the temper of the so-called 'mercantilist' writers and statesmen of the seventeenth and eighteenth centuries, more especially in England and France but later in Prussia and Spain too. The emotional appeal of chauvinism joined with more or less rational economic arguments based on the ideal of a favourable balance of trade and the interests of private individuals and companies, and the result issued in policies of economic nationalism. These aimed to exclude the Dutch from that dominant participation which they had enjoyed in the first half of the seventeenth century, often by adopting methods and techniques learned from the Dutch themselves.

The rapidity of the Dutch expansion in the last quarter of the sixteenth and the first half of the seventeenth century led some observers to discern at an early stage a precarious element in the prosperity of the Republic, barely emancipated from Spain. Was not the occasion of the Dutch expansion largely the distraction of the great dynastic powers, engaged in a bitter struggle for dynastic, religious or political ends? The Dutch economy, wrote Thomas Mun, was 'like a fair bird suited with goodly borrowed plumes; but if every fowl should take his feather, this bird would rest near naked. . .'[1]

The centre of this spectacular economy was without question the city of Amsterdam. When Guicciardini described it in 1561 it was still a modest enough town. Its merchants, as yet men of moderate means only, dealt in fish, Baltic goods – especially grain – and bought wine and salt from France. For Thomas Gresham, it was merely a place where you could buy wainscoting. Half a century later it had become a world metropolis, controlling a great network of trade and shipping that stretched from the British Isles in the west, the Mediterranean and Levant in the south up to Bergen and the Gulf of Finland in the

[1] T. Mun, *England's Treasures by Fforraign Trade* (reprinted by Economic History Society, 1933), p. 78.

north. War and competition had led on the Dutch in turn to expand this European system to the tropics. Following Houtman's voyage to Java in 1595, the East India Company took shape in 1602. In 1600 came the first voyage to Brazil and in 1621 the West India Company was formed. Yet the central core of the Dutch system remained the Baltic trade – the exchange of salt from Biscay and herrings caught in the waters off England and Scotland against Baltic grain. As time went on the stuff of the trade became more varied. Timber, ashes, pitch, tar, cordage and other ships' stores were added to the goods coming out of the Baltic. Wine, textiles, spices, tobacco and other colonial goods lengthened the list of goods sent into the Baltic. But it remained an unevenly balanced exchange. Europe's needs were greater and more pressing than the needs of the Baltic peoples. The Dutch shippers were therefore under a constant necessity to export silver to the Baltic, just as they were to the Indies. This in turn emphasized the importance of restoring trade with Spain, the great source of precious metals through her Central American sources of supply.

What the size of the Dutch merchant fleet at its peak was is a matter of debate. A reasonable estimate in the late seventeenth century suggested that the Dutch controlled nearly half the current European tonnage, and disposed of perhaps twice as much as England and eight or nine times as much as France.[1] Certainly a great part of it was 'utility' shipping, unarmed, slow, cheap to operate – the so-called 'flutes' or flyboats engaged in the carriage of bulk cargo, especially grain.[2] And this in turn illuminates a peculiar circumstance of the rise of the Dutch economy: it is almost certainly connected with the appearance of marginal food deficits in various parts of Europe from England to the Mediterranean. It is possible that these were in part the product of political dislocation but it seems probable that they also reflected the needs of an increased population. Until the European states concerned had expanded their food production by more intensive and scientific cultivation as well as by drainage and forest clearance, the Dutch

[1] C. E. Fayle, *Short History of the World's Shipping Industry*, New York (1933) Especially Chs. 8–11.

[2] Violet Barbour, 'Dutch and English Merchant Shipping in the 17th Century', *Economic History Review*, 2 (1930), pp. 261–90.

shipowners and merchants provided an indispensable service, without which starvation would have followed as a matter of course.[1]

From the beginning the entrepôt system generated not only mercantile profits but employment for sailors, port workers, shipbuilding labour – in short, for those directly concerned with the sale and carriage of goods. But as time went on, other employments grew, as it were, out of the carrying trade. Goods did not merely pass through the entrepôt. They tarried there, to be refined, finished or adapted in one way or another. In this way, a very large part of the activities carried on in the Dutch cities and ports were dependent on the continuous flow of materials into and (since many of them depended on export business) out of the entrepôt. Herrings caught off Scotland and England were cured and barrelled. Timber brought from the Baltic became the basis of the shipbuilding industries of the Zaan area. Grain from the Baltic and East Anglian ports was used for a large brewing and distilling industry. The unfinished woollen cloths from England were finished and dyed at Amsterdam. Unbleached linens from Germany were bleached and finished at Haarlem. The silk industry of Amsterdam bought its raw materials from Italy. The woollen industry of Leiden went to Spain and Turkey for the fine wools which played an increasing part in its manufacture, and an even larger proportion of its dyes came from the West Indies. Finally, there were tobacco curing, sorting and packing industries, and sugar refining became a capital-hungry industry comparable with brewing in the scale of its organization.

In this way, a great part of the economic life and work of the Dutch Republic had become geared to the import and export of goods on a scale unique at this period of history. It was a structure comparable in nature (if not in volume) with that of the British economy in the late nineteenth and early twentieth century. A people numbering perhaps a million souls depended for its livelihood, even for a substantial part of its food, on foreign trade: and this in a time when war was almost a continuous process. In the struggle for political ascendancy in the Republic between the followers of the House of Orange, many

[1] See J. G. van Dillen, *Honderd Jaar Economische Ontwikkeling van het Noorden,* Vol. Vol. VII (Utrecht 1954), p. 317.

of them Calvinist idealists and fanatics, and the merchant leaders of the patriciate, the so-called Regents, it was one of the objects of the Regents to preserve the freedom and property of this small and precariously placed state from unnecessary dynastic or religious imbroglios at home and abroad. But even this realistic pacifism failed to prevent the Republic becoming involved in three naval wars with England and a major war with France in the quarter century between 1657 and 1678. Such wars were not fatal. Their effects – unemployment, distress, bankruptcies, riots, starvation – were short lived and there was enough resiliency to replace losses and seek out new channels of trade. But their cost was high and they demonstrated how easily the lifelines of the Dutch economy – especially that running through the English Channel – might be cut. The relative failure of the Second and Third Dutch Wars and the growing threat from France diminished the threat to the Dutch from England, at any rate, as a military factor.[1] The threat from France remained. And both these great and rising states continued to erect, after 1660, a system of discriminating economic protection that was in origin and intent specifically directed against the Republic. The consequence, apart from the short-term difficulties already mentioned, was to add to the rising costs of production – especially the relatively high level of wages – which was to prove one of the major problems of Dutch industry in export markets in the later seventeenth and early eighteenth century.

The most recent inquiries suggest that there was no sudden, spectacular or general collapse of this economy. The statistics of taxation and shipping movements both point in the same direction: a peak of trading activity in the 1640s, followed in the 1650s by a slackening that persisted till the 1680s. Then a renewed liveliness in the 1680s. Prices, low for a quarter of a century, showed signs of rising again and the 1690s were reminiscent of the golden years of the mid-century, though the volume of shipping scarcely reached the top figures of the earlier period. The early decades of the eighteenth century remained reasonably prosperous in spite of temporary difficulties. As late as 1730 trade was good and optimism

[1] C. H. Wilson, *Profit and Power*, London-New York, 1957, examines the relationship between these wars and the development of Britain and the Dutch Republic.

widespread. It was hardly to be so again in the eighteenth century, though there were scattered years, like 1740–1 and 1749–50, when the economy seemed to show something of its old life again.[1]

How then should the 'decline' of the Dutch economy be understood? Amongst the older generation of historians it was customary to think of the seventeenth century as a period of growth and prosperity that faded steadily but inevitably into the twilight of the next century when the solid Dutch virtues of merchant, manufacturer, shipowner and colonist dissolved into the shady mysteries of speculative finance, and instead of the burgher-entrepreneurs of the Frans Hals gild paintings we have the powder, wig and French manners of the *rentiers* of Cornelis Troost.[2] Clearly this will not do. Like most of the sharply drawn categories of our older history, its satisfyingly neat chronology must yield to statistics and become more blurred and more complex. It will be convenient to summarize the findings of recent studies in regard to seaborne trade, industry and finance.[3]

The aggregate volume of Dutch foreign trade is as difficult to assess accurately from the returns of taxes levied on it as is the equivalent volume of English trade from the English customs returns. There was, for example, a general revision of the tariff system in 1725, the effects of which are difficult to calculate. Comparison of yields before and after this revision raises a number of problems. Nevertheless it can be stated with reasonable confidence that there was, until the effects of the American War of Independence were felt in the 1780s, little falling off in the *aggregate* volume of Dutch trade, and it is possible that the 'invisible' income from the carrying trade may have been larger than might be thought from the somewhat reduced numbers of ships entering Dutch ports.[4] All the same, there were substantial changes in the composition of the Dutch trade as a whole, and

[1] Van Dillen, *op. cit.*, Ch. X. Also 'The Economic Decline of the Netherlands', *Economic History Review*, IX (1939), reprinted in *Essays in Economic History* (ed. Carus-Wilson), London, 1954.

[2] See the excellent chapter on Troost in Sacheverell Sitwell's *The Netherlands* (undated, London).

[3] The fullest and most recent study is J. de Vries *De Economische Achteruitgang der Republiek in de Achttiende Eeuw* (Amsterdam, 1959).

[4] The ships were larger than before. See Van Dillen, *op. cit.*, p. 316.

these proceeded from two main courses, the one, as it were natural, and the other artificial.

The average volume of the Amsterdam grain trade was certainly smaller in the eighteenth century than in the seventeenth. This trade in bulk cargoes in and out of the Baltic was the 'mother-trade' of the Dutch and it was no accident that it had grown up when it had in the late sixteenth and early seventeenth centuries. This was the time when west and southern Europe stood in most need of foreign grain. Dr van Dillen has shown that the best years thereafter – 1649, 1668, 1699, 1709, 1740–1 – were years when harvests failed in west or southern Europe and the victims once again needed grain imports. In general, however, the demand for Baltic grain seems to have become less, presumably because local production was coming more into balance with local needs as farming became more intensive and more efficient. The other Baltic trades in timber and naval stores were less affected and continued prosperous into the mid-eighteenth century.[1]

This decline of a main generative source of national income, employment and profits was attributed by contemporaries and later observers, wrongly as it now appears, to foreign – principally English – competition for trade in the Baltic. There were other branches of trade where the belief that the Dutch economy was being severely affected by foreign rivals was better founded. Whenever political power strongly affected the conditions of trade, the Dutch were not well placed to counter the aggressive economic nationalism of Britain and France, backed as it was by military, diplomatic and – above all – naval power. Thus in the second half of the seventeenth century, the English were beginning to compete vigorously in the Russia trade, the Spanish trade and the Levant trade.

It was in the new colonial trades that the pressure from the growing modern states of Europe was most severe. From the 1620s, when depression had struck England's export trades hard, the demand grew for protection against the competition of Dutch manufacturers and for measures to prevent the Dutch obtaining English raw materials, wool especially, for their own industries. Raw material controls thereafter made their

[1] See also A. E. Christensen, *Dutch Trade to the Baltic about 1600* (The Hague, 1941), esp. Ch. IX.

appearance at frequent intervals down to the Napoleonic Wars and certainly embarrassed the Dutch. In 1651 a combination of interests that included the great English importing companies – the East India, Eastland and Levant Companies primarily – and the shipping interests, secured the passing of the first Navigation Act. The policy of excluding the Dutch from large areas of the import trade into England and from the right to share in the carrying trade for England and her colonies was reinforced and made more efficient in execution by the Acts of 1660, 1662 and 1663 which composed the so-called 'Old Colonial System' of the Restoration. The naval warfare in the West Indies and off the West African coast, together with the loss of New Amsterdam, further removed from the Dutch valuable footholds from which they had carried on a triangular Atlantic trade in European goods, slaves, and colonial goods.[1]

Again, there was something on the other side of the account. It was after 1680 that the Dutch West Indian trade benefited from the growth of plantations on Surinam, providing a principal source of supply of colonial wares down to the mid-eighteenth century. The years from 1680 to 1740 were also a period of prosperous trade and high dividends for the Dutch East India Company.

French methods for countering a Dutch economic predominance intolerable to the Colbertist mind were different from the English. The first phase of anti-Dutch policy was represented by the new French tariffs of 1664 and 1667: the second by the formation of the great trading companies. 'Commerce', said Colbert, 'is a perpetual and peaceable war of wit and energy amongst the nations'. In 1670 he wrote that France had 'conquered' in this economic warfare everyone except the Dutch, whose resources in the northern, eastern and Spanish trades had kept them going. But the *Grandes Compagnies* were, 'like armies', attacking them everywhere and would soon wear them down. The third phase was represented by the war of 1672–8 against the Dutch, the 'mortal enemies' of France who could (it now transpired) only be conquered by physical, political incorporation in the French kingdom. This attempt, like the English attempt at economic hegemony in their war against the Dutch in 1664, misfired. In the 1720s,

[1] C. H. Wilson, *Profit and Power, cit.*, Ch. IV.

both English and French lobbyists were still lamenting to their respective governments the unfair advantages and unduly large share the Dutch possessed in world trade.[1] All the same, the political, diplomatic and military intervention by governments in the field of trade and shipping and colonization clearly imposed a severe strain on a nation as small in numbers and as poor in native resources as the Dutch. The greatest part of the considerable economic expansion of England in the century after 1660 came from trade with the colonies and from the great re-export trades in sugar, tobacco, calico and other colonial wares which were sent on profitably to Europe. The same was true in the eighteenth century of France. Hence the rise of the great ports like Bordeaux, Nantes, Bristol, Liverpool and Glasgow, which looked towards the Atlantic and were well placed for these trades. Amsterdam remained a large distributing centre for colonial wares and for English cloth, but its function was less vital and more precarious than it had been. London and Hamburg were competing for entrepôt business and everywhere in Europe, buying merchants were making direct contacts with selling merchants. The cloth merchants of Exeter and Tiverton who sold their Devonshire kerseys to Amsterdam in exchange for German linens bleached at Haarlem, sail cloth to fit out the Newfoundland fishing fleet and clover seed for local farmers, were beginning to turn to more direct sources of supply in the early eighteenth century. English business houses were setting up their own agencies in Hamburg. Cloth was being sent directly from Exeter to Spain instead of going via a Dutch middleman. Much of this trade therefore bypassed the Dutch entrepôt, though a proportion – what proportion it is not possible to know – may still have been carried in Dutch ships, yielding freight income, and financed by Dutch credits.[2]

Some adjustment, then, there undoubtedly was in the Dutch trading system as it met the new pressures and frictions of the world struggle for power of the eighteenth century. But against the 6–9 millions of England and the 20 millions of France, the Dutch Republic still had a population of under 2 millions. Its

[1] For this phase of French mercantilism see C. W. Cole, *Colbert and a Century of French Mercantilism*, New York (1939).

[2] See C. H. Wilson, *Anglo-Dutch Commerce and Finance in the 18th Century* (Cambridge, 1941), Part I, *passim*.

local market for consumption was therefore limited, its military and naval commitments imposed a heavy burden of taxation on trade and industry, raising costs and inhibiting supplies. Some trades declined, others expanded, but the aggregate volume seems to have remained about the same. Against the might of England and France, the Dutch could only pit their ingenuity and a determination to exploit to the full those advantages of neutrality which still reaped them a rich harvest in the war of the Austrian Succession and the Seven Years War. In general, however, the great expansion of trade, industry and peoples of the eighteenth century left the Dutch behind. Between 1696 and 1772, for example, the Dutch share in the import trade to England sank from roughly 15 per cent to 4 per cent while that in the export trade for England dropped from 42 per cent to 13 per cent. Measured in terms of money, the volume of this branch of Dutch trade remained about the same.[1]

It is somewhat easier to discern the course of industry. Although the picture in the eighteenth century was not one of unrelieved gloom, there can be no doubt that those industries which drifted into utter ruin – and they numbered all the ones that had played a major role in the seventeenth century economy – outnumbered in importance those which sprang up or continued in reasonable prosperity. Of the great traditional industries, a large part was, in Holland as elsewhere in contemporary Europe, textile manufacturing of one sort or another. The most famous was the great woollen and worsted industry at Leiden and its revival and growth in the period between the 1570s and the 1670s were largely the work of immigrant entrepreneurs and artisans who had fled from the Spanish menace in the southern Netherlands. Their enterprise and skill had turned Leiden into the largest concentration of urban industry in the contemporary world, with the possible exception of Lyons. In 1671, the peak year, Leiden contained 72,000 souls and its industries – bays, says, fustians, camlets, arrasses and woollens proper – turned out 139,000 pieces of cloth. Half a century later, total production was barely half the earlier total and a great part of the worsted production had disappeared altogether. By the mid-century Leiden was a stricken city. By 1796

[1] *Ibid.*, p. 24.

its population was less than half the figure of a century earlier.[1] A similar fate overtook the more widely dispersed silk industry. Based principally in Haarlem, Amsterdam and Utrecht, the silk industry had, like the cloth industry, received a new stimulus from foreign immigrants; in this case the Huguenots, who in the 1680s and 1690s brought new techniques and new designs that gave fresh life to trade. At the beginning of the eighteenth century, the industry was still in good heart, but from the 1730s it declined rapidly. The story of the linen-weaving and bleaching industry at and around Haarlem was much the same. A not inconsiderable share in the export trade in the second half of the seventeenth century consisted of German, French or Flemish linens bleached at Haarlem – a typical example of the Dutch flair for gaining control of the most skilled and most profitable phase of an industry. By the earlier decades of the eighteenth century this trade was falling away and from the 1730s the Haarlem industry slowly sank into decline.

In each case the problem was the same: foreign competition from industries enjoying more favourable natural conditions as well as discriminatory legislation by their own governments. The course of events in the cloth industry makes it plain that Leiden faced, from the early seventeenth century onwards, increasingly severe competition from the English worsted industry, which had the advantage of a protected local wool supply, lower levels of rural wages, and a considerable degree of tariff protection in a substantial home market. The Dutch producers were better placed in the woollen manufacture which depended on a supply of fine Spanish wool. Here they enjoyed the advantages of skilled buying that often stood Holland in good stead, lower rates of interest on borrowed capital, and better and cheaper transport. From the mid-seventeenth century, nevertheless, the Leiden industries as a whole clamoured intermittently, and largely unsuccessfully, for protection against the rivalry of an English industry steadily widening its range of products and techniques. It seems unlikely, however, that protection itself could have given much help, for the home market was relatively small. The blast of competition was felt most sharply in export markets where patterns and costs were

[1] N. W. Posthumus, *De Leidsche Lakenindustrie* (The Hague, 1939), Vol. II and Vol. III, *passim*.

the deciding factors. In both respects the Dutch industries seem to have fallen behind their English competitors. From the late seventeenth century French cloths began to be a factor to be reckoned with, especially in the Levant. Finally, and perhaps most serious, came the new threat from imported Indian textiles.

For the silk industry the principal competition was that of the growing French industry, especially active in world markets after the Peace of Utrecht. The linen bleaching industry faced a much wider circle of competitors, from the cheap products of Silesia to the fine 'lawns' of the Irish industry.

Throughout the textile industries there was a steady loss of production and employment as foreign competitors drew level in technical competence and sometimes surpassed the achievements of Dutch producers. The same was true of other important industries, like shipbuilding, where the technical lead of the seventeenth century was lost in the next, as foreign shipbuilders outstripped those who had been, down to the 1670s, their teachers. The decline of the great shipyards on the Zaan was in turn connected with the decline of the great herring and whale fisheries which provided another melancholy feature of the economic scene. Here too were industries which were basic to the most prosperous phase of the Dutch economy. In the case of the herring industry, foreign competition does not provide the whole answer. The total size of the herring catch in Europe as a whole seems to have declined after the mid-seventeenth century.

Against these losses, in part due to the process of 'natural' changes in consumption, the size and movement of population, harvest yields and the like, and in part to the rise of foreign competition, stimulated and subsidized by 'mercantilist' devices, may be set the continual growth of a group of refining industries – sugar boiling and refining, tobacco sorting and packing, cotton printing, diamond cutting, distilling. Some of these – sugar boiling in particular – called for large investments of capital. It seems doubtful whether they made up more than a part of the loss of employment suffered through the decline of the major industries. They were, in any case, necessarily grouped round the ports – Amsterdam and Rotterdam especially – to which their raw materials came. Hence a drift of population from the older provincial cities to these two great ports.

If the commercial aspects of the Dutch economy were doing little more than holding their own and large sections of industry were in decline, the financial institutions of the country were functioning with remarkable vigour. The growth of such phenomena as speculative bargains in commodities and stocks, commercial banking and a complete mechanism of foreign investment was viewed with deep suspicion by many contemporaries who saw it as a cause of the apparent decline of more virtuous, stable and enduring types of economic activity – a quest for easy profits which could only make the situation of the Republic more precarious and capricious than it already was. This view of the relationship has been adopted by many subsequent writers who have seen in it a satisfactory explanation of the subsequent course of Dutch economic history. In reality, the relationship between the new forms of commercial and public finance and the condition of commerce and industry is more complex than this school of 'moral' critics has assumed.[1]

From the early seventeenth century an increasingly complex set of financial and credit institutions had grown up in the Republic against a background of high consumption and thrift providentially combined. The years 1598 to 1616 saw the foundation of such institutions as the Chamber of Marine Assurance, the East India Company, the Bourse, the Bank of Amsterdam, the Loan Bank and the Grain Bourse. The willingness to use a 'transfer' bank, to invest in the share capital of the great trading ventures to the Dutch, the Mediterranean and the tropics was characteristic of a commercially adventurous society. As time went on it was inevitable that the extended foreign relationships of the entrepôt demanded equally extended credit and exchange facilities. Hence the great business in precious metals conducted by the Bank of Amsterdam which bought metal and coin from those traders and companies whose operations won a surplus, for the benefit of those (like the Baltic traders and East India Company) who were net exporters of bullion. Another natural consequence of the reputa-

[1] J. G. van Dillen's contribution to *Nederland Tussen de Natien*, ed. Banning and Bartstra (Amsterdam 1946), Vol. II, pp. 89–97.

tion of the entrepôt was that it became the centre of a large commission trade based on commodity surpluses which foreign suppliers consigned to this central market place. The commission trade, often regarded as a step down from 'active' trading by contemporaries and later writers, was thus not in truth any such thing. But it was true that it was most sensitive to the fluctuations of international trade.

There was also a considerable element of credit-giving inherent in the commission traders' operations. It was quite general for a commission trader to make forward advances of cash to the foreign owner of goods awaiting sale at Amsterdam during the period while his goods were waiting to be sold. In the Franco-Dutch trade, the Dutch agent selling French silks to the West Indies would advance threequarters of an agreed price to the French merchant and charge interest on his 'loan'. He would then get the highest price he could, pocketing the difference, the interest and his commission fee. Some commission agents abandoned their trading functions to become bankers lending capital to foreign commission traders. From there to full acceptance–credit banking was a short step. The growth of this type of banking was one of the dominant features of the eighteenth century and through it Amsterdam financed a large part of world trade, as London was to do in the next century. Most of the acceptance-credit bankers, including the largest – Pels, Hopes and Cliffords – combined their banking and bill business with trading in commodities and precious metals. And in the provision of these services they had the assistance of the rate of interest, which had fallen from its already low level of 3½ per cent at the end of the seventeenth century to a figure of 2½ per cent.[1]

Along with the development of international banking went an extraordinary growth of foreign investments. Even in the seventeenth century the surpluses of private merchants had been left for local investment in England and elsewhere. In Sweden the government had granted mining and trading concessions to Dutch capitalists, amongst whom the de Geers were the largest, in return for capital loans for war purposes. The Amsterdam firm of Deutz were given a monopoly of the silver mines of Idria in return for a loan to the emperor. In the eighteenth

[1] C. H. Wilson, *Anglo-Dutch Commerce*, Part II, Ch. 3.

century these foreign loans became a more and more prominent feature of Dutch finance. Against a local yield of 2½ per cent, a Dutch investor willing to lend abroad could be sure of 5 per cent or 6 per cent and many did. Dutch investors and underwriters supported loans in a number of European countries. Trips, de Geers, Hopes and Horneca Fizeaux specialized in Scandinavian business. Pels lent to Prussia, Hamburg and other German states, Hopes to Denmark, Bavaria, Prussia, Poland, Spain and France, Cliffords to Danzig, de Smeths to Russia. Much larger than any of these was the business which developed in English securities from the time of the foundation of the Bank of England in 1694 and the issue of the first 'Parliamentary' Annuities. The war finance of these years and the union of Stadholder and King in the person of William III brought out a supply of Dutch money in support of the public credit in England; thereafter the stake of Dutch investors on the Funds remained considerable. Precisely what it was has never been accurately calculated and the obstacles to accurate calculation are such that it may never be. Some contemporary estimates were made. They were almost all too high. Nevertheless, the proportion was high enough to be considered of vital interest by those responsible for public finance in England, especially in time of war. Joshua van Neck (later a baronet and his son a peer for services to the government) was, with a small group of Dutch bankers in London, mainly responsible for tapping the resources of the Dutch investors – widows, orphanages, magistrates, and institutions seeking safe placing for their funds – and his correspondence with the Treasury makes it plain that his services were regarded as of great value. Another powerful connection was established through the great Sephardic Jewish financiers headed by Samson Gideon and Joseph Salvadore whose clients included many of the wealthy families of Portuguese Jewish origin. To facilitate Dutch participation in new loans, and to enable investors to buy and sell holdings in existing loans, a complete mechanism developed between Amsterdam and London. The Dutch investor had his agent, with powers of attorney, in London, who sent him regular advice of prices and probabilities on the money market via the packet boat that plied from Harwick to Helvoetsluys. The agent also collected dividends, and bought and sold stock, according to his principal's directions. The most popular channels of investment were the stocks of the great companies – Bank of England, East India, South Sea, and some of the insurance companies – or the Parliamentary Annuities.

These became also the subject of brisk speculation on the Amsterdam Bourse, and in Change Alley. Time bargains and speculation on the margin were known in the early seventeenth century and by the time de la Vega wrote his *Confusion de Confusions* in 1688 a speculative market in shares had developed that lacked no device of a modern stock exchange. Here in fact are the origins of the Stock Exchange as the twentieth century knows it.

Thus, alongside the older institutions of trade and industry, there had grown up a complex mechanism of finance, investment, credit, banking, insurance speculation. Some, but not all, of its operations were connected with the finance of active trade that still passed through Amsterdam. Those which were not were thought by the conservatively-minded merchants to promote direct and rival trading relations between former customers of the Dutch entrepôt. How far such direct relationships were inevitable sooner or later is a moot point. Certainly the tendency of economic nationalism in the growing new states was to eliminate the Dutch from their former position in these nascent economies. In establishing new sources of income from the financing of international trade the Dutch were therefore probably making the best of a situation which they could not hope to control. Certainly it seems likely that these financial operations secured the Republic a new and lucrative source of income.

On the other side of the account, it must be admitted that the new financial elements in the economy did not make for greater stability. The dangers were vividly illustrated by the successive crises of 1763 and 1773. The first, which severely shook European confidence in Amsterdam, came after the end of the Seven Years War and four years of Dutch investment and speculation in English war loans. On her side, England had used the services of Dutch banking houses to transmit bills and specie in support of Prussia, to pay her own troops in Hanover. A credit inflation had developed with new mushroom banking houses granting credits in the form of unsecured finance bills. When the peace was signed, bankers and merchants who had borrowed from each other by chains of bills were unable to meet their obligations and a crop of bankruptcies followed. The most sensational was that of Neufvilles, a relatively new firm, which had been involved in some shady dealings and which failed for 9½ million guilders. From August to November 1763 Amsterdam was paralysed by the depression that followed the Neufville bankruptcy.

This first crisis was the result of unsound methods on the part of the finance houses, perhaps also the excessive outflow of Dutch capital into foreign investments. London, having given steadying support in the crisis, emerged with enhanced reputation, and extended her influence into financial areas, e.g. Russia, where Amsterdam had previously had a monopoly of exchange business.

The crisis of 1773 was somewhat different. It involved some of the large bill-broking houses – Cliffords, especially, which had kept clear of the previous débâcle. The immediate cause of the crisis was the failure of an Aberdeen speculator, Alexander Fordyce, who had close relations with a group of financiers in Amsterdam. Precisely what his relations with Cliffords were is not clear, but late in 1772 Cliffords were involved, together with several other large houses, in an attempt to corner the market in English East India shares. The attempt failed and once again there was a complete collapse of credit on the Amsterdam market. The repercussions were felt throughout 1773 and 1774 and several large houses never recovered. 'The dreadful year 1763 has returned', a merchants' paper wrote, 'but the causes are different and take root in England; the East India Company is the cause . . . our diseased credit is dead, discounting has gone wholly out of fashion, a loan cannot be had except on double security.' Not a merchant in Amsterdam, it added, could raise 50,000 guilders in cash, and many were £700,000 or £800,000 in debt.[1]

The effects of these crises are difficult to assess. They did not in themselves precipitate any further decline in Holland's foreign trade. The northern trades remained substantial, and the West Indian trade in particular improved in the later 1770s. The American War of Independence brought the usual wind-

[1] *Ibid.*, Ch. VI.

fall of profits for the neutral and St Eustatius carried on a lively and remunerative smuggling trade. The older generation did not, however, cease to contemplate uneasily the damage the credit of the city had suffered by reason of the wave of speculation. They inveighed continually against those who 'carried their offices in their hands and pockets' and lived on dry bread and idle fancy, recalling the good old days when the Zwaanenburger Straat, where the grass was now growing, was strewn with casks and bales of merchandise.[1]

The inference was not, so far as the statistics go, warranted, except possibly in the very short term. But it is likely that these speculative crises, in conjunction with the lessened relative importance of Amsterdam in world commodity markets, may have hastened the transfer of some of its custom in financial matters to London. The combination of credit inflation, speculation and share pushing in foreign loans by private banking houses had shown up the dangerous potentialities of the now more financially-biased economy. Nor was there (as there was in London) a central bank to bring stability in times of crisis.

All the same, those dangers and omens must not be exaggerated. The worst dangers were still largely potential in 1780. It was the quarrel with England over neutral rights in that year which inaugurated a series of disastrous decisions – the war against England, the support for the American colonies, the transfer of Dutch capital from the English Funds into French and American investments. Finally came the revolutionary wars when Holland felt the full force of British blockade. In 1805 it was said that half the population of Amsterdam was on the poor rate. Holland emerged from the wars with her colonial empire largely intact. She was to benefit greatly from the fact of her position between Britain and the rising powers of America and Europe and was ultimately to enjoy a renaissance of trade and industry. But the reshaping of the economy was to take time, and in the meantime the Dutch people were to suffer some lean years.

The 'moral' view of Dutch decline – that economic virtue in some way went out of her merchants, that the search for speculative gains and easy profits replaced the hard work and unceasing enterprise of earlier days – has been referred to.

[1] *Ibid.*

Another viewpoint is possible. More recent observers have suggested that the change in the condition of the Dutch economy was merely the necessary consequence of structural changes in the economic life of Europe. It is suggested that the efflorescence of the seventeenth century was possible for this small nation, poor in natural resources, only because *external* conditions were peculiarly favourable – in practical terms, because other states were preoccupied with wars or internal political troubles. If this be accepted, then the course of events in the eighteenth century was merely a natural adjustment to normality when Holland resumed a position in the European hierarchy appropriate to her population, resources and power.[1]

There are the extreme points of historic interpretation. How to choose between them? Plainly the answer must be largely a matter of impressions. The gaps in the evidence are too numerous to warrant more than provisional judgements. Quantitative data are lacking at many points. Most of the necessary measurements, especially as they affect national income and investment, still remain to be done. We can only guess at population trends. Some suggestions can nevertheless be made as to the basic problems facing the Dutch economy in the eighteenth century. Plainly, the major issue of the time was the need to adjust the economy to the changing conditions of the European politico-economic situation. Was the necessary adjustment made? If not, why not? Again, our method must be to look at the problem under the two broad headings of trade and industry.

The merchants and industrialists themselves certainly did not accept the view either that all was well or that nothing could be done. On the contrary, the mid-century saw widespread dissatisfaction with the condition of trade and industry and a crop of proposals for ameliorating and improving the situation. They found their most important and comprehensive analysis in the famous *Propositions* which the Stadholder William IV placed before the States-General in August 1751. The *Propositions* were based on evidence collected from a variety of Dutch business houses and they form a valuable, if not wholly reliable, comment on the Dutch economy of the mid-century. During the preceding quarter century, the document said, the trade of the

[1] J. G. van Dillen (in Banning and Bartstra), *op. cit.*, p. 96–7.

Republic was 'remarkably diminished and in many branches lost'. It stressed especially the loss of the intermediary trades and the establishing of direct trade between former customers of the Dutch entrepôt. Germany was obtaining goods from the north and Mediterranean through Hamburg. Four times as many French colonial exports – sugar, indigo and coffee – were going to Hamburg as to Amsterdam. Northern commodities like hemp and flax were being carried to Mediterranean ports in Spanish, Portuguese and French ships. The Dutch trading houses were disappearing from Spain, Italy and the Levant. And so on. The troubles were ascribed mainly to 'the adopting of our political maxims in trade by foreign powers' – especially by England. The *Propositions* went on to criticize the fiscal policy of the Republic which had saddled Dutch trade with duties much higher than those of Hamburg. (A later writer alleged that they stood in the ratio of 5:1).

On the face of it, the proposals for dealing with the problem were impeccable. The Republic was to become a qualified 'free port'. Goods entering the staple were to be free of duty. Transit traffic in particular was to be allowed and even encouraged by freedom from duty. Raw materials imported for use in industry were to be freed but goods imported for Dutch consumption should be taxed, and competing manufactures should be taxed most heavily of all. This last was (or would have been) a notable concession to industry, although the general undertone of the document was that in any controversy that might arise over the level of duties industry must, as the lesser partner in the economy, give way to trade.

In the event, the *Propositions* came to very little. Significantly, it was recorded that 'a variety of jarring interests did frequently occur'. The moving spirit behind the plan, the Stadholder, died. Then came the Seven Years War, and, as usual, the neutral was presented with favourable opportunities for business with the belligerents. Except for the freeing of the linen trade between Silesia and Spain via Holland from duties in 1752, little else occurred. For this failure there were many reasons, some of them perhaps inherent in the structure of the Dutch economy itself. More immediately responsible than the general deadlock of opinion was the strenuous opposition of the Admiralty authorities who saw their largest sources of income threatened by the proposed reduction in taxes. Thus economic reform was defeated in large measure by the rigidity of the fiscal system itself.[1]

This failure of the attempt at reform may well have damaged such chances as did exist for the Republic to gain a larger share of the expanding volume of world trade. They almost certainly damaged the chances that Dutch industry would revive and have fresh life breathed into it.

It is fairly evident that Dutch industries had suffered from three general difficulties, of which lack of tariff protection was probably the least. The textile industries in particular had been built up largely as export business and they would have gained little benefit from the protection of a home market which provided only a fraction of demand. More serious was the cost of raw materials, mainly imported from abroad. In the earlier period, the Dutch manufacturer (it is reasonable to suppose) had gained by reason of those low freight rates and that comparatively low price of money which were jointly the marvel and despair of Holland's European competitors. As the competing economies developed in the second half of the seventeenth century, the technological lead of the Dutch in shipbuilding and ship management shortened. The rate of interest in England dropped. Capital became more plentiful in other countries – some of it Dutch capital. The specific advantages once enjoyed therefore disappeared. There was now nothing to offset the third disadvantage to which reformers and industrialists alike pointed: the high level of wages. In cotton printing, linen bleaching and the cloth industry, high labour costs were blamed by contemporaries for the decline of the competitive force of these industries and recent students have confirmed their criticisms. The price of labour had increased as the duties on everyday necessities increased. Labour was sufficiently well organized to force higher wages to meet the increased prices of basic food which sprang largely from the high excise duties. Finally the strength of the guilder in relation to other European currencies deprived Dutch export industries of any chance of benefiting from a devaluation.

There was no lack of attempts to get industries going in the years after the failure of the *Propositions*. In the frustration of the

[1] J. G. van Dillen, *op. cit.*, pp. 93–4.

times, with the older utilitarian internationalism dying, younger but not necessarily always better informed minds turned to more parochial solutions for Holland's economic ills. These 'economic-patriots', as they became known, clung to the idea of reviving the old staple market. They denounced with vigour the system of acceptance-credit and commission trade which encouraged foreigners to by-pass the Dutch market. 'A merchant', wrote one of the leading 'economic-patriots', 'should reckon himself unworthy of the name of *patriot* if he charters his ships to Hamburg, Ostend or elsewhere to the damage of our own trade and shipping'.[1] This patriotic, if unrealistic, vision of commercial revival was accompanied by ideas of industrial development. Too much capital had been exported that might have gone into the development of local industry and agriculture. In a way that recalls the English workhouses and spinning schools of the earlier eighteenth century, the 'economic-patriots' conceived the idea of subsidizing special industries for the unemployed and destitute children, instead of merely paying out doles and poor relief. Many of these spinning schools and textile mills were set up in the '70s and '80s. Zwolle, Haarlem, Zutphen, Monnikendam, the Hague, Amersfoort and other cities all had installations, some on a considerable scale, that were the joint effort of philanthropists, poor relief administrators, municipalities and businessmen. One of the most ambitious was at Hoorn where in 1777 the local pastor tried to revive the drooping fortunes of the old West Friesian port by setting up a general commercial and shipping association. It established a textile mill and fitted out a whaling ship. Enkhuizen followed suit in 1780 with a similar association and an 'Economic Workhouse'.[2]

Like their English counterparts, to which one suspects that they owed their inspiration, these philanthropic experiments in industry came to very little, though they may have helped to create a certain amount of temporary employment in a difficult period. In part, their failure was due, as in England, to intractable problems of organization. The idea of organizing hand workers was, in any case, rapidly becoming old-fashioned. But this was not the whole trouble. When the Leiden manufacturer, van Heukelom, set up a cotton mill near

[1] *Ibid.*, p. 94.
[2] *Ibid.*

Utrecht in 1780, using Arkwright's water frame, this too fell on evil days.

The failure of the new industries may have been due, like the demise of the old, to high costs of production. Certainly there can be little doubt that industry bore a heavy burden in the shape of taxation that raised material costs and wages, and that this may in turn be traced back to the cost of defence (and especially naval expenditure) which had to be sustained by a population only perhaps a quarter of the size of that of Holland's principal competitor, England. One is left with the feeling, all the same, that this is not quite the whole truth. Neither material conditions nor the climate of opinion was really favourable to industrial growth. That very coincidence of interests between business and government in which seventeenth-century observers had discerned Holland's peculiar strength and advantage in her time of growth now became a source of weakness in her time of decline. For whereas many saw that reform and renewal of the economy were necessary, none saw the way the world was about to go. Even the proposals of those who wanted to strengthen the element of industry in the economy have an old-fashioned air about them. Most did not even reach as far as that. They looked back nostalgically to the golden age of commerce, hoping against hope for a revival. Statesmen and businessmen alike refused to abandon the hope that the entrepôt might regain its ancient glory and a writer as late as 1824 could remark that the Dutch economy rested on more secure foundations than the British because its trade consisted only to a small extent of industrial products, while 70 per cent of English exports came from factories, which rendered English trade unsteady and changeable.

Such adjustment of the economy as may have taken place to accommodate it to changing world conditions did not relate so much to trade and industry as to finance. Although statistics are lacking, such evidence as exists points to a shift away from the harder competition and falling profits of active trade and industry towards banking, discounting, acceptance-credit, insurance, foreign investment and the like. Certainly the growth of acceptance-credit was largely an eighteenth century phenomenon. The records of private firms and individuals, scrappy though they are, point in the same direction. Just after the mid-century Hopes were signing 89 charter contracts in a year. Twenty years later the figure was 22. In the same period their turnover of bills rose from 800 to 2,159.[1] The evolution of the business of David Leeuw of Amsterdam pointed the same moral. In 1719 Leeuw was a prosperous merchant engaged in trade with England. He imported Devonshire cloths and exported German linens bleached at Haarlem, speculating in colonial goods on the side. In the next thirty-four years he slowly withdrew his capital from active trade, steadily building up thereby a portfolio of some £40,000 in the English Funds – divided between Bank of England stock and Parliamentary Annuities. Why did Leeuw decide to turn *rentier*? Because the opportunities for profitable investment were dwindling? Because he had surplus profits which were not needed to capitalize a business already adequately supplied with funds? Or was he merely an old man preparing for retirement? It is impossible to be sure.[2] His circumstances were individual, but there were thousands of others who followed suit. As the reputation of the English Funds for security grew, Dutch investors were increasingly attracted to them, both for their steady yield of an income larger and easier than they could obtain by investment at home and by the possibilities of capital gains if they chose to speculate. It was only reasonable that the opportunity to earn yields that were safe, favourable and easy should have attracted capital away from local but more difficult ventures. There was, undoubtedly, a considerable expansion of Dutch foreign investment in the course of the eighteenth century. This situation was accurately appreciated in the borrowing centres, where it was realized that the terms of loans to be floated successfully must be such as to appeal to Dutch investors in comparison with alternative opportunities for investment. 'It may be necessary to say', wrote Antony Chamier, the English Under-Secretary of War in 1761, to the Duke of Newcastle, 'that I consider ampler terms as essentially requisite to be given at this time, as it is evident by the decrease of specie in the kingdom that foreign money must come in aid of the large sum wanted. . . . They [the Dutch] will therefore withdraw large sums from their trade,

[1] E. E. de Jong-Keesing. *De Economische Crisis van 1763 te Amsterdam* (Amsterdam, 1939), p. 216.

[2] Wilson, *Anglo-Dutch Commerce*, pp. 118–36.

that can never yield them a profit equal to that that is to be made in our Funds.'[1]

This makes it clear that at any rate in Chamier's calculations (and he was well informed) a significant proportion of available capital funds in Holland was held in forms so mobile as to be switched from trade to foreign investment at very short notice. This may provide a clue to the paradox of an economy 'in decline' that could yet spare a significant proportion of its savings for overseas investment. As the earnings from 'invisible' exports rose – and rise they must have done – earnings became available in foreign currencies for profitable investment. At the same time, it is reasonable to suppose that the decline of Dutch industries such as cloth, linen, silk, and shipbuilding was reducing the need for expensive raw material imports into Holland. There was therefore presumably a saving on the balance of payments, even though it was a saving gained at the expense of local employment. Such an explanation can only be hypothetical but it seems to accord with such of the facts as we know and with the convictions of the 'economic-patriots' that the amount of foreign investment was excessive and at the expense of social welfare. In short, Dutch foreign investment in the eighteenth century represents a voluntary 'diminution of imports' (in C. K. Hobson's phrase). It was therefore in contrast to that considerable proportion of British capital export in the next century which represented an arrangement for financing the sale of British manufactures to foreign countries that lacked the cash to pay for them.

The situation of the Republic in the second half of the eighteenth century was thus not catastrophic, save for the spectacular but temporary crises of financial panic or war. The most recent investigator summarizes it in these terms: industry and the fisheries declined unmistakably, finance and agriculture increased, while commerce remained at approximately its old level. If allowance is made for the probable increase of population, it seems doubtful whether the increase in national income was adequate to avoid a fall in general welfare.[2] But over the longer span of time this represented the unresolved, perhaps in human terms unresolvable, dilemma of a small and far from

[1] *Ibid.*, p. 165.
[2] De Vries, *op. cit.*, p. 167, and Ch. VII, *passim*.

well-endowed people which had, by an earlier opportunism of genius, created a position for itself higher than was warranted in terms of crude power, and was now overtaken by the nemesis of normality. Theoretically, rationally, in the wisdom of hindsight, the Republic should have decided either for full free trade or for a policy of economic protection. The first might have improved its competitive power *vis-à-vis* Hamburg and London, the second might have afforded a better chance to the industrial experiments of innovators like van Heukelom. And if it be objected that the traditions of the Republic were unfavourable to industrial development, it might be answered that this had not always been so and was not to be so in later times. But the question is, in any event, speculative and hypothetical. In reality, the Republic chose neither course: in the manner of human societies, it stumbled on without making any decision at all, and thereby probably got the worst of both worlds. To speak of material collapse is to exaggerate. To speak of 'spiritual' or 'moral' collapse is to exaggerate grossly. The eighteenth century Republic had its achievements – aesthetic, philosophical, scientific – and they should not be underrated. But it would be foolish to pretend that they can be compared with the age of Rembrandt, Grotius and Spinoza. We must leave it that national 'greatness', whether economic, political or cultural, has in it an indefinable element of mystery. To measure it, as to say whence it came or why it faded, calls for the use of imagination as well as statistics.

3

Treasure and Trade Balances: The Mercantilist Problem[1]

When the late Lord Keynes came to write his *Notes on Mercantilism* some thirteen years ago,[2] he felt bound to conclude that the Classical School of economists had been unfair to those writers who for two hundred years had seen 'a peculiar advantage' to their nations in a favourable balance of trade. '. . . we, the faculty of economists', he wrote, 'prove to have been guilty of presumptuous error in treating as a puerile obsession what for centuries has been a prime object of practical statecraft.'[3] His argument, put briefly, ran as follows. The only practical inducement to investment (and therefore to the fuller exploitation of the economic resources of the nation) in the period in question was a reduced rate of interest. That, in turn, depended on increasing the quantity of precious metals in a particular country, which in turn depended on a favourable balance of trade. Lord Keynes was, of course, primarily interested in his inquiries in the relationship between state policy and employment. What he examined was an important aspect of mercantilist thought, though it is doubtful whether it was the most immediate one to those who wrote on these matters in the seventeenth and eighteenth centuries. Re-reading the works of the mercantilists, one cannot avoid an uneasy feeling that employment was seen as a means to increasing bullion supplies rather than vice versa.

[1] This paper was first published in the *Economic History Review*, Second Series, Vol. II, No. 2 (1949), pp. 152–61.

[2] J. M. Keynes, *The General Theory of Employment, Interest and Money* (1936), ch. 23, p. 333.

[3] *Ibid.*, p. 339.

At the same time, others were working on the broader aspects of mercantilism in greater detail. Professor Heckscher's work had appeared in English translation a year or so earlier, and had done much to modify the older view that mercantilist arguments were based – as Lord Keynes put it – 'from start to finish, on an intellectual confusion'.[1] On the particular aspect of mercantilism with which this note is concerned, and which is generally agreed to be of central importance to the whole argument – the importance of precious metals – Professor Heckscher was less satisfied than Lord Keynes with mercantilist logic. In particular he pointed out that little interest was shown in contemporary literature in the practical use of the precious metals, 'i.e. with regard to their final export'.[2] It is the object of this note to suggest that nevertheless they were indispensable practical uses to which precious metals were put in international trade in the mercantilist period, that these uses were sufficiently well known to practical men of trade and government, that they were more or less taken for granted, and that they do in fact form an assumption, largely unspoken and far from clearly stated, in much contemporary discussion. As Professor Clark has remarked,[3] 'the explanation of the mercantilist attitude seems to lie in the commercial conditions of the time, and especially in the needs of traders for capital in a solid and ponderable form'. This argument can be reinforced by reference to such figures and facts as are available concerning the structure and composition of Britain's overseas trade in the period. We have been warned, and rightly so, of the inadequacies of the so-called 'statistics' of trade and the warnings must be heeded.[4] Nevertheless, on certain points relevant to this inquiry, the evidence is so unanimous and the margins so wide that certain basic facts can perhaps be established. We may take Thomas Mun as the starting-point in the inquiry. Chapter IV of *England's Treasure by Foreign Trade*[5] is entitled 'The Exportation of our Moneys in Trade of Merchandize is a means to encrease

[1] *Ibid.*, p. 334. Lord Keynes's conclusions were largely based on evidence provided by Professor Heckscher's study.

[2] E. Heckscher, *Mercantilism* (1935), II, 215.

[3] G. N. Clark, *The Seventeenth Century* (Oxford, 1947), p. 27.

[4] G. N. Clark, *Guide to English Commercial Statistics, 1696–1782* (RHS 1938), pp. 33–42.

[5] Blackwell edition, 1933.

our Treasure'. One of the two prime examples he quotes is the East Indies trade and the facts are too well known to call for more than a brief recitation. The nature of this trade was such that the vent of available exports was insufficient to pay for the quantity of goods available for return. Export of goods therefore must be supplemented by export of bullion, and the answer to criticism of the policy was that re-export brought in more bullion than was needed for the initial process of 'lubrication'.[1] What has received less notice is Mun's inclusion in the same paragraph of a similar case from the Eastland trade.

For I suppose [he writes] that 100,000 *l.* being sent in our Shipping to the East Countreys, will buy there one hundred thousand quarters of wheat clear aboard the Ships, which being after brought into *England* and housed, to export the same at the best time for rent thereof in *Spain* or *Italy*, it cannot yield less in those parts than two hundred thousand pounds to make the Merchant but a saver, yet by this reckning wee see the Kingdom hath doubled that Treasure.[2]

We need not take Mun's word alone in this matter. The difficulties of the Baltic trade were notorious to all seventeenth-century traders. They were especially acute for the English who, whether they were trading to the Arctic or to the tropics, to civilized or to primitive communities, had virtually only one great export commodity to offer – cloth. Even the Dutch had the same problem of balancing their own trade to the Baltic. Their control of the North Sea fisheries, their grip on the Biscay salt trade and their range of colonial commodities might well have seemed to give them the key to world trade, but it was still difficult to find trading cargoes sufficient to pay for their Baltic purchases – largely grain and timber – and there is little doubt that the Baltic was the drain down which disappeared much of the American silver which Spain mortgaged to Amsterdam for Dutch imports. The ultimate destination of much of the contents of the Silver Fleets was the Sound.[3] Dutch dollars were a familiar currency in the Scandinavian and Baltic areas and 'very much esteemed'.[4] At the time Mun was writing, there was probably much to be said for the contention implied in his example that

[1] *Ibid.*, pp. 15–16.
[2] *Ibid.*, p. 15.
[3] See A. E. Christensen, *Dutch Trade to the Baltic about 1600* (Copenhagen, 1941), pp. 367 and 428.
[4] P. D. Huet, *Memoirs of the Dutch Trade (1700)* (Amsterdam, 1718), p. 50.

bullion export to the Baltic could be justified along the same lines as bullion export to the East Indies – as a sprat to catch a mackerel. But there was an awkward catch in the argument. The Baltic trade was not a smooth or regular business. Baltic imports – grains, timber, iron and copper – were apt to be matters of emergency. It was an old story. Dearth was one problem: '. . . if we should have great scarcity of corn within the realm. . . . Then our commodities were in a notable scarcity to counter-value it . . .', wrote the author of the *Discourse of the Commonweal*. The reference can scarcely be to anything but imports from the Baltic, and under these conditions, re-export to recoup losses of bullion was, in the nature of things, out of the question. There was the other emergency – war. From the sixteenth to the nineteenth century, the demands of the navy might call for imports of timber for purely home consumption: and from the sixteenth to the eighteenth century import of Swedish iron for ordnance was a familiar necessity. The query of the *Discourse* must have been repeated by a long line of succeeding generations of men concerned with matters of national defence. '. . . if both war and dearth should come together . . . how should we do? Surely we should be in a very hard case, and much in danger of strangers.'

Now by the time Mun's work was printed in 1664[1] (almost certainly as part of the deliberate propaganda campaign against the Dutch which preceded the outbreak of war in 1665) some changes had overtaken the Baltic trade. Dearth was less a danger, war a greater one. With the agricultural expansion, grain imports were less likely, but the imports of timber and naval stores had become a vital necessity. From Danzig, Riga and Memel came the bulk of the naval timber and masts – oak and fir. From St Petersburg came fir, from Stettin oak. Norway contributed spruce spars and fir timber, while mast fleets came regularly from Gothenburg.[2] These were the main areas, and in the ports the 'factories' or 'colleges' of British agents fought for commercial supremacy with their Dutch rivals. The strategic importance of the Baltic trade was unquestioned: control of the Baltic – *dominium Maris Baltici* – was a prime issue in the Dutch

[1] It was of course written more than thirty years earlier.

[2] See the account in R. G. Albion, *Forests and Sea Power, 1652–1862* (Harvard, 1926), ch. IV.

wars. The standing danger was that Denmark and the control of the Danish Sound would pass to the Dutch. 'If they can shut us out of the Baltic Sea, and make themselves masters of that, where is your trade? Where are the materials to preserve your shipping? Where will you be able to challenge any right by sea or justify yourselves against a foreign invasion on your own soil?' Cromwell's questions to Parliament in 1659 were not mere rhetoric: they were founded on a shrewd appreciation of a very dangerous strategic situation. Mr Albion has shown the perils which followed from the interruptions of the Baltic supply line in the seventeenth century[1], and the anxiety with which Pepys at the Admiralty followed the fortunes of the Gothenburg fleet during the Second Anglo-Dutch War.

This situation helps to explain the strenuous but largely unsuccessful efforts to provide an alternative source of supply of timber from the North American colonies. The policy of obtaining pitch and tar from North America was apparently somewhat more successful.[2] But the Baltic remained the Achilles heel of British strategy, the one area where a trade vital to British defence was wide open to foreign attack. With the shift of the principal menace from the Low Countries to France, the danger abated somewhat, and all through the eighteenth century the Navy drew an ever increasing supply of naval materials from the Baltic.[3]

The strategic disadvantage of the Baltic situation should not be allowed, however, to obscure the peculiar economic difficulties of trade in the Baltic area. Mun's argument about re-export wore thin when the Baltic trade came to consist almost solely of naval materials. Observers were not lacking to pour disapproval on a branch of trade where imports regularly exceeded exports. In his *Trade and Navigation England Considered* Gee wrote:

Norway and Denmark take from England guineas, crown pieces and bullion, a little tobacco, and a few coarse woolens of small value.

England takes from Norway and Denmark vast quantities of deal boards, timber, spars and iron; we pay them a very great balance

[1] *Ibid.*, ch. v.

[2] See the 'Essay' attributed to Oxenford in Clark, *Guide to English Commercial Statistics*, p. 131.

[3] Albion, *op. cit.*, p. 160.

which is greatly increased by the late establishment of ships in the navigation and freight of their timber.[1]

When an inquiry was ordered into the Accounts of the Inspector-General of Imports and Exports, the situation was hardly reassuring. On the basis of the years 1696–9, the entire Baltic area was found to figure in the list of trades where the value of imports normally exceeded exports. Denmark and Norway showed deficits of £93,637; the East Country a deficit of £149,940; Russia £176,373; Sweden £506,677.[2] Culliford, the Inspector-General, himself pointed out that 'Upon the several trades of Sweden, Denmark and Norway, East Country and Russia, the excess is very much on the importation side (which is a demonstration these trades are less profitable to us) and the same may reasonably be supposed to arise from their clandestine carrying away of our milled money instead of our manufactures.' (The export of bullion was of course taken for granted.) The trouble was accentuated, as Gee pointed out, by the fact that a great deal of the trade was carried in foreign bottoms. In the Norwegian trade, for example, 'from Michaelmas 1691 to Michaelmas 1696, there were entered on the Customs House at London 1070 foreign ships from those parts and but thirty-nine English'.[3] The drain resulting from payments for these freight charges to foreign shipowners was clearly recognized from the time of the Navigation Acts onwards.

The result of these disturbing revelations was a recommendation by the Board of Trade that England should be rendered less dependent on the Baltic by turning to Ireland and New England, but the solution was not easy; throughout the eighteenth century, the visible adverse balance of trade with the Baltic remained an intractable problem, and when Oxenford came to write his *Essay* in 1723 he stated that in the reign of Charles II 'as well as ever since, we paid a considerable balance to our sugar and tobacco plantations, to Denmark and Sweden, Russia and the East Country . . .' and went on to inquire pertinently '. . . and from what country then were we repaid these several ballances?'[4]

[1] *Ibid.*, p. 159.
[2] House of Lords MSS. (n.s.), IV, 430–6, 455–7.
[3] Quoted by Albion, *op. cit.*, p. 159.
[4] Clark, *Guide*, p. 122.

The mercantilist argument did not rest only on the peculiar characteristics of these 'difficult' trades. It was also rooted in the views of individual merchants about the requirements of their business. Trading capital *in money* was regarded as an indispensable link in the exchange of goods. The bill of exchange, even in the limited uses permitted by the circumstances of international trade, was conceived as a substitute for coin rather than as a clearing mechanism. For a long time merchants held coined money in higher esteem than pieces of paper which might be (and were) subject to abuse by unsound speculation. In the age of 'Leviathan' it was not unnatural that the analogy should be carried into the whole sphere of political economy.[1] There seemed to be no more reason to dispute the fact that a state with bullion reserves was better off than one without than there was to dispute the fact that a man with a sovereign in his pocket was better off than a man without.

This examination seems to suggest that throughout the period commonly described as 'mercantilist' there were two main branches of trade – the East Indies and the Baltic – where bullion export was a permanent, though an unpleasant necessity. (There were others such as the Irish, Turkish, Italian and some of the Plantation trades where the argument applied, though with less force.) In the first area the trade was defended on the grounds of its ultimate greater profitability through re-export. But the Baltic trade could be defended on no such principle. The defence had to be conducted on the ground of sheer hard strategic necessity. Now given the basic assumption of the mercantilists – and it remained substantially unchallenged from at any rate the time of Mun to the time of Oxenford (roughly a century) – that a visible trade deficit could only be covered by an export of coin or bullion, certain conclusions followed as a matter of course. Overseas trade divided into two types: those in which exports exceeded imports and those in which imports exceeded exports. Clearly the former had to carry the latter. It was therefore necessary to increase to the maximum the yield of precious metal which could be squeezed from the favourable trades in order to provide the bullion or coin necessary to finance the unfavourable. In the Eastern trade the need was for a flow of cash to bridge the gap between purchase and sale – a

[1] Christensen, *op. cit.*, pp. 399–400. See also Heckscher, *op. cit.*, II, 217 ff.

kind of working capital: in the Baltic, it was to provide cash for purchases without which national security was imperilled. And evidently the necessity was held to excuse the unpalatable fact that the transaction was, from any short term or purely economic point of view, a dead loss. Fortunately for the imperial future, the seventeenth and eighteenth centuries did not believe in purely economic points of view.

Given this natural anxiety about trade in those areas which today would no doubt be designated as 'hard currency' areas, the line of argument which followed was a fairly obvious one. Mun had outlined it, in 1702 Brewster was still enlarging on it, and when Oxenford reviewed the position in retrospect he concluded that in the reign of Charles II the nation had lived beyond its means. 'It was the unrestrained liberty in that reign of everyone to consume foreign as well as Empire manufactures which prevented any ballance comeing to England.' Indeed, it was clear to him that the bullion necessary to finance the 'hard currency' areas trade must have been borrowed from strangers (which can only mean the Dutch). All this has a familar ring. If the Baltic and other deficits were an unavoidable necessity, could unnecessary imports from other areas be reduced? Were, for example, wine, or gold and silver lace, really necessary to the national well-being? What could be done to improve the state of Ireland's trade and the deplorable idleness of that nation? Finally, and in general, how could exports which earned favourable balances be increased? Such was, for example, Brewster's thesis: 'That the full employment of all Hands in the Nation, is the surest way and Means to bring BULLION into the kingdom.'[1] Modern as this may sound it was not the policy of full employment in the modern sense so much as an intermediate stage in a policy which balanced social welfare in the same scales as national defence. Similar considerations had lain behind the seventeenth-century attempts to wrest control of the herring fisheries and the colonial trades from the Dutch. There was shrewdness as well as jealousy in Sir George Downing's observation that 'The herring trade is the cause of the salt trade and the herring and salt trade was the causes of that country (i.e. Holland) having, in a manner, wholly engrossed the trade of the Baltic Sea. . . .' The Baltic countries might

[1] F. Brewster, *New Essays on Trade* (London, 1702), p. 45.

not be good customers for cloth: they were usually ready to take fish.

Always bearing the 'hard currency' areas in mind, the mercantilists turned to another aspect of the problem. The appointment of the first Inspector-General of Imports and Exports proceeded from consideration of 'the Great usefulness of Keeping a Distinct account of the Importation and Exportation of all Commodities into and out of this Kingdom; and to and from what places the same are Exported or Imported, *in Order to make a Ballance of the Trade between this Kingdome and any other part of the world* . . .'.[1] The last phrase has been italicized because it is important to note that the idea of individual areas of trade with individual balances, favourable or unfavourable, was carefully preserved. Like their descendants in the 1940s, the mercantilists had more reason than the classical economists to know that overall trade balances are not always a satisfactory answer to the problem of international payments; to know that an account of a nation's trade which *in toto* shows a favourable balance may yet contain within itself hard cores of individually unbalanceable trades. The solution to the problem lay then, as now, in the formation of a system of multilateral payments, but that entailed an international credit and currency structure which was unthinkable to seventeenth-century Englishmen. Until that became practicable, a store of precious metals remained the principal and often the only link between a series of channels of trade each of which was essentially bilateral. If the link was missing, imports from any area of trade might well be limited to an amount which could be paid for by direct export of commodities.

Nor was this the only reason for looking askance at the overall trade figures revealed by the Inspector-General's inquiries. When Brewster came to examine the figures for exports and imports from Michaelmas 1697 to Michaelmas 1698[2] he found that the balance stood as follows:

Exports	£6,361,108.	10*s.*	7*d.*
Imports	£4,732,360.	5*s.*	6*d.*

The favourable balance on visible trade thus came to £1,628,748. 5*s.* 1*d.* and, as Brewster very reasonably observed

[1] Clark, *op. cit.*, p. 3.

[2] Brewster, *op. cit.*, p. 29.

'... if it did, this kingdom would be like *Solomon's*, have Silver as plenty as the stones of the Street'. But he was not so easily deceived. The question of real (as distinct from official) values he ignores. He does, however, note the effects of smuggling, and, more important, he raises the question of foreign borrowings. Rejecting the notions of those who regarded *Foreign Money in our Publick Funds* as clear gain, he points out that these foreign proprietors had to receive interest on their money. 'But suppose here may be', he continues, 'but *five* or *six* Millions of Foreign Money, when *that* and the *interest* is carried *out* of the kingdom, it will make a great hole in our 12 Millions.' (His estimate of the money in the kingdom.)

Brewster may have exaggerated the amount of English borrowings from abroad but he was quite correct in drawing attention to the facts. Throughout the war, the government was borrowing fairly extensively from Dutch lenders on the security of malt tickets, salt tallies and tallies on impositions. It was the beginning of the Dutch stake in the national debt, which was to grow to considerable proportions in the course of the century.[1] He was probably right also in arguing that these borrowings brought in no bullion. For most of the expenditure financed in this way went on military charges on the Continent. Government expenditure abroad was another item which (just as today) had to be borne in mind as a debit against the visible trade balance. Most interesting of all, Brewster quotes Baltic purchases as amongst those financed by foreign borrowing. 'We cannot think', he writes, 'that all our imports (of naval stores) especially from the *Baltick*, are on Englishmens' Accompts.'[2]

It was presumably in answer to this kind of charge that Oxenford[3] wrote the long-winded and obscure, but very important *Essay towards finding the Ballance of our whole Trade Annually from Christmas 1698 to Christmas 1719*.[4] That England had borrowed heavily from the Dutch he admits freely. The procedure was for correspondents to subscribe to 'lotteries, annuities, or other publick funds', paying by bills of exchange.

[1] Brewster, *op. cit.*, p. 22.

[2] I am accepting Professor Clark's suggestion that Oxenford was the author of the 'Essay'. Clark, *op. cit.*, p. 25.

[3] Printed in Clark, *op. cit.*, pp. 69–134.

[4] Charles Wilson, *Anglo-Dutch Commerce and Finance in the eighteenth century* (Camb. Univ. Press, 1941), pp. 88–95.

In this way some £10 million may have been raised. The obligations outstanding for the war he calculates at £14 to £15 million, and he concludes that the difference was met by the overall favourable annual balance which worked out at between half a million and a million.[1] Upon this balance rested one permanent charge – the bullion necessary to 'lubricate' the trade with 'hard currency' areas.

That this much was recognized is quite clear. Smuggling, freight charges, the cost of foreign wars, and the interest charges on money borrowed for those wars, made nonsense of arguments based on the so-called 'statistics' of visible trade. Other 'invisibles' do not appear to have been so clearly recognized. (It would be interesting, for example, to know what the cost of the upkeep of foreign embassies and Company 'factories' abroad amounted to. What, too, was the cost in bullion or foreign currency of the Grand Tours, of gentlemen's purchases of *objets d'art* in Italy or of the residence of Scottish and English Nonconformist students at continental universities?) The balance on visible trade was in better fettle by 1700 than it had been in the dark days of the mid-seventeenth century, when the value of imports was calculated to be almost twice the value of exports,[2] but the margin was throughout the eighteenth century a slender one to bear the burden of all these assorted charges, most of which can never be accurately calculated. It is not really surprising that foreign borrowing continued to be necessary up to the last quarter of the eighteenth century.

All this is evidence that until well into the eighteenth century Britain's financial position remained far more critical than the apparently favourable 'statistics' of visible trade would seem to suggest. It was, above all, the demands of war finance which kept statesmen nervous and maintained a general respect for precious metals. It remained as true in the eighteenth as it had been in the sixteenth century that, as the *Discourse* put it '. . . money is, as it were, a storehouse of any commodity you would have'.[3] Bills of exchange might grow in use, but there

[1] *Ibid.*, pp. 118–19. [2] B.M. Add. MSS. 36785.

[3] The idea is far from dead in the twentieth century. Addressing the TU Congress at Southport on 3 September 1947, Mr Ernest Bevin referred to 'this balance of payments business, and to America's failure to redistribute the Fort Knox gold. 'I am quite sure', he went on, 'that is one of the readiest ways to assist in increasing the purchasing power of the devastated areas of the world.'

were many who, Cobbettwise, preferred the more solid forms of purchasing power – and, on the whole, with good reason.

That the broadly bilateral character did give way to some kind of multilateral system of trade and payments in the eighteenth century seems to be undeniable. Its centre was not yet London but Amsterdam. In the early seventeenth century trade with the Netherlands seems to have been regarded as labouring under some of the disadvantages later attributed to the trade with the Baltic. That at any rate was the opinion in 1618 when the Privy Council was in favour of compelling Dutch merchants to employ their balances to buy British goods under the terms of the Statute of Employment. This, it was held, was the most likely means of redressing the scarcity of coin.[1] More than thirty years later the situation still remained unfavourable and an Amsterdam correspondent could observe: '... your expense for foreign goods is twice as much as the goods you export and this in a few years will drain all your stock and not leave you a penny. We have more English gold in Amsterdam than you have.'[2] That this particular mercantilist nightmare did not materialize may have been due to an increasing willingness amongst Dutch merchants after 1660 to leave their balances invested in London. Goldsmiths and bankers were alleged to have in their charge considerable quantities of Dutch money lent out to other merchants at from 5 to 7 per cent.[3] Here in embryo may be seen the beginnings of a mechanism of international finance which in time was to relieve the pressure on capital in its 'solid' forms. For at the same time there was growing up at Amsterdam a highly organized system for international investment and acceptance-credit which was no less useful to Britain than it was to the continental nations. For example, no exchange rate was quoted between London and St Petersburg until 1763: payments for Anglo-Russian trade were made through Dutch banks.[4] It was common knowledge that a large part of the volume of bills in circulation in Europe issued from Dutch merchant bankers and ran at a commission

[1] A. Friis, *Alderman Cockayne's Project and the Cloth Trade* (1927), p. 215.

[2] *State Papers, Dom. 1651–2.*

[3] Hist. MSS. Comm. Appendix to 8th Report, p. 133.

[4] J. G. van Dillen, 'De Beurscrisis te Amsterdam van 1763', in *Tijdschrift voor Geschiedenis* (1922), p. 253.

of ½ per cent. It would perhaps be permissible to discern the early use of this system from Brewster's remarks about foreign participation in Britain's Baltic purchases. Britain's direct trade with Holland normally showed a large visible favourable balance, and it may well be that this was used as a basis for credit in the unfavourable areas such as the Baltic and the Mediterranean. When this proved insufficient – and war expenses were apt to render it so – resort was had to loans at Amsterdam. The Dutch advanced credit for the maintenance of British forces abroad and took payment in various forms of government stock, most frequently in annuities. These loans, estimated in 1776 to account for £59 million out of a total national debt of £143 million, represent the extent to which the British government of the day was enabled by a new system of international lending to live beyond Britain's own resources. Where their predecessors had been limited in their ambitions by the amount of hard cash they could raise, the governments of the period after the Glorious Revolution exploited with increasing success the possibilities of living beyond their income. With the borrowed profits from Holland's Golden Age, Britain gambled on an imperial future, and gambled successfully.

The advent of a system of international lending and credit, and of multilateral payments, may help to explain the lessening of anxiety about bullion resources in the course of the eighteenth century, though the anxiety was only lessened and not wholly removed.[1] The new machinery creaked continually and from time to time broke down completely – as in 1763 and 1773.[2] These periodic revelations of weakness in the credit mechanism may well have had the result of prolonging the life of the old prejudices. Certainly they died hard, and even the coming of fully convertible currencies and multilateral payments did not entirely banish them. As Lord Keynes observed: 'The majority of statesmen and practical men in most countries, and nearly half of them even in Great Britain, the home of the opposite view, have remained faithful to the ancient doctrine.'[3] If, in the

[1] I cannot entirely agree with Professor Heckscher that the need for reserves was of little consequence to seventeenth-century mercantilists. It is certainly implicit even in Oxenford's *Essay* in the eighteenth century.

[2] See Wilson, *op. cit.*, ch. VI.

[3] Keynes, *op. cit.*, p. 333.

interval since those words were written, a high proportion of the dissident half have been converted, the reason must be sought in the disturbing tendency of international trade to revert to conditions which in some ways resemble those of the seventeenth rather than those of the nineteenth century.

4

'Mercantilism': Some Vicissitudes of an Idea[1]

The basic concepts which in recent years have come to be called 'mercantilism' owe less to historians than they do to economists. Economists it was who were exasperated (as Adam Smith was) by the contrast between the truth that was economic logic and the error that was economic policy: or beguiled (as the German historical economists were) by the vista of a future made bright by the conjunction of national political institutions with economic enterprise. Thus, from time to time, economic science, refashioned by the exigencies of time and place, has produced new interpretations of a useful phrase, often by what seems like a process of casual inversion. Ideas have been stood on their head but the name by which they go has been retained. The historiography of mercantilism came in this way to resemble a set of still pictures rather than a motion film. Virtually unnoticed, the meaning of mercantilism turned some sharp corners. As continuity of interpretation was lost, intelligibility was lost also: until one historian could complain, and with some justice, that by being made to mean everything, the word had come to mean nothing. It had become 'a positive nuisance' and if it could not be abolished it should be avoided.[2] Yet it is not easy to

[1] This paper was first published in the *Economic History Review*, Second Series, Vol. X, No. 2 (1957), pp. 181–8. When this article was already in the press a review by Mr D. C. Coleman of *Heckscher and Mercantilism* appeared in the *Scandinavian Economic History Review* (1957). Although the purpose of the two articles is quite different, they have some ground in common. The author therefore feels it is desirable to state that the article printed here was written without any knowledge of Mr Coleman's review.

[2] E. A. J. Johnson, *Predecessors of Adam Smith* (New York, 1937), p. 4. More judiciously Prof. T. H. Marshall (*Econ. J.*, XLV (1935)) remarked that e.g. Professor Heckscher 'has not established beyond dispute the validity and utility of the term which is the title of his work.'

abolish a phrase which is itself so essential an ingredient of economic thought and has in no small measure helped to fashion economic policy. The purpose of this note is to see whether the *curriculum vitae* of mercantilism can help to clarify its real characteristics: whether the clamant disagreement obscures any basic, if reluctant, harmony amongst scholars.

The inquirer might do worse than begin with a recent re-definition by Professor Viner.[1] Professor Viner has questioned what he calls 'certain stereotypes' that have been accepted by students of mercantilism. The one to which he devotes most attention is the notion that mercantilism was a 'system of power', that 'power' was for mercantilists the sole or overwhelmingly preponderant end of policy, 'opulence' being a means to this end. Refuting those scholars who, be believes, have propounded such doctrine, he concludes that practically all mercantilists would, in fact, have agreed on four interdependent propositions, viz. (i) that wealth is essential to power, (ii) that power is essential to wealth, (iii) that wealth and power are each proper ultimate ends of national policy, (iv) that there is 'long run harmony' between these ends though there may well be times when military security demands economic sacrifices. It is very far from the purpose of this note to quarrel with Professor Viner's propositions. On the contrary, both his evidence and his conclusions are convincing: so convincing that one wonders how other analysts and critics of mercantilism could have wandered so far from the obvious truth in disregarding or suppressing one or other of the inseparably twin ends of policy. The question is: did they?

The phrase 'the mercantile system' first acquired significance, Professor Heckscher has said, at the hands of Adam Smith. It had appeared sporadically in the writings of the physiocrats but from the publication of *The Wealth of Nations* it passed into common usage. Its first purpose in Adam Smith was uncontroversial: there were (he wrote), 'two different systems of political economy, with regard to enriching the people'.[2] The one was the system of commerce, the other that of agriculture. But from definition he passes swiftly to castigation. The system had

[1] Jacob Viner, 'Power versus Plenty As Objectives of Foreign Policy in the 17th and 18th Centuries', *World Politics* I, No. I (1948).

[2] Adam Smith, *The Wealth of Nations* (ed. McCulloch, 1863), Book IV, p. 187.

nurtured a confusion between wealth and money which had come to be considered in common language as synonymous. Restrictions designed to hinder bullion export had been exchanged gradually for an anxiety over the balance of trade as the occasion of gain or loss of treasure. This was merely to exchange one fruitless care for another. In defence against a mere chimaera an enormous apparatus of control had been set up to encourage exports and discourage certain types of imports. Thus from Thomas Mun had sprung a system first perfected in England but imitated later by 'all other commercial countries'.[1] We are not concerned here with the merits or otherwise of Adam Smith's attack on the mercantile system but with his definition of it and his interpretation of its origin. It is enough to say that, like so many economic writers of the eighteenth century, Adam Smith was little bothered by any real sense of historical change. The effects of those alterations in the nature of money and credit and the structure of the British trading system which he describes so vividly elsewhere are entirely ignored in his section on the mercantile system. The possibility that the obsession with bullion might have rational historical roots is scarcely examined. His explanation of the way the system originated and developed is quite unequivocal. It was the result of arguments 'addressed by merchants to Parliaments and the Councils of Princes, to nobles and country gentlemen . . .'. And between the gentlemen who did not understand trade and tradesmen who did not grasp the nature of the national welfare, the attention of government had been diverted to a misguided end. In this way a conspiracy of traders and manufacturers had been able to victimize the nation in part and in whole. The linen manufacturers, for example, had secured their own enrichment at the expense of both the consumers and 'the poor spinners'. Adam Smith's verdict is a last trump of expiring physiocracy and a fanfare to socialism emergent:

'It is the industry that is carried on for the benefit of the rich and powerful that is principally encouraged by our mercantile system. That which is carried on for the benefit of the poor and the indigent is too often either neglected or oppressed'.[2]

Here as so often in *The Wealth of Nations* there recurs the echo of that physiocratic antipathy which would have virtually ex-

[1] *Ibid.*, pp. 188–90. [2] *Ibid.*, p. 290.

cluded merchants from respectable society. The economic conspiracy was, besides, an offence against the natural course of social justice – the *droit naturel* of the physiocrats – and 'to hurt in any degree the interest of any one order of citizens for no other purpose but to promote that of some other, is evidently contrary to that justice and equality of treatment which the sovereign owes to all the different orders of society'. In the absurd and mischievous ban on the emigration of artisans, liberty itself was sacrificed to 'the futile interests of our merchants and manufacturers'. And so to the grand peroration: consumption, the sole end and purpose of all production, was itself subordinated to production and the interests of producers. And amongst the contrivers of the system 'our merchants and manufacturers have been by far the principal architects'.[1]

Whatever one may feel about the merits of this exposition of the mercantile system, there can be no doubt that Adam Smith chose his title aptly. It *was*, for him, a system devised by merchants for ends mercantile, if illegitimate. One might be tempted to conclude that here the pursuit of opulence has been allotted such an indisputable role in policy-making that considerations of power are virtually excluded. Such a conclusion would be quite wrong. The famous defence of the Navigation Acts puts Adam Smith back with the equivocators. From an economic point of view, the Acts were indefensible, the product of 'national animosity' (against the Dutch). Yet deliberate wisdom could not have done its job better than this stout, if economically irrational, patriotism. Defence was more important than opulence: the Act was 'perhaps the wisest of all the commercial regulations of England'.[2] Nothing is said, of course, of the machinations of the great companies which, as Mr Ashley has since shown, preceded the passing of the Act and prove that it had economic as well as strategic aims.[3] Until very recently most historians followed Adam Smith's interpretation and justification of the Acts as primarily if not solely strategic in character.[4]

There was, then, even in Adam Smith, a dualism, which

[1] *Ibid.*, pp. 295–8. [2] *Ibid.*, pp. 203–4.

[3] M. P. Ashley, *Financial and Commercial Policy under the Cromwellian Protectorate* (1934), Ch. XIII.

[4] e.g. J. A. Williamson, *Cambridge History of the British Empire* (1929) I, Ch. VII.

needs to be recognized. But it is on the other hand true that the main statement of his *credo* attributed the mercantile system as a whole to economic motives, and it was this stream of thought which had most influence in England down to the twentieth century. The theory that official intervention could be beneficial in the national interest became, for most writers, an impossibility and any practice based on such an idea – whether by Edward III, Elizabeth or the Stuarts – a sham. 'I think', wrote George Unwin, 'the part played by state power in history has been very largely evil.' It was not strange that a pacific Manchester anti-imperialist should stand so clearly in the direct line of succession. It is a larger tribute to the strength and pervasiveness of Adam Smith's influence that even an imperialist and Chamberlainite like Hewins could muster up very little more patience with the mercantile system than Unwin. 'As a measure of national prosperity, the balance of trade', wrote Hewins, 'was inadequate and untrustworthy.' It led to errors of commercial policy, encouraged the pursuit of treasure for its own sake, appealed to base prejudice, played into the hands of the landed classes and led to the 'mischievous corn laws'. Trade and industry were cramped and distorted, not in the general interest but to satisfy the demands of 'ignorant and self-interested cliques of merchants and manufacturers who feared without reason the competition of foreign rivals'. Even when the circumstances which had led, misguidedly, to the theory of the balance of trade had passed away, the protectionist system inspired by that theory continued to overshadow English commerce. Birmingham and the London School of Economics were, it seemed, no more friendly to the mercantile system than Manchester. But like Manchester they still regarded it as essentially *mercantile* in character, even if wickedly monopolistic.[1]

It is from the 1880s onwards that the old interpretation begins to jostle competitively with a new one – what Professor Viner has defined as the 'stereotype' that mercantilism was a system aimed exclusively at national power. And like a good many things that arose to compete with established English products in the eighties, this one also came from Germany – specifically, Professor Viner thinks, from von Heyking. Von Heyking's *Zur Geschichte der Handelsbilanztheorie* (Berlin, 1880) has a short lead

[1] W. A. S. Hewins, *English Trade and Finance* (1892), Introduction *passim*.

in time over Schmoller's *Studien über die Wirtschaftliche Politik Friedrichs des Grossen* which appeared in 1884 and contained a long section on the Mercantile System which had already appeared as an article in the previous year.[1] The relation between political institutions and national prosperity and power was the common stock of German historians of the day. The idea can claim no single inventor. In the event, and certainly as regards English opinion, Schmoller was probably its most influential protagonist. Schmoller's strength lay in his distrust of abstractions. In an age of oversimplification he had the merit of recognizing and accepting the complexity of historical change. He was oppressed (Professor Gay once wrote) 'by the mystery of the human spirit that moved behind the interlacing tangle of social and economic change'.[2] And that, at any rate, was something. Schmoller's theme in his essay on the mercantile system was the connection between economic life and the essential, controlling organs of social and political life. Economic institutions were dependent on political bodies; individual economic action could not go on in a political vacuum. Hence, while politically organized states had advanced their economies, Germany had lagged behind. Yet Schmoller did not, in fact, advance the 'stereotype' that mercantilists subordinated economic ends to those of power or strategy, and the criticism that his interpretation depicts mercantilism as 'primarily a system of state-building'[3] disregards the very important qualifications Schmoller attaches to *Staatsbildung*. Economic and political interests, he insists, went hand in hand.[4] Mercantilism '. . . in its innermost kernel is nothing but state-making – not state-making in a narrow sense but state-making and national-economy-making at the same time'.[5] This insistence on the dual character of mercantilism reappears throughout the essay. 'In all ages, history has been wont to treat national power and

[1] With the exception of the first four pages this is the same as *Das Merkantilsystem in seiner historischen Bedeutung*. It appears as Chapter I in *Umrisse und Untersuchungen* (Leipzig, 1898) which was republished fourteen years later. This was also the same essay which appeared in English translation in 1896 as *The Mercantile System and its Historical Significance* (New York and London, 1896). See below.

[2] Edwin F. Gay. 'The Tasks of Economic History', *Journal of Economic History* I (1941), 9–16.

[3] Viner, *op. cit.*, p. 1.

[4] Schmoller, *The Mercantile System*, p. 50.

[5] *Ibid.*, p. 69.

national wealth as sisters; perhaps they were never so closely associated as then.' In other places Schmoller seems even disposed to regard power as subordinate to economic gain in mercantilist policy. The long wars of the seventeenth and eighteenth centuries, he writes, 'have economic objects as their main aim'.[1] And while it is true that there is a hint of contempt for what Brie later stigmatized as the 'kaufmännisch gefärbte Imperialismus' of the English, Schmoller was objective enough to recognize the merits of methods pursued by rivals: '... it was precisely those governments which understood how to put the might of their fleets and admiralties, the apparatus of customs laws and navigation laws, with rapidity, boldness and clear purpose at the service of the economic interests of the nation and state, which obtained thereby the lead in the struggle and riches and industrial prosperity.'[2] In this way they had given the economic life of their peoples a necessary basis of power and an impulse to economic movement.

Schmoller's account of the central features of mercantilist thought and his description of the apparatus of legislation and enforcement of policy does not differ greatly from Adam Smith's: it is only that he applauds where Smith condemns. He does not even desert the phrase 'mercantile system' for 'mercantilism'. Both are used interchangeably. But what had previously been regarded by *laissez-faire* economists as a discreditable conspiracy of trade against the nation now assumes the aspect of a national campaign for prosperity and power, often brutal in execution but ingenious in conception and efficacious in method. Its ideas, says Schmoller, 'were nearer reality than the theory of Adam Smith, as also were the main ideas of Frederick List'.[3] A note on the rise of the Prussian silk industry appended in 1892 supplies further proof, if any were needed, that Schmoller retained an inclination towards an 'economic' and even liberal interpretation of mercantilism. Not the least merit of Frederick the Great's economic policy, he wrote, was that it constantly laboured towards a double end: to create a flourishing industry 'by state initiative and political means, and then, as quickly and as completely as possible, to set it on its own feet and create thriving private businesses – and so render itself superfluous'.[4]

[1] *Ibid.*, p. 72.
[2] *Ibid.*, p. 72.
[3] *Op. cit.*, p. 60.
[4] *Ibid.*, p. 89.

Where private initiative was available, it was left to itself. The final ideal was 'that economic forces, while living for themselves should yet entirely serve the state, and that the state, pursuing its own ends, should at the same time place all its might and all its members in the true service of the national economy'.[1]

Thus rehabilitated under Prussian guidance, the mercantile system found its way back into English economic history, mainly through the writings of Cunningham. The first edition of *The Growth of English Industry and Commerce* appeared in 1882, just when Schmoller had succeeded to Adolf Held's chair at Berlin. And as edition succeeded edition, the number of footnotes which referred to the researches of Schmoller, von Heyking, Schanz, Pöhlmann, Pauli, Ratzinger and others multiplied. The distinction drawn by the German historical school of economists between theory and historical reality informs Cunningham's whole philosophy:

> '. . . the very sphere we are about to study is conditioned by political circumstances which have extended or diminished the area over which the English Government and the English race have held sway at different times . . . History must trace out the conscious efforts . . . to develop the resources and expand the commerce of the realm: such deliberate endeavours were made through political institutions for political objects and affected our progress for good or evil.'[2]

Cunningham's emphasis on the political objectives of the mercantile system probably owed at least as much to the older Coleridgean tradition of anti-utilitarianism as it did to the new authoritarian nationalism. Both derived partly from German sources. Whatever the origins, it brought down on him the ridicule of the other leading economic historian who, politically, shared Cunningham's Chamberlainite views: W. A. S. Hewins. To Hewins, the mercantile system was still (in the Adam Smith tradition) a mercantile affair. To credit merchants with political and abstract ends was merely absurd. Cunningham does not appear to have replied to Hewins in print.[3] To Unwin, who attacked his whole conception of national policy, he gracefully

[1] *Ibid.*, p. 91.

[2] Cunningham, *op. cit.*, 5th Edition, I, 22.

[3] Viner, *op. cit.* It will be seen from the earlier account of Hewins's views that it is not entirely correct to say that he was 'sympathetic' to mercantilism (see Viner, p. 3).

gave in, acknowledging (as Professor Tawney has said) that there was no foundation for his original contention that Edward III had followed a consistent policy.[1] On this sort of theoretical issue, Cunningham was not at his best. He invited, as Professor Viner says, the charge of ambiguity.[2] In several places, he retreats from the 'power' interpretation: thus. 'To some extent plenty is a condition of power and the two policies may have much in common.'[3] Yet in this and similar statements, Cunningham is hardly more equivocal than Schmoller – or for that matter than Adam Smith. It is only that he was less cautious in allowing himself elsewhere to lapse into monolatry.

Thus far there had been two contrasting interpretations of the mercantile system. Classical economists had interpreted it in a primarily economic sense and been compelled by their principles to condemn it. The German historical economists had deflected it in the direction of power and approved it as strongly as their opponents had denounced it. But neither school of thought had ever entirely lost sight of the dual aims and origins of the system though each had tended to give a bias to its interpretation. Heckscher's *Mercantilism* (1931), like earlier analyses, was not free from inconsistencies where the objectives of the system were concerned. It appears to admit here and there that mercantilism – the older English phrase was now finally abandoned for the Germanic abstraction – had economic as well as political ends; even, occasionally, that power was sometimes sought as a means to prosperity. Yet on the whole Professor Viner's conclusion, that, in Heckscher's view, mercantilists subordinated all else to considerations of power as an end in itself – seems just. Mercantilism was (Heckscher wrote) 'primarily a system for forcing economic policy into the service of power as an end in itself'.[4] It therefore differed (he thought) from both earlier and later systems of thought and policy and contrasted especially with what Heckscher deemed to be the indifference of *laissez-faire* towards power.

[1] G. Unwin, *Studies in Economic History* (1927). R. H. Tawney's Introduction, p. lix, Note 1.

[2] Viner. *op. cit.*, p. 3. It is perhaps a little hard to call it 'hopeless contradiction'.

[3] Cunningham, *op. cit.*, p. 471. See also Professor Viner's own similar quotations, p. 3, n. 5.

[4] Heckscher, *Mercantilism* (1956), II, 17. The *addenda* (pp. 358–9) do not really carry the argument any further.

The controversy had thus been given a new twist. Adam Smith had interpreted the mercantile system as a conspiracy for economic ends and condemned it accordingly. Schmoller had seen it more particularly as a system of power and approved it for that reason. Now orthodox economic principles combined with a political interpretation to produce an unfavourable verdict. Nor is the unspoken logic of Heckscher's argument difficult to divine. A process of authoritarian interference with economic policy so long continued and so absurdly misconceived (by orthodox standards) was difficult to explain except on the principle that its authors were principally concerned with non-economic ends. At times, it is plain, the mere suggestion that mercantilist policy might represent an approach to contemporary problems containing some element of economic rationality put a strain on his patience. An awkward question nevertheless remained: if it was true, as Heckscher himself said, that 'mercantilist writers were mostly connected with trade in one form or another',[1] it was not easy to understand why they should have formulated theories or originated and supported policies aimed solely at increasing the power of the state and not at all at expanding the general prosperity of society or even their own share of it. Except on the assumption, which might be dismissed as improbable, that they had an abstract altruistic concern which obliterated their private economic interests: alternatively, and surely more probably, that 'the power of the state' represented in their minds a necessary adjunct to their private welfare.

It was the fate of Heckscher's extremely 'political' and unfavourable interpretation to provoke another, equally unilinear, and as favourable as Heckscher's was critical. Keynes's *Notes on Mercantilism*[2] were, no doubt, by way of being a *jeu d'esprit* and there was something in Heckscher's contention that 'the bent of his [i.e. Keynes's] mind was not historical, however interested he was in historical information'. One might go farther and agree that the projectors of the fishery companies, the Cockayne project and the Navigation Acts would have been puzzled by the sophisticated argument which related balance of trade policy to investment and employment theory. Yet in broad

[1] *Economic History Review*, 2nd. Ser. III (1950).
[2] *The General Theory of Employment, Interest and Money* (1936), p. 333.

outline the argument was not derisory. By trying to isolate the purely economic element in mercantilist thought and policy, Keynes was perpetrating an anachronism. Mercantilism was always something more and something less than 'economic'. But his refusal to treat concern for the balance of trade as merely 'a puerile obsession' was a useful stimulus to students compelled to read economic history still rooted in orthodox theory but doomed to live in an age when nine out of ten governments pursued policies which resembled suspiciously those mercantilist devices dismissed as absurd by economic logic.

The student who tries to follow the history of controversy about the basic aims and character of mercantilism must often feel that the jousting is over words rather than over historical realities, that it is more a matter of semantics than of historiography. Yet the task of unravelling the complexities of national economic policies cannot be abandoned merely because we have been confused by premature dogmatizing. Obviously there have been failures of communication. Under contemporary ideological pressures, arguments have become distorted and what was said was not always (one suspects) what was intended to be said. The nature of policy has hardly anywhere been related sufficiently closely to the resources, geography, politics and social structure of the different states. Policy, as Professor Marshall has observed, 'has no meaning, no character, apart from its context. The same coincidence of items may recur at different periods, without having the same historical significance'.[1] The so-called 'uniform body of doctrine'[2] had itself tended to mislead: for it cloaked a variety of motives and objects, some biased towards economic, some towards strategic ends. Professor Viner has put us in his debt by clarifying the debate and opening the way to further inquiries into this interdependence of economic and strategic objectives. A continuous survey of the work of those scholars – mostly economists by training – who have successively formulated the concepts of mercantilism suggests, nevertheless, that a dualistic theory has always been latent in the historiography of mercantilism. Not until Professor Viner's study had it ever been made so admirably explicit.

[1] Heckscher, *Mercantilism* (Revised Ed.), I, 21.
[2] *Economic Journal, loc. cit.*

5

The Other Face of Mercantilism[1]

'In England', Sir John Seeley once wrote, 'it is our custom to alter things but to leave their names unaltered.'[2] Anyone who wished to test the truth of the dictum historiographically might examine the history of the word 'mercantilism'. It has borne many, sometimes oddly conflicting, meanings, but they have had at any rate one thing in common: they have all been in some degree unpalatable to those reared in the traditions of English liberal thought. It was as the conspiracy of a mercantile minority out to line its pockets at the expense of the rest of the community that the system was first depicted by the classical economists.[3] The interpretation of the German school of historical economists a century later was certainly no less distasteful to the liberal mind. To Bismarckian Germans it might appear seemly to condone the pursuit of aggression and covet its rewards. But even Chamberlainites – like W.A.S. Hewins – amongst English historians had their doubts, and to George Unwin state 'policy' was simply a sham – the supreme illustration of the evils of bigness. The economic actions of the political body were not even the early thrustings of a lusty infant, but the morbid twitchings of disease. And Unwin, who believed that historians should be concerned with the life of communities, not with the actions of states, found more sympathizers in his profession (one suspects) than Cunningham, who was nearer to the German tradition. Others, misliking what they took to be the moral and intellectual confusion of mercantilists and their works, agreed to deny any

[1] This paper was presented to the Royal Historical Society on 10 May 1958, and published in the *Transactions of the Royal Historical Society*, 5th Series, Vol. 9 (1959), pp. 81–101.

[2] Sir J. Seeley, *Science of Politics* (1896), p. 298.

[3] A. Smith, *The Wealth of Nations*, book iv.

title of coherence to folly so diverse and deplorable.[1] Thus the history of national policy was persuasively represented as a series of contests from which greed and stupidity emerged monotonously victorious.

No period or society came out of the inquiry with fewer honours than that of Restoration England and the century that followed: the years when (according to Adam Smith) the principles of the mercantile system were devised and applied in legislative form. When the inquiring beam lighted and focused on the ruling classes, it found them treating the wage-earners – I am quoting from Professor Tawney's *Religion and the Rise of Capitalism* – in the same way as coloured labour was treated by the less reputable colonists, consigned to 'collective perdition'. This, Professor Tawney explained, was 'partly the result of the greatly increased influence on thought and public affairs acquired at the Restoration by the commercial classes, whose temper was a ruthless materialism, determined at all costs to conquer world markets from France and Holland and prepared to sacrifice every other consideration to their economic ambitions'.[2] Professor Tawney's verdict was echoed by Mr Beloff when he came to write his study of *Public Order and Popular Disturbance 1660–1714* in 1938. Again, ruthless mercantile ambition is linked in guilt with the destruction of the central machinery of welfare: the Privy Council. The Civil War brought social *laissez-faire*, and the Restoration failed to restore an independent social policy. 'Rarely indeed', writes Mr Beloff, 'can national wealth, as opposed to welfare, have predominated to such an extent as it did in the minds of the ruling class of the period.'[3]

The picture that has been created is that of a ruthlessly materialistic ruling class which did not merely neglect but actively exploited the poor. 'Mercantilists,' an authority on economic thought writes, 'if they held any wage theory at all, believed in an economy of low wages.'[4] For Miss Margaret James the social legislators of the Restoration 'aimed at nothing less than making the poor a source of profit to the state by forcing

[1] See A. V. Judges, 'The idea of a mercantile state', *Trans. Roy. Hist. Soc.*, 4th series, xxi (1939).

[2] R. H. Tawney, *op. cit.* (London, 1926), p. 268.

[3] M. Beloff, *op. cit.*, p. 18.

[4] E. Roll, *A History of Economic Thought* (London, 1939), p. 99.

them to work for reduced wages'.[1] The presence of a few nobly philanthropic exceptions to this general rule was not enough to soften the indictment. Firmin, the London mercer of Socinian leanings, who experimented in social reform or the Quaker, Bellers, whose *Proposals for a College of Industry* (1695) showed deep concern for social welfare, emerge as entirely exceptional figures, quite untypical of their age. How far is all this a just and representative account of the aims and attitudes of the governing classes of Britain in the years that followed the Restoration?

There is no reason to question the belief that the wealth and power of the state represented the twin objectives of much of the thought and policy of the time, inseparably joined in the contemporary mind. It was deemed by most writers the function of government to intervene in the operation of the economy to secure economic ends that could, they thought, be secured in no other way, and the great majority of those who have made a study of mercantilism would, I think, agree with Adam Smith that the apparatus of legislative intervention consisted of those 'two great engines', the manipulation of exports and imports according to certain principles which would nourish native manufactures. The motive principle of both 'engines' was the same: the balance of trade. The efficacy of the entire system was to be measured by the condition of the 'balance'. Recent over-elaboration of the concept of mercantilism has reawakened old scepticism, raising afresh the question whether it is not merely an arabesque woven by the imagination of historians upon the facts of history. It seems to me as dangerous to deny that certain principles informed both thought and policy in this period as it is to apostrophize those principles and exaggerate their effects. It is equally fallacious to suppose that thought and policy were distinct activities that can and should be treated separately. No body of economic literature was ever more closely related to interest and policy than the writings of the mercantilists. Much (though not all) of it represents the skirmishings of interested parties round the political lobbies; and of all the writers mentioned in this paper I can think of only two of whom it could be said that they did not in their own persons exercise some practical influence on economic policy or institutions. The mercantilist

[1] M. James, *Social Policy during the Puritan Revolution* (London, 1930), pp. 344–5.

writers were neither scribblers nor idealists. They were not sophisticated or labyrinthine. Even their *Utopias* were earthy ones and it was not accidental that they frequently spelt the word as *Eutopia*, meaning a place where all was well.[1] They felt no call to disguise the material character of their aims. They have little relevance to any times but those in which they lived. Unlike the Diggers, the Levellers and the other social revolutionaries, they have not attracted the devotional attentions of those historians whose preoccupations are really political rather than historical. If they sin, it is not in being heartless or materialist, but in being a bit dull.

In the early formulations of policy, the virtue of a favourable balance was held, quite uncomplicatedly, to reside in the net influx of bullion which was assumed to be its necessary consequence. This doctrine was still powerful in the period of which we are speaking. Indeed, Mun's classical statement of it, though written perhaps forty years earlier, was published for the first time in 1664. It was in the following year – the year of the Plague – that there was sketched out the first draft of an economic tract which, in its various revisions, was to exercise a powerful influence on thought and policy, not only in England but in many European states also, especially in Italy, France, Germany and Austria. This was Josiah Child's *New Discourse of Trade*, as it became known in later editions. When it first appeared in print, in 1668, it was as a very short affair under the appropriate title of *Brief Observations*, and it dealt principally with problems of interest rates and usury. Attached to it by way of appendix was a note by Culpeper on the problem of usury which contained a section on the relief of the poor. Its general theme will be evident from this text: 'He that is weary of his life fears neither axe nor gibbet: and to prosecute such by the methods of Justice I will not say it is like the Excommunication of Rats but I am sure it resembles the Outlawing of Tories.' Child's work, which is not mentioned by Professor Tawney, went into five editions between 1668 and his death in 1699. As edition succeeded edition, two themes grew in importance: the relief and employment of the poor, and the relationship of employment to the national welfare as reflected in the balance of trade. From Culpeper's text,

[1] Harold Child, 'Some English Utopias', *Transactions of the Royal Society of Literature*, iii (1933).

Child develops the theme that it is man's 'Duty to God and Nature to provide for and employ the poor, whose condition is sad and wretched, diseased, impotent, useless.' In the later editions, this crystallizes into his famous proposal for an assembly of 'Fathers of the Poor', endowed with powers to buy land, build workhouses and hospitals and to set the poor on work, with a special *non obstante* to overcome obstructive patents. Simultaneously, Child modified the existing conception of the balance of trade. Sharing the doubts of that considerable body of persons who despaired of ever measuring accurately the volume of imports and exports, Child came to the conclusion that the balance might be judged better by measuring the general volume of trade with reference to the 'number of hands' employed. The juxtaposition of ideas might well begin to look suspicious: on the one hand, proposals for organized charity; on the other, a theory that comes near to equating national prosperity with the effective value of its labour. Add that Child was a City merchant with a reputation for tough and none-too-scrupulous bargaining, who hated competition, Dutch or English, and did not conceal his contempt for the booby squires who muffed the nation's affairs at Westminster, and the liberal mind is prepared for the worst. What emerges, somewhat surprisingly, is an impeccable exposition of the virtues of high wages on the Dutch model. 'Wherever wages are high, universally throughout the whole world, it is an infallible evidence of the riches of that country; and wherever wages for labour run low it is proof of the poverty of that place.'

That the views of Child and his followers did not by any means extinguish the older view of the trade balance or the hopes of those who believed it could be calculated is seen from the contemporary debates on the establishment of the Board of Trade and the Inspector-General of Customs, and from the title of Brewster's *Fifth Essay* of 1702: *That the full employment of All Hands in the Nation is the Surest Way and Means to bring Bullion into the Kingdom* – a theoretical umbrella under which all shades of opinion might happily sit. But Child's proposals proved to be a matrix of opinions and policy on both of his two main counts. Over the wisdom of providing workhouses and similar institutions, many took issue sharply with him. The great debate on the poor raged for over half a century, between those who believed in workhouses and those who did not; and under interrogation by the liberal historians, neither side could escape the fate of the witness who is asked whether he has stopped beating his wife. To believe in workhouses was to invite suspicions of exploitation; to disbelieve in them is to invite the charge of callous indifference to suffering. Consider, for example, Daniel Defoe, spokesman for what he himself called 'the Middle State or – the Upper Station of Low Life', the author of *Giving Alms no Charity* (1704) and the stoutest opponent of organized charity, often condemned as the arch exponent of selfish, middle-class prejudice. Defoe was too passionate, too inquisitive an observer of the human scene to be guilty of much consistent theorizing. Yet if he had a theory to solve the contemporary and social problem it was a theory of a large population and high wages. To this extent he followed Child: 'All the wealth of the nation and all the trade is produced by numbers of people', he wrote. His observations of the habits of workmen might be thought to point to the dangers of conspicuous consumption by the poor: he describes how he saw workmen take their wages to the ale-house, 'lie there till Monday, spend it every penny and run in debt to boot and not give a farthing of it to their families, tho' all of them had wives and children'.[1] Yet he did not draw the conclusion that the remedy lay either in lower wages or in poorhouses. Defoe wobbled on many things: on one he was rigidly consistent – that England's commercial prosperity depended on the quality of her export goods. To lower wages would reduce 'the value and goodness of the manufacture' and make them less competitive. 'If you expect the poor should work cheaper and not perform their work slighter and more overly (as we call it) and superficially, you expect what is not in the nature of the Thing – This therefore is beginning at the wrong end of trade . . .'[2] He objected to workhouses for the same reason: their subsidized inferior products would damage that reputation for quality on which English prosperity rested. Logically, he raised no objection to welfare schemes that provided for destitute women or half-wit children. It would, of course, be as false to suggest that everything that was said in the debate of the poor can be regarded

[1] Quoted in J. Sutherland, *Defoe* (1950), p. 130.
[2] Defoe, *Plan of the English Commerce* (1728 edn), p. 60.

as pointing to the welfare state of the mid-twentieth century as it would to condemn the speakers for consigning the poor wilfully to universal pauperdom and Gin Lane. The 'hard tone' presaging the dismal science at its most arid, which even Cunningham detected in the opponents of charity in these years, is not wholly imaginary. 'When a man is perfectly content with the state he is in,' said Locke, 'what action, what industry, what will is there left but to continue in it?' One of Mandeville's works bore the title *Content the Bane of Industry*, while his *Essay on Charity* (1723) made a bitter attack on those tradesmen, like Firmin, who sponsored charitable institutions out of the hope of gain and that satisfaction 'which delights mean people in governing others'. It will be noticed, all the same, that it is not the merchant writers but the philosophers who speak in the sharpest tones. Here, as not uncommonly, it was logic – the logic of clerks who believed that they had discovered the *spiritus movens* of economic action in human egoism – that put the acid into contemporary social thought. When Pope celebrated the new principles of domestic policy and human conduct in the *Essay on Man*, he learnt them not from his father, a devoutly Roman Catholic linen draper, but from Bolingbroke and Christchurch. Yet it would be as presumptuous to withhold from the poet and philosopher his claim to sincerity as it would be uncharitable to exonerate the merchant *ex officio* from the charge of compassion. While the spiritual fathers of *laissez-faire* were busily proving the mischief of supposing that anything should or could be done, the tradesmen – Child the Grand Cham of the India Company, Firmin the London mercer, Cary the Bristol sugar merchant, Bellers the Quaker clothier, Nelson the heir to a Levant Company fortune – were pressing on with their schemes for institutions, and helping to foot the bill. And if some, like Mandeville, impugned their motives, there were others, like Davenant, who remarked contrariwise on the 'malignant temper in some who will not let a public work go on, if private persons are to be the gainers by it . . .'[1] Not all private vices, it appeared, conferred public benefits.

Historians have underestimated the gravity and oversimplified

[1] C. Davenant, 'An Essay upon the Probable Methods of Making a People Gainers in the Balance of Trade.' *Collected Works*, ii. 214.

the complexity of the great debate of the poor. Faced by the difficulty of analysing the relation between states of mind and private interests, between thoughts and actions, they have too often been satisfied with what are fundamentally *a priori* conclusions. It is now apparent that between the Restoration and (say) the end of the Seven Years War England faced a chronic problem of poverty which affected severely somewhere between a quarter and a half of the whole population. It was not only the large number of real paupers but the high proportion of casual part-time workers in the nation's leading industry, clothmaking, that constituted the problem.[1] Gregory King's Tables included a figure of over a million and a quarter for 'cottagers, paupers, vagrants, gypsies, thieves, beggars' out of a total of five and a half million in 1688. Population growth and industrial change had faced seventeenth-century England with a social problem that the Middle Ages had never known: an army of workers partly or wholly dependent on a great but unstable manufacturing export industry. One of the motives behind the mercantilist urge to diversify the nation's industries had been the consciousness that fluctuations in the demand for cloth might (as Mun put it) 'suddenly cause much poverty and dangerous uproars, specially by our poor people'. Politics and Nature had combined to endorse his warning. At home and abroad wars had continually disrupted markets and it is at least arguable that at two points – 1652 and 1665 – the decision to fight the Dutch may have been influenced by the belief that the trade depression might thereby be relieved. Vigorous industries in Holland and France were now competing for Europe's shrunken cloth markets and Colbert had placed the forces of the state in the balance. By the end of the century, the structure of the industry was adjusting itself to the stresses of the times. The less competitive areas of the west country were yielding ground to East Anglia, as both these areas were in the eighteenth century to yield to the Yorkshire industry. On an industrial pattern already distorted by human violence must be superimposed the effects of the disastrous harvests which supervened from time to time. 1649, for example, a year of regicide, mutiny, disorder and upheaval, was also visited by an appalling harvest that drove up

[1] D. C. Coleman, 'Labour in the English Economy of the 17th Century', *Economic History Review*, 2nd series, VIII (1956).

grain prices to famine heights and added to the grievous trade depression.[1] On top of the French wars of the '90s came especially bad harvests in 1692, 1693, 1695, 1698, 1708 and 1709. The severity of the hardship created by these conjunctions of normal and exceptional stresses undoubtedly helped to deflect the course of economic thought. The very confusion of 1649 made it an *annus mirabilis* for the literature of social criticism and reform, much of it pivoting upon the problems of poverty. The only one to have achieved any kind of notoriety is Winstanley's *Declaration from the Poor Oppressed People of England* denouncing 'particular property'. For Winstanley, the rebel against reality, there was no question of compromise; to that extent he is less important in this inquiry than others less intransigent – Hartlib, Rice Bush, Chamberlen or Goffe, for example. Theirs was not the pure milk of utopianism. They were, on the contrary, anxious to come to terms with social reality. Hartlib, the friend of Milton and many of the revolutionary leaders, educationally the disciple of Comenius, had already published in 1641 his *Description of the Kingdom of Macaria, shewing its excellent government, wherein the Inhabitants live in great Prosperity, Health and Happiness*.[2] This remarkable work which followed in the footsteps (as Hartlib said) of More and Bacon, and foreshadowed Mandeville and the physiocrats, was followed in 1649 by *London's Charitie stilling the Poor Orphans' Cry* and in 1650 by *London's Charity Inlarged*. Here he outlines a scheme of Parliamentary provision of workhouses to employ poor people and educate poor children. This in turn reflected the influence of a pamphlet by Rice Bush called *The Poor Man's Friend* which described the efforts of the 'many worthy citizens of London' to provide for the poor and was dedicated to a group of 'eleven gentlemen' (including Hartlib) who were said to have been

[1] For an account of the depression of 1649 see evidence of Thomas Violet given before Parliamentary Committee of enquiry. *State Papers Dom., 1650*, p. 178, no. 61. The evidence of depression is discussed in C. Wilson, *Profit and Power* (1957), pp. 147–9. For the depression of the late seventeenth and early eighteenth centuries see Beloff, *op. cit.*, ch. III, esp. pp. 56–8. For a general discussion of the intellectual ferment of 1649 see Gooch and Laski, *English Democratic Ideas in the 17th Century* (Cambridge, 1927), esp. ch. VIII.

[2] *Harleian Miscellany* (London, 1744), i. 567. I am much indebted to Dr Leon Fuz for allowing me to see the text of his doctoral thesis submitted at the Rotterdam Hoogeschool in June 1951, in which he examines English welfare economics from Francis Bacon to Adam Smith.

active in this work.[1] Peter Chamberlen, the author of *The Poor Man's Advocate, or England's Samaritan,* which appeared in the same year, was, like Samuel Hartlib, of immigrant stock.[2] Here again were proposals, mercantilist in character, for a general increase in wealth which would also provide for the poor and narrow the socially dangerous gap that divided them from the rest of society. It is more difficult to put a certain date to William Goffe's *How to Advance the Trade of the Nation and employ the Poor*, but internal evidence suggests that it appeared at about the same time as Chamberlen's work.[3] Like Chamberlen, Goffe proposes measures by the state of a kind a Keynesian generation was to describe as 'priming the pump'. The principal object was to re-employ the poor, whose numbers he estimates at half a million. 'The poor', wrote Goffe, 'ought to be encouraged and mercifully dealt with and kindly used, until their slow hands be brought to ready working and ought at first to have the highest price the commodity will bear to themselves.'[4] Most of the reformers were strongly influenced in this, as in so many other matters, by the example of the Dutch, whose provision for the poor offered an obvious model for others.[5]

The profusion of welfare economics of 1649 seems to me to form the basis of almost all later economic thought for more than a century. The recognition that the problem of poverty, employment and national welfare are all linked together was never subsequently lost sight of. It was to appear again whenever bad times provoked men to brood on social remedies. 1659, a bad year, brought forth Cornelius Plockhoy's *A Way Propounded to Make the Poor in This and Other Nations Happy*.[6] Between then and the crisis of the '90s writers like Child, Matthew Hale, Robert Harford, Firmin, Davenant, Yarranton, Locke and others

[1] See G. H. Turnbull, *Hartlib, Drury and Comenius* (Liverpool, 1947), pp. 65–6.

[2] See W. Schenk. *The Concern for Social Justice in the Puritan Revolution* (London, 1930), pp. 279–80.

[3] *Harleian Miscellany*, iv. 366–70.

[4] Quoted by T. E. Gregory in 'The Economics of Employment in England, 1660–1713', *Economica*, i (1921–2). The pamphlet is, as stated above, of an earlier date than the Restoration.

[5] See, for example, *The Dutch Drawn to the Life* (1664), ch. iv, esp. pp. 55–6.

[6] Plockhoy is often referred to as Peter Cornelius (see Gooch and Laski, *op. cit.*, pp. 117–8); Schenk (*op. cit.*, p. 153) describes him as Peter Cornelisz Plockboy.

developed the theme.[1] The debate was resumed at full length between 1692 and 1709 with the new editions of Child's *Discourse.* John Bellers published his *Proposals for a College of Industry* in 1695, and two years later his *Epistle to Friends Concerning the Education of Children.* There is a strong general resemblance between these and other writings of the '90s – Dudley North's *Discourses* (1691), *Britannia Languens* (1696) and John Cary's *Essay* (1696).

Some might support and others oppose the idea of parish factories, as Defoe opposed Sir Humphrey Mackworth's Bill for those institutions in 1724, but one idea had come to be firmly established in the popular mind: the potential value of the labour represented by the nation's poor. Nor can the general approach to the problem be dismissed as merely cynical or self-interested. It had become too plain that poverty was the dominant social problem. Post-Restoration mercantilists were no longer so absorbedly preoccupied, as their predecessors had been, with state welfare measured in the narrow terms of the net amount of bullion gained or lost via the balance of trade. This traditional obsession was now blended with a concern for the social needs of the community which had its roots in the ideas of 1649. The obstinate core of mercantilist thought can nevertheless be seen in the belief that some activities were beneficial and some harmful to the community and that it was the state's task to discern and separate the two.[2]

At this point I can imagine the critics moving to their second line of defence. 'We may' (they might well say) 'have omitted to count one or two heads, neglected one or two principles. But does this affect the argument? Does not the story remain one of neglect and harshness? Even granting that their motives were less blameworthy than has sometimes been supposed, did not deeds lag a long way behind intentions?' Certainly there is no lack of evidence to substantiate the gloomiest view of society in the hundred years under review. The originals of Tom Nero, Mother Needham, Tom Idle and the rest may all be discovered in the fearful annals of St Giles, Shoreditch, Drury Lane and

[1] E.g. Sir Matthew Hale, *Discourse Touching Provision for the Poor*, 1683. R. Harford, *Proposals for Building in every Country a Working Almshouse or Hospital as the Best Expedient to perfect the Trade and Manufactory of Linen Cloth, etc.*, 1677.

[2] See John Cary, *Essay on the State of England, etc.*

Alsatia. This last century before the Industrial Revolution is near enough the present to invite comparison of its social and moral standards with those of a later day. Even now that it is a commonplace to say that the civilization of the Augustan Age was but a veneer, it comes as something of a shock to read the Report of the Commons Committee on the Care of the Poor in the Parish of St Martin-in-the-Fields in 1715. Three-quarters out of the twelve hundred babies born every year in the parish died, many being exposed or overlaid by 'nurses'. Money was stolen, accounts were falsified, paupers were starved and in some cases murdered. Consider the later inquiries of Jonas Hanway, Russia merchant and social reformer, founder of the Marine Society, the Magdalen House and the Foundling Hospital, and one of the most indefatigable and splendid bores of English history. His seventy-four separate works on charitable problems seem, again, to underline the failure of private enterprise to find any solution to the social problem. In the fourteen parishes investigated by him he calculated that the death-rate amongst infants entering or being born in the workhouses that had sprung up since 1720 was 88 per cent. Some parishes (it was said) acknowledged that 'no infant had lived to be apprenticed from their workhouses'.[1] Under the system by which the poor were hired out to a contractor, the workhouse had become a place of vice, a catch-all for the infant and the infirm, the able-bodied idle and the criminal alike. Some of this may have been exaggerated but much was undoubtedly true. Is the true explanation to be found (as some historians have suggested) in a decline of charity, in a harsher and more censorious attitude towards poverty and misfortune? The title of Professor Tawney's chapter on this period – 'The New Medicine for Poverty' – gives a suitably sinister twist to the theme. Statistical comparisons of virtue, whether of individuals or societies, are not a promising branch of historical inquiry. But there exists one source of information as to the extent, if not the quality, of charity in England which has not (so far as I am aware) been analysed. Under the provisions of Gilbert's Act of 1782, the Ministers and Churchwardens of the parishes of England and Wales were required to make a return of all the charitable trusts then existing, with the date of creation, the name of the donor, the object, the capital

[1] See J. H. Hutchins, *Jonas Hanway 1712–86* (London, 1940), pp. 47–75.

and annual income, and the title of the trustees responsible for administering the charity.[1] In all, some sixty or seventy thousand separate donations, mainly of seventeenth and eighteenth-century origin, were recorded. They yielded a total annual income of £258,700 spread over all the counties of England and Wales. All but £6,236 came from English returns – a capital value all told of some £5 million in the ratio of £5 worth of land for every £1 of other types of investment. The majority of the benefactors defined their intentions only in general terms: food and clothing or fuel for the poor. A few were more specific. These poor were to have beef, those herrings; some got linen, others woollens. Poor men were to have coats, or shirts and shifts, poor women to have gowns. There was to be provision 'to marry poor maidens'. The poor here were to have Bibles, the poor children there to have books. This village was to have an almshouse, another a charity school. Mr Tomkins of Abingdon would relieve 'poor Dissenters (but not Papists)'. And so on. Obscurities abound. Many charities have no date. Many no doubt were omitted. There are hints at misappropriation. Of many a benefaction the authorities could only observe: 'but we do not apprehend that it was ever received'.

To interpret reliably the enormous volume of information contained in the returns calls for an intimate knowledge of local economic and social history. But by a combination of random sampling and parochial analysis some pretty reliable impressions can, I believe, be obtained. The incidence of charities is related broadly to the size and character of the geographical areas, the density of the population and the general prosperity of the town or parish. As one might expect, the City of London, the Home Counties and Midlands were relatively generously endowed. Large areas like the West Riding and rich counties like Kent come top of the income-by-county analysis. To prepare any definitive analysis would require far more study than I have been able to give for the purpose of this paper. The brief survey that has been undertaken does not, however, provide any warrant for supposing that the well-to-do were left any less charitably disposed by the social, economic and religious changes in the half-century that followed the Restoration. There was

[1] *Abstract of Returns made by Ministers and Churchwardens of the Several Parishes and Townships of England and Wales. Ordered, by the House of Commons, to be printed, 1816.*

undoubtedly some gradual decline – perhaps 10 per cent to 20 per cent – between the *average* number of trusts created in the half-century before, and the half-century after, 1660. A similar fall occurred in the following fifty years. Josiah Child has himself remarked that 'formerly in the days of our pious ancestors the work was done but now charity is decreased'; but he goes on to explain that this did not proceed from any decline in charitableness, so much as from doubts whether it was proper that private gifts by the benevolent should reduce the poor rate levied on those with less tender consciences.[1] It could indeed hardly be expected in a period when the yield from the poor rate was raised from £665,000 to £900,000 in fifteen years (1685–1701) that private donations should not in general be affected.[2] We have seen the same phenomenon in our own day as the welfare state has extended its functions. But even this trend was not universal. Suffolk, which comes after the West Riding in the volume of charity endowment, was not amongst the largest shires and was if anything less densely populated than a number of surrounding areas.[3] Is it unreasonable to suggest that its position was probably related to the presence of those *entrepreneurs* of the local draperies, Old and New, of whom Unwin himself wrote so eloquently? And what of Bristol with its noble record of over six hundred charities? A high proportion – almost a third – date from the half-century after the Restoration. It was no accident that Cary was a Bristol man: Bristol was surely the most benevolent place in England. The City of London had well over a thousand trusts, of which about one-third were created between the Restoration and the Peace of Utrecht. At Norwich, too, nearly a third of the 160-odd trusts likewise dated from this period. The collective charge that a whole class was through several generations guilty of social irresponsibility must, I think, be rejected as non-proven. The social conscience of the trading classes seems to me to have been no less tender than that of their feudal predecessors in office and may in some respects have been more sensitive. For the merchant did not move in society with the unselfconscious ease of the landed magnate nor speak with

[1] Child, *New Discourse* (1694), p. 84.

[2] Figures from Beloff, *op. cit.*, passim.

[3] H. C. Darby, *Historical Geography of England before 1800* (Cambridge, 1936), p. 524, fig. 83.

the confident voice of the learned clerk. He was in general a little more anxious than they to stand well with his fellow men, and for this, less fortunate members of society had cause to be thankful. Charity might go on breaking in. His habit of discriminating between deserving and less deserving beneficiaries may register a spiritual decline when compared with that medieval almsgiving which aimed only at the moral betterment of the donor; but it is by no means certain that the change brought any one material loss.

Amongst the many uncertainties in the returns of charities one trend emerges clearly: the growing proportion of donors who felt moved to endow some form of active apprenticeship or instruction for the juvenile poor, as distinct from the passive forms of relief common in earlier periods. It is a reminder that these were the early years of that remarkable movement for charity schools which was co-ordinated from 1699 by the SPCK. Hundreds of thousands of children, for whom no other means of education existed, received in the thousands of such schools the rudiments of education, religion and practical training that gave them a chance to earn a living.[1] At the peak of the movement the boys went as apprentices into every kind of trade, the girls became sempstresses or domestic servants. Again, it is easy to put a cynical motive to the work, to point to the drift away from literary and religious studies to technical training and utility. Some falling away of standards there may have been. Yet the charity schools remain a notable instance of that principle of voluntary association which historians like Unwin and Tawney have rightly enjoined on us to behold and admire as a vital element in social development. No previous age had faced such a formidable social problem and none certainly had attempted to relieve, employ or educate an army of poor already alarmingly enlarged by natural increase. These improvisations in social service failed or fell short of their object not because of a shortage of good intentions or of money, but because the supply of those capable of organizing and administering them with reasonable efficiency, honesty and compassionate understanding was totally inadequate. To read the replies made by parish governors to Hanway is to realize how appalling were the

[1] M. G. Jones, *The Charity School Movement: A Study of 18th Century Puritanism in Action* (Cambridge, 1938), *passim.*

difficulties encountered in the organization of poor relief, how rarely a parish could find a treasure like the splendid Nurse Howe of St Mary Whitechapel, how few were the Humphrey Clinkers, how numerous the Tom Neros. To endure the continual proximity of the poor a man needed to be either especially saintly or especially impervious to human suffering, cruelty, filth and corruption. In such a situation it was not unnatural that men should lose faith in the efficacy of high principles and take refuge in the reflection that 'whate'er is best administered is best'. Yet the art of administration was equally elusive. Administration, as the modern world understands it, is a Victorian invention resting on Victorian values: it ran counter to much that was characteristic of eighteenth-century society. Enough of the bad old days remained in 1857 to provide Charles Dickens with material for his classic satire on bureaucracy: the Circumlocution Office in *Little Dorrit*.[1] He would not have been entirely at a loss for material a century later.

The apathy, indifference and chaos of the eighteenth-century poor law was the product not of a new capitalist ethic, but of the frustration, failure and occasional panic of a generation faced by a problem beyond its power to control. The heart of the matter was contained in the title of Defoe's famous pamphlet: *Everybody's Business is Nobody's Business* (1728). This applied not only to the condition of the institutions, but to the Settlement Laws themselves. Few historians today accept Adam Smith's famous strictures in the Laws at their face value, but it was a fact that they gave local authorities powers of ejectment that at first might appear ruthless. Yet here again, the preamble to the Act which explains why the powers were deemed necessary puts the problem in a different light.[2] The provision of relief for the unemployed differed greatly between one parish and another and those parishes 'which endeavoured to do their duty in this respect were inundated by distressed paupers'. In short, what came to be regarded by later critics as a system of calculated brutality and repression arose in the first place not from unconcern or harshness, but out of a desire to protect the efforts of

[1] See Leo Silberman's introduction (1957) to *The Statesman*, by Henry Taylor, especially pp. xx to xxv. The original title of *Little Dorrit* was to have been *Nobody's Fault*.

[2] E.g. E. M. Hampson, *The Treatment of Poverty in Cambridgeshire* (Cambridge, 1934), pp. 125–6.

those local authorities who were trying hardest to improvise remedies.

Those who do not trust interventionism are apt to inveigh alternately against its wickedness and its futility. It cannot have been both. The influence of 'policy' on the labour situation in the seventeenth century may have been exaggerated;[1] certainly 'policy' was to an important extent a reflection of social facts. Yet it seems an oddly misplaced modesty in scholars to disown the historical importance of ideas. The great Debate of the Poor conducted in press, pamphlet and Parliament had helped to elucidate the importance of labour – skilled labour in particular – to the community. The facts of unemployment and poverty had joined with the ideas of educational reform that stemmed originally from Comenius and Milton and the junction stimulated a new emphasis on apprenticeship, training and skill. Later theories of labour value have their roots in these years. Yet though the debaters had broadened and socialized their criteria of the nation's economic welfare, they remained mercantilists to a man. Hartlib, for all his precocious concern with technology, monetary substitutes and the like, was not free from the orthodox preoccupation with shipping and 'dominion on the sea and thereby the strength and renown and flourishing estate of the nation'.[2] Defoe has sometimes been credited with precociously free trade views on the strength of the part he played in Harley's *Mercator*, but in fact his views remained conventionally mercantilist and protectionist.[3] Firmin was amongst the stoutest opponents of the import of French textiles. Mandeville, for all his scorn of bullionism, remained firmly anchored to the old principles, enjoining upon politicians that 'above all, they'll keep a watchful Eye over the Balance of Trade in general and never suffer that all the Foreign Commodities together, that are imported in one year, shall exceed in value what of their own growth or manufacture is in the same exported to others'.[4] The principles of *Machtpolitik* had no more single-minded disciple than Jonas Hanway, who dedicated one of his

[1] Coleman, 'Labour in the English Economy of the 17th Century', *Economic History Review*, viii (1956).

[2] Samuel Hartlib, *Legacy of Husbandry* (London, 1655), p. 292.

[3] See especially *An Humble Proposal to the People* of England in the *Works* (Oxford, 1841), xviii. 27, 41, 45.

[4] B. Mandeville, *The Fable of the Bees*, ed. F. B. Kaye, 2 vols (Oxford, 1924), i. 116.

principal works to Anson, the victor of Finisterre.[1] John Cary, the great Bristol merchant and philanthropist, exemplified perfectly the union of mercantilist principles with ideals of social reform. The theme of his famous *Essay* of 1695 was that some trades were profitable to the nation and should be encouraged; others were harmful and should be discouraged. In making its decisions between the two, government should be guided not so much by the net effects on the bullion flow as by the results in terms of manufacture and employment. As an economist, Cary was heir to the ideas of Child – balance-of-trade-mercantilism modified by considerations of employment. His influence was exercised equally on trade policy and on social reform. But it was not only in England where his writings were widely distributed and read down to the mid-eighteenth century. This type of mercantilism – what might not unfairly be called 'social mercantilism' – was the most powerful formative influence on continental mercantilism in the eighteenth century. Two of the founding fathers of German *Kameralwissenschaft* – Becher and von Schroeder – were resident in England in these years (J. J. Becher fled to England in 1680 and remained here till his death in 1685; von Schroeder lived in London from about 1663 to 1674 when he returned to Germany) and the resemblance between the 'equilibrium of occupation' of Schroeder's *Fürstliche Schatz und Rentkammer* (1686) and the ideas of Child and Cary is too close to be accidental. From this, three-quarters of a century later, came Sonnenfels's theory of the two trade balances by which economic health must be judged: the 'monetary' and the 'employment' balance. The genealogy of mercantilism in Italy is equally clear. When Genovesi came to establish a flourishing school of economics at Naples in the 1750s, he began by translating John Cary's *Essay* for his pupils' benefit, while relegating Mun's earlier work to an appendix. His own doctrine that distinguished between the 'useful commerce' which exported manufactures and the 'harmful' which brought in foreign manufactures, was the word precisely as Cary had preached it. There can be little doubt that the social and economic policy of enlightened despotism in Eastern Europe owed most of its theoretical foundations to English 'social mercantilism'. Even in France, the new synthesis was not without influence. De

[1] *Historical Account of the British Trade over the Caspian Sea* (London, 1754), i. 421.

Gournay, then an *intendant* for commerce, who stood between the extremes of mercantilist and physiocratic dogma, published in 1754 a French edition of the works of Child and Culpeper.[1] In some sense, England was only paying back an intellectual debt owed to Europe. For it is a remarkable fact that not a little of the 'welfare' element in that doctrine may be traced to thinkers of European origin. Hartlib was a Pole, something of a cosmopolitan who spoke several languages including Dutch.[2] Comenius, the source of much of the educational controversy of these years, was a Czech. Chamberlen was by origin French; Plockhoy, a Zeelander. Mandeville came from Rotterdam. That the debate which had begun round the theme of wealth and conquest had broadened into a debate on social ends was not a little due to their intervention. It was not only English economic and technological organization that was leavened by immigrant influence, but English social ideas too.[3]

At their weakest, the criticisms of the social arrangements in the post-Restoration age to which I have referred imply that at that time human nature amongst the ruling classes took a distinct turn for the worse. More charitably, we might take the theory to be that in the social situation of that time the worse side of human nature found more opportunities to exhibit itself. The evidence of the creation of charitable trusts seems to me to dispose of any sweeping allegations of this kind. It is rather evident that, on the contrary, local experiments and experiences grew into something like a social philosophy which grafted new social ends on to the older strategic and monetary objectives of mercantilist thought. There was no unanimity about the means to be employed: there was indeed a bitter and protracted debate between those who believed, with Child, that the problem of poverty demanded direct treatment – the workhouse and the spinning school – and those who believed, with Mandeville and Defoe, that this was a problem which could be dispersed only through an accelerated rate of economic activity in general. The alignment of supporters, it is plain, can in no way be

[1] A. Oncken, *Die Maxime Laissez Faire et Laissez Passer* (Berne, 1886), pp. 87–9.

[2] Turnbull, *op. cit.* See the same author's *Samuel Hartlib. A Sketch of His Life and Relations to J. A. Comenius* (Oxford, 1920); also Brit. Mus., Sloane MSS. 654, fos. 345–8.

[3] For the influence of immigrants on technology, etc., see, e.g., W. Cunningham, *Alien Immigrants* (Cambridge, 1897).

explained in terms of economic interest; and the ranks of those who took what has often been regarded as the tough line included many (like Dr Johnson) who qualify neither as capitalists nor as puritans and who can hardly be accused of inhumanity. Both sides recognized that the employment of the poor – and especially their skilled employment – was an objective to be pursued as a means to the prosperity of individuals and of society; but many recognized that it was, besides, a social and religious duty. Here was, in fact, not the monotone of repression, but the antiphony of a genuine debate in which the claims of material interest and social welfare were mixed in proportions not discreditable to the age. To administrators and thinkers in the less fortunate, more backward states of middle and south Europe, such arguments seemed to be the talisman of English progress. Writing later in the eighteenth century Hannah More described the period we have been examining as 'an age of benevolence'. Perhaps the *Bas Bleu* was predisposed in favour of the paternalism for which her native Bristol was famous. But her verdict is entitled to respect, especially as it seems that the opposite conclusion has been reached by the device of peopling the post-Restoration scene with selected cartoon figures more appropriate to the comedy of Congreve or Wycherley than to serious historical study. As historians we might do well to ponder what an eminent critic has written of this technique of caricature as it was employed by the dramatists of the Restoration: 'It is in a sense prig-drama. It flatters the vanity of the spectator for whose amusement the weaknesses of his friends are held up'.[1] It is true that there is weighty authority for the view that it is the historian's task to sit in judgement. 'Morality,' said Sir Thomas Browne, 'is not ambulatory', and Acton invoked his support for the view that the historian should err on the side of severity rather than risk the moral perils of leniency.[2] But Acton also saw the dangers that arise from haste and prejudice. The 'weighing of testimony' was for him the vital part of the historian's task.[3] There is not, after all, much fundamental difference between that and Professor Butterfield's injunction: 'to surround the man with all that can be gathered in the way of

[1] Bonamy Dobree, *Restoration Comedy 1660–1720* (Oxford, 1924), p. 11.
[2] *Lectures on Modern History* (1930 edn), p. 28.
[3] *Ibid.*, p. 16.

historical explanation'.[1] When Acton spoke,[2] the impact of the social sciences on the study of history in England was but recent. When historians spoke of moral judgements they still thought of the actions of individuals, and principally of rulers and statesmen who were conceived to have shaped the course of events. It is different with the sociologized history of our own day which is less concerned with individuals and more with men as members of social groups. It is curious that the socially-scientific historians began by glibly ordering men's characters according to their occupations and ended by dispatching to collective perdition whole classes of men throughout several generations on the strength of evidence which the late Judge Lynch might have hesitated to regard as adequate. So far from reducing the need to weigh the testimony, this new sociological trend in historical technique makes it all the more imperative, lest history should sink to the rough justice and intellectual shallowness of a standardized political conflict.

[1] *History and Human Relations* (1951), p. 119.
[2] June 1895.

6

Cloth Production and International Competition in the Seventeenth Century[1]

'. . . the whole World as to Trade, is but as one Nation or People, and therein Nations are as Persons'.[2] Pronouncements such as this, backed by the faith that it was peace, industry and freedom, not 'policies', that brought trade and wealth, were to make Dudley North a paragon to the later classical economists – 'an Achilles without a heel' as McCulloch described him.[3] To contemporaries, North's views must have sounded more like the triumph of hope over experience. There was, however, one respect in which North could claim that his conception was actuality and not merely wishful prophesying. For all the mercantilist barriers that criss-crossed them and bedevilled the fortunes of individual producers, the cloth markets of the seventeenth century formed something like a single theatre of economic operations, within which technology, patterns and fashions were borrowed (or purloined), raw materials bought, sold and smuggled, and finished products marketed, all on a massive scale. So that when in the next century the author of the *Chronicon Rusticum – Commerciale* compiled his devotional history of the English woollen industry, he found himself compelled to trace out the interlocking complexities of the Italian, Dutch, French, Polish, Silesian and German industries as well as those of his own.[4]

Even more than the conscientious Smith, the student who

[1] This paper was first published in *The Economic History Review*, Second Series' Vol. xiii, No. 2 (1960) pp. 209–21.

[2] *Early English Tracts on Commerce*, ed. J. R. McCulloch, Discourses (1691).

[3] *Ibid.* p. xiii.

[4] John Smith, *Chronicon Rusticum – Commerciale or Memoirs of Wool* (1747).

follows in his footsteps at the present time must share the view that the world's cloth markets and the industries that supplied them need, like a jig-saw puzzle, to be seen as a whole: taken apart, the component bits do not altogether make sense. This is particularly true of the English industry. Fortunately for the clothier, less so for the historian, the industry did not suffer from the attention of the exciseman, its raw materials did not, for the most part, pass through the Customs House, and much of its output was sold on home markets unchecked and untaxed by bureaucracy. The evidence regarding the volume of production and the ebb and flow of trade is therefore more than usually scanty, and Smith could censure, quite rightly, the 'Spirit of Romance . . . and Credulity' that enveloped most writings on the subject. 'Extravagance and Ignorance' had produced merely 'a Heap of *Falsehood* and *Chimera's* . . .'[1] The Dutch cloth industry, contrariwise, is richly documented and valuable statistical evidence of the Italian industry has recently been uncovered. The process of comparing and correlating this local evidence yields, it is suggested, a sum total of information greater than can be obtained by examining each parcel of evidence in national isolation. And because the dynamic of these industries was to a considerable extent international competition, important local developments that cannot be satisfactorily explained by local evidence can be illuminated by evidence of developments elsewhere.

The broad outlines of the English cloth trade, and the evolution of the industries that supplied it, have become tolerably clear in recent years. From 1615 at the latest the old broadcloth industry that had been a bright jewel in the earlier Tudor expansion ceased to glitter, and during the next quarter of a century its gleam became ever duller. This depression of the woollen industry proper was increasingly offset by the rise of a buoyant new industry, or rather a series of industries, which made many different fabrics. The broadest distinction between the old and the new was to be seen between the 'pure' cloth of the old order and the 'stuffs' of the new. The former, in which short carded yarn provided both warp and weft, was a fabric thick, fine and costly. The latter, in which both warp and weft were of the long, combed wool, was in general lighter, coarser

[1] Smith, *op. cit.* pp. xi–xiii.

and cheaper. Between these two technological limits there stood, however, a third type of fabric in which the weft consisted of carded yarn (or cotton or silk) while the warp was of combed yarn. Thus while the 'says' of Elizabethan fame came into the category of 'stuffs', the 'bays' and serges were a 'mixed' woollen and worsted cloth.[1] In general, the difference between the pure woollens on the one hand and the stuffs and mixtures on the other was that in the latter the pattern of the weave could still be seen in the finished fabric, while it disappeared from most, at any rate, of the fine thick woollens.[2]

While newer stuffs and mixtures – the so-called New Draperies – were rising, the manufacture of woollens stagnated or even declined. It may be going too far to say that, by the eve of the Civil War, the trade in the newer fabrics almost equalled in value that of the old,[3] but the trend was unmistakably in that direction. The curves of the first four decades can without risk be extrapolated through the rest of the century and into the next. The trade in new worsteds and mixed fabrics introduced by the 'strangers' in the 1560s was putting the older manufacturers under severe competition by later Elizabethan times. By the mid-seventeenth century the old broadcloth industry of Suffolk which had supplied a major share of Ipswich export cargoes was in decline, and a similar trend was observable in the west and later in the north.

'It surpasseth my skill', confessed Thomas Fuller, the antiquarian, 'to name the several stuffs. The nimble woof, its

[1] This technical fact seems to invalidate the statistical assumption of Miss Deane [P. Deane, 'The Output of the Woollen Industry in the Eighteenth Century', *Journal of Economic History*, xvii (1957)] that the output of the woollen and worsted industries respectively was in direct proportion to the supply of short and long wool. Such an assumption must surely exaggerate the output of the woollen manufacturers who used only short wool and underestimate the output of the makers of mixed fabrics who used a variety of yarns. In the early decades of the 18th century, the export of woollens proper was only a fraction of that of worsteds, stuffs, mixed cloths etc. See below, p. 98 n. 2.

[2] See, e.g. Lipson, *Woollen and Worsted Industries*, pp. 128–30; Astrid Friis, *Alderman Cockayne's Project and the Cloth Trade* (1927), pp. 1–3.

[3] F. J. Fisher, 'London's Export Trade in the Early 17th century', *Economic History Review*. Second Series, Vol. III, No. 2 (1950). Mr R. Davis, 'English Foreign Trade 1660–1700 in *Economic History Review* Second Series, Vol. VII, No. 2 (1954), has commented that the figures of London trade, used by Professor Fisher, would naturally reflect the City's larger interest in Southern European markets (which took a higher proportion of the newer fabrics than the Northern markets). But see below p. 107 n. 3.

artificial dancing in several postures about the standing warp, produceth infinite varieties in this kind.' Fuller's 'infinite varieties', confusing to a contemporary, have become even more difficult to identify and classify with the passage of time, the corruption of names, the changed meaning of technical terms and the loss of identifiable samples. Yet without some attempt to identify, we shall lack the clues to the fortunes, good or ill, of the cloth industry, which was not a single industry but a *congeries* of industries whose relationships and fortunes were the result of continual competition for markets between their varied and changing products. East Anglia was the original home of the 'stuffs' proper. Norwich specialized in fine worsteds, or worsteds mixed with silk or cotton, the so-called bombazines widely used by middle class persons – as Clapham used to say, 'respectable women not of the first elegance'. Suffolk specialized in 'says', a hard-wearing worsted often used for men's dress. In Colchester, and along the Essex-Suffolk borders, the strangers had set up to make not only says but bays, a cheap unfulled mixture of worsted warp and woollen weft commonly used for cloaks. The 'perpetuanas' were not unlike bays. Lavenham made 'callimancoes', a light worsted in striped colours much in favour with Eastland traders who sold them to Russia where they were used by 'the Tartars and Siberian tribes for sashes'.[1]

Similarly, though more slowly, the west and north were turning over to the new fabrics. The earlier export trade from both these areas had been in the cheaper types of woollens – dozens or kerseys. The kersey was not, as is often said, a worsted but a coarser, thinner woollen which shared one characteristic of the worsted: it carried a visible pattern of weave. In the latter decades of the seventeenth century, Yorkshire was moving away from kerseys and dozens towards bays, serges and shaloons. Serges were, like bays, a mixed woollen and worsted. Shaloons, much used for coverlets and linings, grew mightily round Halifax. Such were to be the articles handled by Joseph Holroyd at the turn of the century and, a few years later, by Sam Hill.[2] Devonshire had changed tack equally decisively. By 1700, cloths and kerseys had made way for serges and perpetuanas, and

[1] *Report on Hand Loom Weavers, 1840*, Vol. XXIII, p. 302.

[2] *Letter books of J. H. Holroyd and S. Hill* (Halifax, 1914). Also H. Heaton, *The Yorkshire Woollen and Worsted Industries* (Oxford, 1920), p. 268.

Exeter's exports of serge represented a value not far short of half a million sterling, or 28 per cent, of the nation's cloth exports.[1]

By 1700, then, there could be no question that the new fabrics had established a predominance in the nation's woollen exports. Of the outport exports, Exeter serges and Norwich stuffs alone accounted for 60 per cent of the total.[2] The origins of this change are less certain. Professor Fisher has seen it as an essential part of the shift of emphasis in British trade from northern to southern Europe. The ending of the war with Spain opened up prospects of trade with Spain and the Mediterranean while the Thirty Years War darkened them in the north. He sees the 'New Draperies' as the response of industrial enterprise to a changed political and commercial situation, yielding 'a range of fabrics admirably suited for the warm but non-tropical Mediterranean'.[3] The conjunction of quality with a greater measure of commercial freedom than existed in the more northerly and older markets ensured the success of the new trades. More recently, Mr Bowden has put forward another explanation of the supersession of woollens and one which differs, superficially at any rate, from Professor Fisher's. The dynamic of the change, he believes, was not commercial but technological. Of the several factors which explain the change of fortunes in cloth 'the most important . . . was the changing character of the English wool supply'.[4] The main influence on the nature of wool, he suggests, was the pasturage itself. The area producing the finest wools was the area most susceptible to sixteenth and seventeenth century enclosures, and with enclosure came a heavier fleece and a longer staple: but the wool was coarser, less suited to the needs of woollens and more suited to the newer fabrics. The short staple wool, suitable for carding, which was produced was, he has argued, inferior to the imported wools from Spain. Hence the one spectacular success amongst genuine woollens in the seventeenth century was the 'Spanish' cloth of Wiltshire, to

[1] W. G. Hoskins, *Industry, Trade, and People in Exeter 1688–1800* (1935), pp. 66–74.

[2] Davis, *op. cit.* See also the appendix to *The Answer of Robert, Earl of Oxford* (1715) which suggests that the pure woollens accounted for only a fraction of export values by the early eighteenth century.

[3] Fisher, *op. cit.*

[4] P. J. Bowden, 'The Wool Supply and the Woollen Industry', *Economic History Review* Second Series, Vol. IX (1956).

which Mr Ramsay has already drawn attention in his study of the Wiltshire industry.[1] Originally, Wiltshire clothiers had made principally undressed and undyed broadcloth. In the first decade of the seventeenth century, they turned to these so-called Spanish 'medley' dyed cloths, achieving a measure of success which alarmed their Dutch competitors, so that the merchant adventurers who imported the new fabric into Holland were forced out of their then staple, Delft, to the nearby and more complaisant city of Rotterdam. The fuller significance of this will be examined later.

If reference is made to the nature of European competition for the cloth markets, which it is the main purpose of this article to explore, it will emerge that the commercial and technological explanations of the trends of the English industry are less alternative than complementary explanations. The evolution of other industries, the Italian and the Dutch in particular, illuminates both the elements of enterprise and technological change in the situation, suggesting at the same time that neither 'explanation' is without limitations.

In the Mediterranean markets the main new factor was the decline and virtual disappearance of Italy as a leading producer. The great Italian cloth-making cities – Milan, Florence, Como – had all suffered vicissitudes in the sixteenth century. But in 1600, Italy still remained an advanced economy. By 1700 that was all changed. In the course of the seventeenth century the woollen production of the leading urban producers had dropped from somewhere between 70,000 and 80,000 cloths a year to a few thousand. The woollen and silk textile industries were all in final decline.[2] Venetian industry was most successful in postponing the end.[3] It had reached its peak somewhere between the 1580s and the 1620s, but as late as the 1640s, it could still rise to levels of production reminiscent of palmier days. Thereafter the decline was slow but inexorable. Its sources were the failure of Venetian industry to hold its markets, export markets especially, against foreign competition. The most recent

[1] G. D. Ramsay, *The Wiltshire Woollen Industry* (1943), Ch. VIII *passim.*

[2] C. M. Cipolla, 'The Decline of Italy', *Economic History Review* Second Series, Vol. V, No. 2 (1952).

[3] D. Sella, 'Les Mouvements Longs de l'Industrie Lainière à Venise', *Annales*, No. 1 (1957). Dr Sella's figures are taken from material recently discovered in the *Archivio di Stato.*

and thorough inquiry suggests that the reason for this failure lay in the high costs of the industry and its inability to follow the caprices of fashion. Northern competitors in the Levant – England and Holland – produced fabrics 'more pleasing and less costly' which apparently seduced Turkish customers, as a report to the Senate explained in 1668.[1] The Turks wanted cheap, light cloths. The Venetians offered dear, heavy ones. Apart from the rigidity imposed on the industry and the characer of its products by gild regulations, it is plain that raw, material costs were a major problem. Venetian cloths were traditionally pure woollens comparable to English and (as will be shown later) Dutch woollens. They were made exclusively of fine Spanish wool, and the supply of this had fallen into the hands of a small group of monopolists. It seems, therefore, that raw material supply may have created something of a problem for the Venetian industry – Venice did not apparently attempt a 'New Drapery' – but the prime source of trouble was the appearance of the northern 'Stuffs'. The twenty English 'houses' at Constantinople in 1600 boded ill for the future. By 1631 Venetian output dropped to 8,000 pieces – between a third and a quarter of the volume of thirty years earlier.[2] It was nearly a century since it had gone so low. This diminution and ultimate disappearance of Italian competition left the way open for the northern traders, whose ships had been appearing in the eastern Mediterranean regularly since the 1570s.[3]

The consignments of textiles which formed a principal weapon of the English and Dutch traders in the battle for the Levant trade were thought of by the Venetians as of one kind, and as constituting a single threat: they were cheap, they were light and they were northern. It is a salutary reminder that though the English and Dutch industries were rivals, and though, under the pressure of competition in the seventeenth century, they were to develop along different lines, they stemmed in origin from precisely the same roots. Cloth-making in Holland, as in England, was carried on in many places – Amsterdam, Haarlem, Delft, Gouda, Utrecht – and a score of smaller towns all

[1] *Archivio di Stato, Senato Rettori*, 30 December 1668. Quoted by Sella, *op. cit.*

[2] Sella, *op. cit.*, Tables.

[3] See F. Braudel, *La Méditerranée et La Monde Méditerranéen à l'epoque de Philippe II* (1949), esp. pp. 479–81.

had their cloth industries: but the most intensive concentration was at Leiden, and it is the Leiden evidence that has survived in greatest abundance and been analysed most thoroughly. By the middle of the seventeenth century Leiden, with 63,000 inhabitants, was a half to a third as large again as Bristol or Norwich. It represented the largest single industrial concentration in Europe, and was turning out cloth to a total annual value of nine million guilders[1] – say about half the value of the total British cloth exports at the time. Probably the largest part of this was exported, and the competition with English textiles both at home and abroad was direct, sharp and continuous throughout the century. The structure of both industries was shaped in considerable measure by that competition and so were the patterns of their production.

Both these major competitors for the world's cloth markets owed their position to the revivifying stream of skill and energy that flowed from the southern Netherlands in the 1560s and 1570s. The same Flemish refugees who brought the New Draperies to Norwich, Colchester and other towns brought the '*nieuw draperie*' to Leiden. They had presumably settled in East Anglia not only because it was their nearest refuge but also because it was already the centre of a worsted manufacture. In 1577 a small group of Flemish refugees at Colchester, bay and say makers, were enticed back to the Low Countries by the privileges offered them by the Leiden town government to settle in Leiden and set up their manufacture of stuffs.[2] From these small beginnings, there grew in the next half century an extensive and thriving industry which dwarfed the stunted remains of the old Leiden woollen industry, the '*Oude Leidsche Draperie*'. The products of this group of manufactures corresponded pretty closely to those of the industries which were growing up at the same time in England: there was, especially in the first half of the century, heavy production of bays (a mixed woollen and worsted as in England), says (a hard wearing stuff) and cheap mixed fustians. As the figures given below show, the output of pure woollens (*lakens*) was very small in these years. The balance of the Leiden industries, and their changing fortunes through

[1] N. Posthumus, *De Geschiedenis van de Leidsche Lakenindustrie* (1939), Vol. III, pp. 882, 941.

[2] Posthumus, *op. cit.*, pp. 12–14.

the century, are apparent in the following tables showing production of the different branches of Leiden industry by pieces.[1]

(total to nearest 000 cloths)

	Woollens	Worsteds or mixed cloths					Total
	lakens	bays	says	camlets	arras	fustians	
1620	1,500	17,000	50,000	—	6,000	22,000	97,000
1640	11,000	19,000	33,000	—	10,000	17,000	90,000
1660	20,000	16,000	34,000	38,000	3,000	7,000	118,000
1680	21,000	10,000	19,000	34,000	—	1,000	85,000
1700	25,000	6,000	8,000	37,000	—	6,000	82,000

Thus the outstanding feature of the period from 1620 to 1700 at Leiden was the rise of a new woollen manufacture, and the protracted but inexorable decline of the worsted and mixed cloth industries, with the exception of one – the *grein* or camlet industry. In short, the fortunes of the Leiden industries were exactly the reverse of those of the English textile industry, where the worsted group was in the ascendant and woollens in decline.

The explanation of this is not far to seek. For reasons, some of which are clear and others less clear, the Leiden *laken* manufacture reached a good competitive footing with its English counterpart; the Leiden worsted group did not: indeed it seems to have lost whatever advantages it began with. One of the original blessings bestowed by the Flemish innovators at Leiden in the 1570s was their emancipation of the industry from its dependence on imported English wool at a time when the volume of protest from English interested parties against the export of wool and ancillary materials was becoming ominously loud, and the revolt against Spain cut off the supply of fine Spanish wool. The 'New Draperies' could use the long *kamwool* (combed wool) from domestic sources – north and south Holland, Brabant, Friesland and elsewhere – or from Pomerania. This was not, even for the less exacting requirements of the worsted group, of the best quality, and much of it evidently fell below the standard of the supply which had formerly been obtained from England. But it sufficed, in a period when the New Draperies in England were also having teething troubles, to establish the newer fabrics, for they owed their international reputation less to the quality of their raw materials than to the skill which was employed in dyeing and finishing them.[2] Such

[1] Constructed and adapted from data in Posthumus, *op. cit.*, Vol. III, 930–1.
[2] For the technical details see Posthumus, *op. cit.* Vol. II, 257–79.

were the circumstances in which the large and flourishing manufacture of bays, says, fustians, and arras prospered in the early years of the seventeenth century, while the Old Drapery appeared to be dragging out a lingering death, deprived of its supply of both English and Spanish fine wool.

Then the trouble began. From the 1620s, bays and says began to run into difficulties, largely because of English competition, and especially, it would appear, in the Mediterranean markets. Leiden kept up a continual demand for protection in the home market and succeeded in 1643 in having dyed says and kerseys placed under the ban which had been introduced on dyed woollens during the Cockayne crisis in October 1614. Further demands continued to be raised whenever times were bad.[1] This was only one example of the trouble Dutch industry was to run into time and time again: it was far from easy to counter successfully the arguments of the powerful mercantile interests whose business consisted in importing English cloth.[2] More serious, perhaps, was the prohibition of English wool export. It seems reasonable to suppose that as the English makers acquired new skills in worsted making and finishing, the previously marginal importance of wool became crucial. Drebbel's cochineal and tin dye came into use at Bow: a Portuguese immigrant, Devora, brought the anil blue dyes in 1643: Bauer, 'a Fleming', added his unspecified but highly regarded contribution after the Restoration.[3] Petty, Boyle and Hooke all presented papers on the subject to the Royal Society in the 1660s. The English, said the governors of the woollens and bays industries in 1663, had stolen the technique and market for says from them.[4] The competition for obtaining supplies of appropriate wool thus became important. Since 1614, when the Anglo-Dutch disputes sharpened, and especially since 1622, when the commission on the

[1] See below n. 4 for the results during the depression of 1663.

[2] Amsterdam's trade with Exeter and Topsham, for example, consisted in trading German linens bleached in Haarlem for Devonshire cloth.

[3] See J. S. Burn, *History of the Protestant Refugees* (1846), p. 258. Also G. N. Clark, *Science and Social Welfare in the Age of Newton* (1937), p. 44, n.l. Roger Coke calls him Brewer, says his parents were English (victims of Laud?) and claims he brought fifty Walloons with him who instructed the English how to 'make and dye fine woolen cloths cheaper by 40 per cent than they could do before . . .' (Smith, *Memoirs of Wool* (1747), Vol. I, p. 229).

[4] *Bronnen tot de Geschiedenis van de Leidsche Textielnijverheid* (1918), Vol. V, 1651–1702, No. 29.

depression had drawn particular attention to the need, successive statutes and ordinances had tried to put teeth into the now traditional ban on wool export from England. There were prohibitions in 1622, 1630, 1632, 1634, 1639, 1647, 1649, 1650, 1651, 1652, 1660, 1662 – preliminaries to a code of legislation which remained in force till 1825. Scottish export, a convenient backdoor supply for the Dutch, was tackled by an Act of 1652. One of the excuses for the attack on New Netherland in 1664 was that the Dutch colonists were illegally purchasing large supplies of wool from their New England neighbours. The efficacy, and even more, the wisdom, of such legislation, has been much debated by later generations. One should not entirely neglect the view of contemporaries, English and Dutch, that the ban had important consequences. The neglect of the prohibitions, wrote the author of *The Golden Fleece* in 1656, would bring Holland and England to an equality or even benefit the Dutch. Their enforcement would damage the Dutch by forcing them 'to procure the wools through many Hands and several voyages'.[1] A few years later Leiden clothiers said the same thing: '... England, spacious and rich in sheep (*schaepryck*), forbids the export of wool and has it better and in greater abundance (than us) so that our wool must be imported and pass through more merchants' hands, bearing freight and toll, and is necessarily dearer in price....'[2] Although the Acts never wholly stopped the export of English wool, they reduced it to an insignificant trickle in the seventeenth century – perhaps some 3–4 per cent of a total foreign supply to the Dutch cloth industry, most of which came from Spain.

Only one branch of the Leiden worsted industries made any real progress in the seventeenth century (as the figures eloquently show): the manufacture of *greinen* (camlets),[3] which began in the third or fourth decade. The reasons for this fall are to be considered below. Bays held up better than the rest, but even they did not resist the sharper decline that set in after the Third Dutch War in the 1670s. By 1700, the entire worsted group, with the single exception of camlets, was at a low ebb.[4]

[1] W. S. Gent. *The Golden Fleece* (1656). [2] *Bronnen*, Vol. V, No. 29, para. 14.

[3] But see below p. 106 for the difference between Dutch *greinen* and English 'camlets'.

[4] The decline continued in the eighteenth century. The say and fustian branches virtually disappeared. Posthumus, *Tables*, Vol. III, 1098.

The evolution of the Dutch woollen industry proper in Holland in the seventeenth century stands in strong contrast to the decline of the worsted group. Turning the Cockayne crisis energetically to advantage, the woollen manufacturers of Leiden used their better protected position to build up an expanding production of *lakens*. The industry did not escape its ups and downs, but, as the table shows, it was the only branch of the Leiden industry which enjoyed a fairly steady increase through the years from 1620 to 1700 and whose output was greater in the 1690s than at any other period of the century. Here again, we have the reverse situation from that in England, where the makers of pure woollens were in difficulties, save for the 'Spanish' cloths of Wiltshire and, later, of neighbouring counties.[1]

Closer examination of the evidence leaves little doubt that these contrasting situations in the two major European textile industries were the result of direct competition, product by product, between them; and that the special achievements of the woollen and camlet branches of the Leiden industry must be related to the exploitation of the unique advantage these industries (and they alone) possessed in regard to raw material supply. The surviving figures for the first two months of 1661 show clearly the pattern of Anglo-Dutch competition in cloth. There had come, in two months, and from London alone (the governors of the *laken* and bay Halls at Leiden complained), the following:

7,377 pieces of 'woollens'.
158,073 pieces of 'manufactures' (worsteds).[2]

[1] Gloucestershire Clothiers only began to use Spanish wool in the eighteenth century, *V. C. H. Gloucestershire*. Also E. Moir in *Gloucestershire Studies* (ed. Finberg).

[2] See *Bronnen*, Vol. V, No. 30, para. 5, and No. 33, para 18. The detailed list is as follows:

7,377	cloths.
6,446	bays.
1,043	kerseys.
1,964	says.
11,967	serges.
8,366	perpetuanas.
10,494	hose.
110,316	'sayettes'.

It is not quite clear what was included in the very large item called 'sayettes'; presumably it is a generic term for cheap, possibly unfinished, worsteds of a cheap kind.

Presumably the larger part of the woollens were undyed, for the import of dyed woollens was forbidden: Wiltshire Spanish cloths may have escaped this ban if dyed in the wool, but even so they would have paid a stiffish tariff after 1651. The main threat was obviously to the Leiden worsted group, which bore the brunt of this English competition: to be precise some 96 per cent Northern Kerseys from Yorkshire competed with cheaper Leiden bays and (it was said) drove them off the market. Four times as many English bays were said to be sold in Holland as were made at Leiden. Blankets were likewise threatened. The price of 'gentlemen's says' (*heerensaaien*) dropped by 25 per cent between 1660 and 1670 and production fell by 50 per cent in face of English competition.[1] The valuable markets offered by the monastic establishments of Italy and Spain – monks and nuns were conspicuous consumers of cloth for habits – were invaded by the English makers of says, kerseys and long ells.[2]

How then did the camlet and woollen industries manage to fare so well in this competitive stress? The answer would seem to be a combination of circumstances involving raw materials, marketing and pricing.

The *greinen* of Leiden evidently differed considerably from those rough English 'camlets' which appear to have been the last refuge of a cloth district in decline.[3] They were the work of a group of Leiden makers, mostly of Walloon origin, who began about 1630 to manufacture a new kind of camlet, not unlike says. It was made partly of camel hair (Turkish yarn) or goats' hair, later mixed with wool or silk.[4] These 'Leiden Turks', as they came to be known, swiftly established a large market in both northern and southern Europe, and they sold especially well in France. Their main use was for men's clothing. With the camlet, Leiden had lighted on a worsted type of fabric, to the raw materials for which she had access at least as good as, if not better than, the English, and selling in markets where the Dutch

[1] The detailed effects of English competition on prices and wages are fully described in the Leiden petition printed as No. 30 in Vol. V. of the *Bronnen*.

[2] The cheaper 'natural' says of Leiden known as *monnikensaaien* went largely to the Carmelite monasteries of Italy. Compare Defoe, *A Plan of the English Commerce* (Edn. 1928), p. 138: 'In Italy the clergy wore black Bays, the Nuns were vail'd with fine says and Long Ells'. By this time they were English worsteds.

[3] J. H. Clapham, *Concise Economic History* (1949), p. 242.

[4] *Bronnen*, Vol. IV, No. 223. See also Posthumus, *op. cit.*, pp. 272–9.

were not worse burdened than their rivals. Little wonder that the English cast envious eyes on the camlet business. Sir George Downing, plotting as always for a favourable balance of trade and a greater volume of employment, wrote to the Lord Chancellor, Clarendon, from The Hague early in 1664: 'I have this day given a pass to an Englishman to goe for England, who is a weaver of camlotts and moohaires. He tells me yt. there are at least 500 weavers of such kind of stuffs and such as work under ym, yt are gone from yt place for want of worke within these 2 months, some for England, and others for other parts —'.[1] Evidently the slump was but temporary. The English manufacturers do not seem to have succeeded in producing a competitive product, at any rate for some time.[2]

For all that has been said about the greater saleability of the new fabrics in semi-tropical areas, Leiden woollens enjoyed wide markets in the Mediterranean and Levant, and even in Africa and the Caribbean.[3] Only the English market was virtually closed to them by a tariff of ten shillings a yard. This the Leiden manufacturers regarded as intolerably high, and it remained a constant source of indignation.[4] The rising production of fine woollens at Leiden was based on the steady supply of Spanish wool that gradually became available after the truce. Of the total quantities of wool imported into the Republic to supplement home production, it appears that in the second half of the century roughly four-fifths came from Spain. Indeed, as well informed a technical writer as de la Court (himself a Leiden clothier) thought that the Dutch entirely monopolized the Spanish wool supply, to the detriment of the English woollens industry. Significantly, this supply began to assume real proportions in the 1620s, about the same time as the Leiden woollen industry proper began its remarkable seventeenth century renaissance. The vital character of Spanish wool to the growing *lakenindustrie* explains the full significance of a scheme that

[1] Downing-Clarendon, The Hague, 14 Feb. 1664. O.S. T. H. Lister, *Life and Administration of Edward, First Earl of Clarendon* (1837), Vol. III, 361.

[2] The author of *Englands Advocate* (1699) says that England had 'before the War' replaced the former import trade in 'Hair Camblets' from Brussels and Holland by English manufacturers and was exporting them to France too (p. 11).

[3] Posthumus, *op. cit.*, p. 825. It is possible to exaggerate the relationship of woollens to northern markets and worsteds to southern. The sale of callimancoes in Russia has been mentioned above.

[4] *Bronnen*, No. 29.

appeared on the eve of the First Dutch War. The English author (or authors) of *Considerations of the Advantages to the Commonwealth of England, by getting all the Spanish Cloth wools into English Hands – etc.* (1651) saw that while the ban on the export of wool from England might embarrass some branches of Dutch industry, it did nothing to hinder the most valuable of all: the fine woollens. The Spanish wool supply blunted the edge of English strategy by providing the basis for the most valuable of all the Leiden industries. As part of the economic warfare strategy of England, therefore, there should be established a private company to pre-empt all the wools of Segovia and Castile.[1] Nothing, so far as is known, came of the idea, but a similar scheme was revived in 1661–2 when another slump descended on the English cloth industry while its Dutch rivals were said to be enjoying a boom.[2]

Evidently the success of both woollens and camlets at Leiden was closely related to raw material supply: in the first case, Spanish, in the second, Turkish, wool. The industries concerned ran only one risk – insecurity in wartime, and that had to be accepted.[3] The progress of the *lakenindustrie* was related also to the notable advances made by experimenters like Cornelius Drebbel and Kepler, his son-in-law, in the arts of dyeing with indigo and cochineal. Here as elsewhere the mercantile and technological precocity of the Dutch went hand in hand. (It was no accident that colonial textile dyes were amongst the first articles of trade to be 'enumerated' under the Navigation Acts of the Restoration.) The result was, in the case of camlets and woollens, two commodities of high value and quality which stood up to foreign competition better than the cheaper varieties,

[1] J. Thurloe, *A Collection of State Papers* (1742), Vol. 1, p. 200.

[2] *State Papers Domestic*, 30 July, *Calendar 1661–2*, p. 449. As so often happened the Dutch held quite a different view of their condition which they regarded as unprecedentedly depressed. *Bronnen*, Vol. V, *passim*. A later proposal to revive the pre-emption of Spanish wool appears in *A Treatise of Wool and Cattle* (1677). Smith, printing it in *Memoirs of Wool* (1747) (Vol. I, 311), dismisses it as 'wild and weak'.

[3] Downing wrote from the Hague to Clarendon: '. . . . their grogrim yarne, by reason of the sinking of ye ship *King Solomon*, and the stop of ye rest of their Smirna fleete from Cadix, is risen within this month 24 stuivers a pound, which is a mighty rise. He saith also, yt, the sayd weavers doe complain infinitely yt their trade is lost; and yt in a little time, if this warre goes on and y ye Turky yarne and Spanish wooles be kept from coming in hither yt will be but a very thin towne' (14 Feb. 1664. O.S. *Lister, ibid.*)

where the high ratio of labour costs to raw material costs put Leiden at a disadvantage.[1] A quality *laken*, dyed and finished, would sell at anything from 5½ to 12½ guilders per ell. The next most valuable type was the camlet, at perhaps half this price. A say was not worth more than a third of the price of a camlet. Bays fetched a little more. Fustians were only worth half the price of says.

These prices put a different complexion on the Leiden production figures. While the worsted group produced a large output, its value (always excepting the camlets) was relatively smaller than that of the woollens. The total value of the Leiden industries rose from about 4 million guilders in 1630 to a peak of 9 million guilders in 1654. Thereafter there came a steady fall to 5–6 million guilders in 1700. Taking the peak year values, it becomes clear that fine woollens account for nearly half the total value and camlets for another third. Together they represented 77 per cent of the total. Bays and says together, represented only 16 per cent; fustians, arras, etc. the remainder. Thus the two branches mostly closely linked to fine imported materials and the most skilled techniques represented an economic activity of much greater value than might be deduced from the production figures. In 1655, camlets and woollens accounted for less than half the total pieces produced (some 50,000 out of 106,000) but they represented more than three-quarters of the total value of Leiden's production.

The high values of fine woollens and camlets, associated with

[1] The author of the proposals for pre-empting Spanish wool (Thurloe, *ibid.*) has an illuminating passage on the nature of competition for the fine cloth market. 'One Pound of English Wool of 12d price, is improved in a mixed [English] Cloth to 4s. so as ¾ of its value is merely made out of the Labour, and that Labour of Carding, Spinning, Dying, Weaving, Fulling and Working, does not cost us above ½ of what the *Hollander* pays, by reason of their high rates of Houses and Victuals, to which all Labourers' Wages are proportioned. But now, in fine *Spanish* wool that costs three times as much as our *ordinary* English *Wool*, that Advantage in the Labour doth not hold for us; nor can the most judicious Eye guess so near the true worth of fine Cloth, but that the Maker may at most times advance 10 *per Cent.* on the Fancy of the Buyer, which on coarse Cloths cannot be done; and therefore they paying no Import or Excise on the Manufacture, from the Sheep's Back to their own; and ours paying Customs here, and freight and Insurance thither, and a great Excise there, we cannot recover the Vent of our fine Cloth in *Holland*, (if we should be reconciled) nor in other Parts, nor get our Workmen home, but by keeping the *Hollander* from Spanish Wools.' The effect of taxation – excise especially – in raising wages and thereby costs, remains to be investigated. Contemporaries made much of it.

high quality, help to explain why these types of cloth maintained their position better than cheaper types. Under pressure from English competitors, operating at lower costs both of material and labour, prices of Leiden cheaper worsteds dropped to a point where Leiden manufacturers could no longer compete. The conditions of English rural cottage industry, where part-time wages were low and labour easily stood off in slack times, placed the English clothier at a distinct advantage in the cheaper lines. In the pure woollens and camlet markets, on the other hand, profit margins were higher, the high wage costs of an urban labour force more easily absorbed, and it seems as if the English manufacturers found it difficult to offer a competitive article. Perhaps this was partly because their access to the special imported raw material supplies required was less good: English writers were apt to stress the advantage that Dutch buyers overseas enjoyed in such matters by reason of the easier credit and lower interest rates on borrowed capital available in Holland.[1] In turn, the high cash value of the Dutch trade in fine cloths made of Spanish wool may help to explain the vigour with which the Dutch reacted to the import of the Wiltshire Spanish cloths.[2]

The end of the seventeenth century found the major part of the woollen cloth supply to world markets still in the hands of the English and Dutch clothiers. Their combined competition in southern European markets had finally dispatched an Italian industry structurally ossified, its enterprise and competitive power paralysed by the dead hand of local gild regulation.[3] The French were trying to break into the Levant trade with the medium quality ranges of Languedoc manufactures (where they were to do well in the eighteenth century) but their threat was not yet serious.[4] Downing could speak in the 1660s of a danger that Silesia might monopolize the coarse cloth trade while Holland would make the fine, and England would be driven back to her old status of wool producer;[5] but this was largely the

[1] Josiah Child, *A New Discourse of Trade* (1694), pp. 22, 23, 51, 52. Roger Coke, Barbon and Davenant all make similar points.

[2] Above, p. 106.

[3] Sella, *op. cit.*

[4] R. Paris, *Histoire du Commerce de Marseille 1660–1789* (Le Levant) (1957), pp. 543–5 and Cinquième Partie, Ch. II. *passim.*

[5] Thurloe, *op. cit.*, Vol. VII, p. 848.

language of rhetoric. Some growth of cheap textile manufactures in east Europe there certainly had been, and this, combined with the currency problem,[1] probably created difficulties for both English and Dutch exporters. The 'broad lists' of Yorkshire – a cheap and inferior kersey – were one casualty.[2] Leiden fustians probably another. The local manufacture of cheap says in France later in the century found other victims. But Anglo-Dutch competition remained, it would appear, the major force shaping the new division of markets. Caught in a vice between inexorably rising costs and inexorably falling prices, the major part of the Leiden worsted group making cheaper lines slowly gave up the struggle. In face of English competition, their earlier advantages in raw materials and technical skills disappeared. Only the more costly camlets and woollens survived to maintain Leiden's reputation for quality. Changes of taste and fashion may have helped here, while hastening the decline of the cheaper worsteds.[3] The result was that, in a world of falling prices, Leiden's total production at the end of the century was valued at some 5–6 million guilders, or not more than 60–70 per cent of the figure of half a century earlier. The next half century was to see a general decline. Leiden was a dying city, and against its losses could be set no countervailing growth of textile finishing industries at Amsterdam or elsewhere.[4] Industrial decline was general, and to this many factors contributed, including high costs that derived from heavy taxation on food and necessities, and the failure to devise a satisfactory tariff policy. A large volume of British exports, including cloth, continued to find its way to world markets via the Dutch entrepôt, though with the slow spread of the skills in the English dyeing and finishing trades, the Dutch function became increasingly restricted to one of distribution. An increasing percentage of the west country serges, Norwich stuffs and Yorkshire kerseys, shaloons and camlets found their way to their customers by direct

[1] See B. E. Supple, 'Currency and Commerce in the Early 17th Century', *Economic History Review* 2nd Series, Vol. X, No. 2 (1957).

[2] Coke *MSS.* I. 465 (1632). See Heaton, *op. cit.*, pp. 193, 198.

[3] Posthumus, *op. cit.* (p. 928) speaks of the 'declining demand for says in spite of new processes of manufacture'. The contemporary P. de la Court said that many of the New Drapery products had 'fallen into disuse'. *Welvaren van Leyden* (ed. Driessen), Ch. VI.

[4] H. Brugmans, *Opkomst en Bloei van Amsterdam* (1944), pp. 219–20.

routes.[1] Whatever may have been the 'selling points' of the worsted types of cloth that commended them to southern buyers in 1600, they were now finding a large market amongst the more sophisticated urban middle classes and rural gentry of western Europe.

It seems probable that the competition of Leiden's fine woollens was sufficiently obstinate and protracted to underline the attractions of the worsted market to an English woollen industry whose ancient advantage in point of fine wool supply had long since disappeared. The new threat which developed steadily from 1660 onwards to Europe's woollen industries generally came not from traditional types of woollen and worsted manufactures but from oriental textiles imported in increasing quantities by the great trading companies and swiftly imitated by local manufacturers. Thus the European textile industries entered the latest phase of the long transition from fairly uniform, heavy, costly woollen fabrics to lighter, brighter, and markedly cheaper fabrics of mixed materials. The details of this changing pattern of consumption still need far more attention than they have yet received.

In the third decade of the eighteenth century, Defoe sat down to confound the pessimists who mistook the misfortunes of one part of industry and trade for the decline of the whole. The characteristic of the woollen textiles trades, he declared, was '. . . that if one Place sinks, another rises; and if one kind of Manufacture declines, another advances'.[1] Defoe's habit of remedying his shortage of statistics by liberal use of the imagination does not always make him a reliable guide, but here his comment seems perfectly valid. During the preceding century, the pattern of the cloth trade and manufacture had been not fixed but kaleidoscopic. It was determined not by one factor but by many interdependent ones including raw material supply, the vagaries of fashion, the exigencies of climate and the forces of social change. In the contests for world markets that ensued,

[1] *Archief Brants* (Fol. 403. Gemeente Archief, Amsterdam) contains much evidence of the growth in direct trade between Exeter, Topsham and Spain and Hamburg. See the correspondence David Leeuw–George Poe, John Elwill. The decline in serges was, it seems, partly a question of fashion. See also Hoskins, *op. cit.*, pp. 74–8.

[2] D. Defoe, *A Plan of the English Commerce* (1928 edn. Oxford, following the 1728 edn.), p. 188.

much depended on the degree of flexibility that an industry could achieve in adapting itself to changing demand. Costs of production varied between one area and another, between – especially – urban and rural industries. So long as defence costs remained high in Holland, so did wages and costs of production. Equally, English government could do little directly to reduce the cost of loan capital to the entrepreneur, however much Restoration publicists might propose and counter-propose. They could, on the other hand, manipulate economic conditions to a debatable extent through protective tariffs, subsidies and raw material controls. In a situation where 'natural' advantages and disadvantages were pretty evenly distributed, the kind of intervention urged by writers from Mun to Downing may well have had an important influence on the pattern of cloth production in both Holland and England. It is difficult to avoid the conclusion that their generally weaker position compelled the Dutch to concentrate on products based on wools from Spanish, Turkish and local sources and to exploit those markets where such products were saleable.

7

Taxation and the Decline of Empires, an Unfashionable Theme[1]

During the past half century, the subjects and methods of historical inquiry have alike undergone radical change. Some branches of history, e.g. pure constitutional history, are less popular than they were formerly. Such declining interests are offset by the newer branches of economic and sociological inquiry and explanation. A phenomenon which still retains in full the fascination it exercised on the generations of Machiavelli or Gibbon is the rise and decline of the great civilizations of the past, as recent academic tourneys between Professor Geyl and Toynbee amply witness. Yet, even here, the methods of the twentieth century historians differ markedly from those of their predecessors. The older, and in the broad sense, liberal school of historians was largely content to explain these phenomena in political terms – by the qualities, great or foolish, of those who were held to govern the destinies of nations, or by the moral strength or decadence of peoples. This allowed economic factors to operate mainly as a function of political wisdom or political folly. Wars, for example, brought great financial burdens in the shape of taxation, debt, debased currencies. These in turn obstructed or destroyed material progress. This line of argument logically placed taxation in the forefront of the explanation of national decline. In Samuel Dill's classic study of *Roman Society in the Last Century of the West* (1898), the burdens of taxation and the problems of the *curiales* are the central point in the explanation of material decline. A fine

[1] This paper was presented as a lecture to the General Meeting of the Historical Association at Utrecht on 2 November 1962.

rhetorical chapter in volume IV of the original *Cambridge Modern History* (1906) on Spanish decline in the seventeenth century centres on the *alcabala* and the *millones*, whose catastrophic effects are placed alongside the exploits of decadent kings with actresses, court brawls and intrigues, as the root cause of Spanish decadence. The volume on the coming of the French Revolution in the same series had only one economic chapter: it was on taxation and public finance, and its writing was, significantly, entrusted to an official in H.M. Treasury.[1] And generations of English students were brought up to interpret the collapse of the absolute monarchy in England in terms of ship money, to explain the American revolt by reference to 'No Taxation without Representation' and the Boston tea-party.

The coming of economic history as a separate branch of inquiry and the rise of so-called economic interpretation has changed all this. Historians, no longer content with older explanations, have re-written these chapters of history in terms of a growing variety of economic and social phenomena – demographic change, economic fluctuations, technological change, price movements, and the like. An influential re-interpretation of the English Civil War hinges on the economic decline of the gentry. The revolt of the American colonies is seen as the result of the workings of the old colonial system, mixed with domestic social change. The decline of Spain is explained by Professor Hamilton as an effect of the influx of Spanish American silver and the resulting price rise in Spain. The new eighteenth-century volume of the *Cambridge Modern History*, I notice, will contain several chapters on economic and social factors that helped to bring about the French Revolution. In all these revisions, little attention seems to be given to the subject of public finance and taxation. One reason for this swing of opinion is not far to seek. E. H. Carr has recently told us that before assessing the merits of any historical interpretation we must look at the historian himself, at his background, at his prejudices. There has indeed been a change in our attitude to taxation. In the world of democracy and the welfare state, taxation has come to be accepted as an unavoidable and necessary adjunct of welfare. It is no longer the grievance it was for

[1] Henry Higgs, M.A., of H.M. Treasury, 'Finance,' ch. III in: *Cambridge Modern History*, vol. VIII 'The French Revolution' (Cambridge, 1904), pp. 66–78.

liberal historians writing of an age of dynasticism or tyranny: it is at worst a nuisance. And great historical principles are not easily manufactured out of nuisances. An excellent survey of modern research on Spain recently published by a Cambridge colleague, Dr Elliott, mentions taxation only as one of many factors.[1] His conclusion remains that the root trouble lay with the habit of Spanish governments in consistently trying to take on tasks beyond their powers. In an earlier generation, I have the feeling he would have crystallized his reasoning into a *critique* of Spanish fiscal policy.

The question I want to examine is whether we have, in the reaction against the older view of the importance of government actions, gone too far. Did the conscious actions of governments, so often expressed in terms of fiscal policy, have more fundamental effects than we allow? In particular, how does the question look in terms of the history of the Dutch Republic and its so-called decline in the eighteenth century?

We are fortunate in having an authoritative survey of the classical and recent literature of the Dutch rise and decline provided by two eminent Dutch scholars in the *Algemeene Geschiedenis der Nederlanden.* In volume VII (1954) Dr van Dillen gives a masterly summary of the economy at its peak. In volume VIII (1955) Dr de Vries provides the most comprehensive account so far of the eighteenth century decline, and this is expanded in his book *De economische achteruitgang der Republiek in de achttiende eeuw.*

The picture that emerges may be very briefly summarized as follows. By the mid-seventeenth century, the Dutch staple market had come to be the directing centre of European trade. Within the economy, great industries – textiles, shipbuilding, refining and finishing processes – had arisen employing technologies far in advance of those known elsewhere. Leiden, as an industrial town, had only one superior: Lyons. The Zaan was the greatest shipbuilding centre in the world. Yet by 1700, the strength of this famous system was being sapped by the emergent economic nationalism of other countries, England and France in particular, which set up tariffs and restrictive barriers like the Navigation Acts. Yet 'decline' can be exaggerated. It cannot

[1] J. H. Elliott, 'The Decline of Spain', in *Past and Present*, vol. XX (1961), p. 52–75.

be established with any certainty before 1730. Down to the 1790s there was no long term *quantitative* decline of trade or shipping. Foreign investment and financial activities actually grew. Only for manufacturing industry was there positive and quantitative decline, even collapse. At Leiden, output was halved and unemployment widespread in the second half of the eighteenth century. The textile industries generally were in a poor way; so was shipbuilding. Pauperism was everywhere in evidence.

What were the reasons for this state of affairs? Did they lie in a psychological or moral change in the people, in a decline of energy and enterprise, or did they spring from a change in the material world context in which the Dutch economy perforce had to operate? Dr van Dillen has put the answer quite explicitly: decline, he says, was '... the consequence of *international* factors, of a structural change in the economic life of Europe'. This conclusion need not, I believe, be questioned. But it calls for further interpretation. This is, I believe, suggested in part by comments made by Dr van Dillen and Dr de Vries. But I think they would agree that so far, the logic of these comments has not been fully explored. They apply with special force to the decline of *industry*, though I believe they also affected trade and shipping too. At the core of this problem lies the level of wages in the Republic, more especially in the larger towns. The competitive strength of Dutch industry, Dr van Dillen has written, 'was restricted above all by the relative height of wages, caused partly through the high excise on foodstuffs ...'.[1]

Dr de Vries has likewise referred to the frequent complaints of the cost of wages, especially in the province of Holland, the most industrialized area. This was clearly connected intimately with fiscal policy, which laid heavy burdens on food. Higher food prices meant higher wages.[2] Now it is not uncommon for employers to make this kind of complaint, and the case should not be accepted uncritically. But, as Dr de Vries goes on to show, the argument that wages were *relatively* high seems to be established. Cotton printers' wages, for example, were about

[1] J. G. van Dillen, 'De economische ontwikkeling van Nederland, in: J. S. Bartstra and W. Banning (ed.), *Nederland tussen de natiën*, vol. II (Amsterdam, 1948), p. 96.

[2] Joh. de. Vries, *De economische achteruitgang der Republiek in de achttiende eeuw* (Amsterdam, 1959), p. 107.

three times those paid in similar employments in Germany and Switzerland. Other historians have shown that even in 1690 it was asserted that Dutch wages were 16 per cent higher than in England.[1]

The evidence of Leiden suggests that the level of wages in Holland had risen sharply during the first half of the seventeenth century, following a sharp rise in the cost of living. This must presumably have presented a problem to the exporting industries at a time when European price levels were beginning their long decline and when competition for markets, textiles especially, was sharpening everywhere. When the cost of living rose again between 1740 and 1795, wage levels followed suit – but not fully. Although the Leiden manufacturers kept wages down, they were apparently still too high to enable them to offer prices competitive with those of foreign rivals. Thus the Netherlands got the worst of both worlds; a grave social problem of widespread unemployment and poverty, combined with falling sales at home and overseas.[2]

How were these problems related to the policies of governments? How far was it possible to have avoided or modified them? I should like at this point to refer to some evidence from contemporary seventeenth century English observers of the Dutch scene. They found, as you know, very little to comfort them when they surveyed the various advantages of commercial skill and technology which seemed to give their Dutch rivals such a lead in the struggle for wealth and power. One spark of comfort they nevertheless almost all discerned. The Dutch, they declared, bore an almost unbelievable burden of taxation. Here is a striking passage from a letter written by George Downing, then English agent in The Hague, in January 1658–9. In many ways a repulsive character, Downing was a shrewd observer of economic matters.

'. . . . its strange to see [he writes] with what readyness this people doe consent to extrerordinary taxes, although their ordinary taxes be yett as great as they were dureinge the warr with Spaine, and indeed such as would make any man admire at, a barrell of ordinary beere payeinge 40 stivers excise, and 5 stivers for bringeing in, each stiver

[1] J. en A. Romein, *De lage landen bij de zee* (Utrecht, 1949), p. 289.

[2] N. W. Posthumus, *De geschiedenis van de Leidsche lakenindustrie*, vol. III (The Hague, 1939), p. 851, 1010 *et seq. et seq.*, 1089 *et seq.*, 1172.

beinge more than an English penney, and every man payes the 6 penney of the rack rent of his lands, besides an infinity of other taxes, so that I have reckoned that a man cannot eate a dish of meat in an ordinary[1] but that one way or another he shall pay 19 excises out of it. This is not more strange than true.'[2]

A similar comment occurs in the classic description of the Netherlands written a decade or more later by Sir William Temple. A fish dish eaten in Holland, he remarks, paid 30 excises.[3]

John Ray, who travelled through Holland in 1663, was a different kind of observer, a casual visitor. Later to be famous as a pioneer of scientific botany, he too was a shrewd and accurate observer. 'All manner of victuals both meat and drink [he wrote] are very dear, nor for the scarcity of such commodities, but partly by reason of the Great Excise and Impost wherewith they are charged. . . .'[4]

Such are a few of the stray comments made by visitors on the spot. They could be multiplied many times. The evidence about the nature and incidence of taxation in Holland was collected and printed in a different way by another late seventeenth-century English writer. Gregory King may justly claim to be the father of national income studies, and his survey of the income and expenditure of the different classes that composed English society is a mine of information for the economic and social historian. In recent years, his methods and conclusions have been subjected to searching tests by several modern economists and social scientists, notably Miss Phyllis Deane in Cambridge and Professor Glass at London. They have stood up to the trial very well. I doubt whether the figures I am about to quote can be regarded with the same confidence as those which refer simply to the English situation. They are nevertheless of great interest and should not, I think, be dismissed as wholly implausible. In 1696, King set out to estimate the relative

[1] An inn.

[2] C. H. Firth (ed.), *The Clarke Papers*, vol. III (Westminster etc., 1899), p. 175.

[3] Sir William Temple, Observations upon the United Provinces' (1672), in: *Works*, vol. I (London, 1720), p. 70; in the edition by G. N. Clark (Cambridge, 1932), p. 153.

[4] John Ray, F.R.S., *Observations topographical, moral and physiological made in a journey through part of the Low-Countries etc.* (London, 1673), p. 51. Ten years elapsed before Ray recorded his note

strength of the French, English and Dutch economies in so far as the current war might affect them and its issue be in turn influenced. Holland, a country whose population he estimates at 2·2 millions, with a total national income of £17·7 millions or £8 a head, had spent £22 million on the war in seven years. Yet so great was her trade that she, alone of the three contestants, was richer than at the start of the war. The most striking statement in relation to our problem, however, is his estimated comparison of public expenditure and taxation between the three countries for 1695:

	Population	Annual Income per cap.	Public Revenue £ million	Taxes per cap.	Consumption per cap.
England	5,450,000	£7.16	6.5	£1.4.0	£7. 3.0
France	13,500,000	£5.18	17.5	£1.5.0	£4.18.2
Holland	2,240,000	£8. 2	6.9	£3.1.7	£4.13.9

If these figures were accurate, one would conclude that Holland, with a population less than half that of England, and perhaps one sixth that of France, raised a public revenue larger than that of England and over a third that of France. The fictitious Dutchman-in-the-street, however, had less to spend on himself than his neighbours, because he was required to pay in taxes nearly three times what the average Frenchman or Englishman paid.[1]

The figures quoted are not indisputable. They are the guesses of an intelligent and discerning statistician, accustomed to handling this kind of problem. I think they merit serious attention. At the very least, they emphasize the persistent, underlying problem of the Republic: the cost of defending not merely her territory but her peculiarly vulnerable economy, with its enormous trade routes stretching out over the oceans of the world. This in itself is enough to explain the weight of taxation falling on trade and industry. But of course the costs of defence were too great to be met by even extraordinary taxation alone. Like many other states before and since, the Republic had to fall back on the device of anticipating revenue, of living beyond

[1] Gregory King, 'Naturall and Politicall Observations' (1696), reprinted in: J. H. Hollander (ed.), *Two Tracts by Gregory King* (Baltimore, 1936), p. 54–6.

her immediate means, in short, of contracting a debt to her own citizens. To calculate the size of these evolving, growing debts, provincial and federal, is not easy. The territory called public finance is not well charted. Moreover, the technical problems of measurement are complex. We can, nevertheless, obtain some impressions. Temple suggests that it was Venice and Holland – both rich but small states – which inaugurated the era of professionalized warfare in modern Europe and thereby created the need for public debts. Ships, standing mercenary troops and frontier garrisons were beyond the pocket even of the Republic, with an annual revenue which he estimated at 120 million guilders or over £10 million. The Province of Holland alone had a debt which he calculates at over 65 million guilders. Paying 4 per cent interest this meant an annual charge of over two and a half million guilders. The service on the debt was provided mainly from excise and customs.[1]

It is both easier and more helpful to think in terms of interest charges rather than capital values. Thus, Temple thought the annual cost of the Republic's debt was another 13 million guilders. This is not difficult to reconcile with Dr Houtzager's calculation that Holland's debt alone in 1667 stood at 131 million guilders.[2]

In 1728 the annual charges stood at over 13 million guilders. Between 1728 and 1750 the debt rose again by over 70 million guilders and in that year expenditure exceeded income by nearly 3 million guilders.

Opinions differed, and may still differ, as to how far such debts were necessary, how far economies could have been made. But the fact remains that the system of state and federal debts meant that a growing block of permanent obligation was steadily built into the fabric of the Republic. Repudiation was unthinkable; total repayment impossible. Fortunately, interest rates were lower than elsewhere and falling. Nevertheless, the cost was a grievous burden on people, industry, shipping and trade. Indirect taxes were heavier than direct – a contrast with England, where direct taxation on land was, even in 1700, still the largest single source of revenue. There were many local

[1] Sir William Temple, *Observations etc.*, p. 70.

[2] D. Houtzager, *Hollands lijf- en losrenteleningen vóór 1672* (Schiedam, 1950), pp. 85, 86, 107.

variations. But at Leiden the salt tax was levied at a rate of 100 per cent on value, beer at 60 per cent, bread at 25 per cent, meat 14 per cent. Vinegar, sugar, cattle, fish, oil, tobacco, butter, paper – all these and many other articles paid their toll. Customs at the great ports were probably not yet unreasonable, but internal tolls, vehicle and canal dues were heavy.

Modern research has revealed that long before the Industrial Revolution, economic life was marked by fluctuations, sometimes violent and far-reaching in their social and economic consequences. As the room for manoeuvre lessened, the recurrent depressions in trade and the chronic malaise of industry (especially textiles) provoked complaints about the effect of taxation on production costs. As Dr de Vries has shown, the economy of the Republic did not suffer a uniform decline. Industry was hit harder than trade or agriculture. He has added that it was those industries whose product represented primarily the accumulation of labour value – what he has called *arbeidsintensieve* industries – that suffered most. Industries employing large aggregation of fixed capital – brewing, distilling, sugar boiling etc. – fared much better. I would go further than this. Even within the *arbeidsintensieve* industries, of which the outstanding example was the textile manufactures, it is possible to discern substantial differences. Take, for example, the Leiden cloth industries. I have pointed out elsewhere[1] that the fortunes of the Leiden industries and their English rivals followed quite different courses in the seventeenth and eighteenth centuries. At Leiden, the cheaper worsted industries – *baaien, saaien, fusteinen* – declined rapidly in the later decades of the seventeenth century and thereafter. The much more expensive *lakens* survived better, and even grew down to 1700. In England, the most striking feature is the rise of the worsted manufacture. Invert, that is to say, the fortunes of Leiden and you have those of Norwich or Exeter. This was not accidental. The reasons were analysed by an anonymous writer as early as 1651. The price of an English cloth (he says) represents, to the extent of 75 per cent, the labour it embodied – carding, spinning, dyeing, weaving, fulling and working. Wool only represented 25 per

[1] Charles Wilson, Cloth Production and International Competition in the Seventeenth Century,' in: *Economic History Review*, second series, vol. XIII (1960–1), p. 209–21.

cent. The labour cost only (this is his estimate) about half 'what the *Hollander* pays, by reason of their high rate of Houses and Victuals, to which all Labourers' wages are proportioned'. But it was different with fine cloths. Here the Spanish wool cost three times as much as English wool. And a customer could be persuaded to pay 10 per cent more on what he calls 'the fancy of the Buyer', which could not be done with cheap cloths.

The explanation sounds plausible: and it accords perfectly with the later evolution of the Dutch and English industries. It seems that as labour costs rose, the profit margins of the Leiden makers disappeared. Their products were no longer competitive. I need not labour the importance of this. At its peak the value of Leiden's output may have been nine million guilders a year (or nearly half the value of England's total export trade). By 1700 it had fallen by a third or more. Its population and employment fell catastrophically. Now I do not want to suggest that high taxation and high wages are a *deus ex machina* that explains everything. Other factors were important. But if, for example, monetary factors, the high circulation of money, the strength of the guilder, or even the growth of economic nationalism elsewhere, had been the *dominant* cause of decline, one might have expected industries would have suffered more uniformly than they did. The selective character of industrial decline, and the special problems of these *arbeidsintensieve* industries, suggests strongly that labour costs were of fundamental importance.

Their effects were not, of course, limited to industry. The effects of high costs in shipbuilding must have been reflected in higher freight costs. Likewise seamen's wages, which affected shipping and fishing costs. Trade was therefore not immune. Docks, warehouses, weigh-houses, victualling stores all employed labour on a vast scale. Hence the costs of shipping, of buying, selling and transport would all be susceptible to the rising costs of labour.

The consciousness of the problem grew in the eighteenth century. The literature of protest and of proposed reformation is familiar to us. I will only select and comment on three sources which underline in quite different ways the fundamental and intractable nature of the problem. The crisis of 1751 was temporary: but it provoked an important attempt to analyse the reasons for the Republic's economic problems. When the merchants presented their analysis to the Prince of Orange, they selected two broad sets of causes, one external, one internal. The first was the rise of economic nationalism throughout Europe. The second was 'the oppressive taxes' which had been imposed upon trade. As merchants they were naturally concerned more with those which affected them most directly i.e. customs, trade and transport dues. Their remedy – lower and more uniform duties – failed for a number of reasons. But a major reason was unquestionably the purely fiscal one. The opposition of the Admiralties was not merely obstructive: it reflected the difficulty of paying for what they had to consider the unavoidable expenses of state.

The nature of the state finances and the problems they posed were clearly set out in the sketch written by the statesman Van de Spiegel in 1782 which Dr de Vries has edited for us.[1] This is a dispassionate view of the Republic's situation in a radically changing world. For more than a century and a quarter, Van de Spiegel explains, the Republic's debt had been increasing, and alongside it, the burden of taxes. Now the costs of war themselves – of ships, weapons, equipment – were all rising steeply. War, in fact, was a luxury the Netherlands could no longer afford. Hence an empirical, even opportunist view of diplomacy that contrasts with De la Court's statement of policy of the previous century. An Englishman living in 1962 can see the point. Realism itself suggested new and different answers in a world where great neighbours were becoming greater while Holland remained the same size. One sentence I will quote. The author is referring to the financing of war by borrowing. Wars are no longer fought (he says) 'at the charge of the present generation, but at the charge of posterity'.[2]

Finally, a writer of very different kind. Luzac's *Hollands Rijkdom* is not a wholly reliable book. It is long-winded and repetitive. But it is full of shrewd insights. He was passionately concerned with the effect of food taxes on the economy, and especially with the auction of labour that results from higher

[1] Joh. de. Vries, 'Van de Spiegel's "Schets tot een vertoog over de intrinsique en relative magt van de Republyk"' (1782), in *Economisch-Historisch Jaarboek*, vol. XXVII (1958), pp. 81–100.

[2] *Ibid.*, p. 97.

wages.[1] But he connects the problem with another phenomenon that is once again being inquired into today. The demographic history of Holland, Dr van der Woude wrote recently, 'is still the great *terra incognita* of our national history'.[2] Van der Woude's own conclusions, and those of other scholars, notably Dr Simon Hart, suggest that the rise of population in Holland in the later eighteenth century – if indeed there was a rise at all – was insignificant compared with the spectacular rise which may be found in many other areas in Europe.[3]

In England, though the terrain is more explored, the problem of why the increase took place after 1760 remains obscure and controversial. In the last thirty years, much attention has again been devoted to studying the supposed relation between an expanding economy and the rise of the birth-rate, or at least its maintenance at a high level. Luzac's comment on the social situation in the Netherlands acquires interest in the light of these studies.

> The flight of skilled workpeople [he says] is one of the disadvantages which spring from the influence of taxes, because it is apparent that parents will not put their children to a task or craft where there is (as the saying goes) no dry bread to be earned; that small parishes fear to see marriages contracted; that thereby prostitution is encouraged; whence springs in turn the lack of suitable apprentices, from whom in time skilled artisans must be trained; and thus finally a lack of skilled hands to carry on work properly, while diligence and energy diminish and the lower orders of society are reduced to a kind of indifference, indolence and idleness. . . .[4]

All this must of course be guess-work. But it does suggest the interesting possibility of a relationship between high indirect taxation, a declining economy, and a falling birth-rate.

As I see it, the situation might be summarized thus: in the eighteenth century, the increasing burden of state expenditure and of debt piled up on an economy that was stagnant or declining. This was a powerful force driving wages up and production down. From the point of view of social welfare, neither

[1] E. Luzac, *Hollands Rijkdom*, vol. IV (Leiden 1783), p. 82–4.

[2] A. M. van der Woude, 'De weerbare mannen van 1747 in de dorpen van het Zuiderkwartier van Holland als demografisch gegeven,' in: *A. A. G. Bijdragen*, vol. VIII (Wageningen, 1962), p. 35–76.

[3] *Ibid.*, p. 44.

[4] E. Luzac, *Hollands Rijkdom*, p. 84.

the growth of agriculture nor of finance and overseas investment afforded any adequate compensation for the decline of industry and the halting of trade. Let me advert for a moment to other countries, of which England is the best documented example, though France or Prussia could equally be quoted. Everywhere, eighteenth century economic writers were obsessed by the problems of employment, or rather, of under-employment and poverty. In the period immediately preceding the Industrial Revolution, a high proportion of the people – in England perhaps a third or more – were in a chronic condition of poverty. Hence the schemes for workhouses and compulsory or charitable industry which proliferated.[1] The Netherlands problem was unique only in its severity, and in the apparently insuperable problems that obstructed its solution. At the heart of the problem lay not only the structural changes in the world *economy*, but also the change and relative degeneration in the *political* situation of the Netherlands in Europe which placed on her people an impossible burden.

The phenomenon of decline has also a wider importance: we have heard in the last few years much about economic growth, and the stages by which such growth and evolution is said to proceed. In the discussion it often seems to be assumed that any nation that places its feet on the upward path of growth will inevitably reach the top, and stay there.[2] Maybe. The lessons of history can be misleading. But the case of Holland shows an example of a society and an economy that reached a high degree of maturity, only to falter, halt and in some respects decline for a century or more before reconstruction could begin. In the so-called *Memoirs* of De Witt, the writer could use as his text the slogan *Ab furore monarchorum libera nos, Domine.* History was to show that though the Dutch nation could rid themselves of their own dynasts, they could not rid themselves of those of other nations. Against the Spaniard they conquered, only to fall victim in the end to the extravagant *machtpolitik* of the *ancien régime* itself.

I conclude that we economic historians have in general been

[1] See Ch. 5.

[2] See P. T. Baeur and Charles Wilson, 'The Stages of Growth', a review article on W. W. Rostow, 'The Stages of Economic Growth' (Cambridge, 1960), in *Economica*, new series, vol. XXIX (1962), p. 190–200.

too anxious to pigeon-hole the problem of taxation and public finance, because it is thought to be irrelevant, difficult or perhaps just dismal. I believe we shall have to re-examine it. Indeed, there are already signs that this is happening. In a recent paper, Professor A. H. M. Jones of Cambridge has reinstated taxation as a real factor in the decline of the Roman Empire.[1] Professor Mousnier has pointed the way for a new approach in France and I believe others are following it up.[2]

The history of the Dutch Republic, which contains the seeds of all modern public finance, should provide a fruitful source of inquiry into problems whose better understanding would illuminate many larger aspects of economic and social development.

[1] A. H. M. Jones, 'Over-Taxation and the Decline of the Roman Empire', in *Antiquity*, vol. XXXIII (1959), p. 39–43.

[2] R. Mousnier, L'évolution des finances publiques en France et en Angleterre etc., in: *Revue Historique*, 75e année (1951), vol. 205, pp. 1–23.

8

Canon Demant's Economic History[1]

'Of all varieties of history', wrote Sir John Clapham, 'the economic is the most fundamental. Not the most important: foundations exist to carry better things.' The idea – a superstructure of civilization built on economic foundations – has been used often enough. The character of the relationship has not always been so modestly expressed – by economic historians anyway. For this reason, and because it is the idea underlying the Holland Lectures recently delivered by Canon Demant, it has seemed a useful gambit for an examination of the use made of economic history and ideas in those lectures.

Canon Demant has called his lectures *Religion and the Decline of Capitalism*, thus inverting the title (though accepting in many respects the ideas) of Tawney's famous lectures in the same series in 1922. Capitalism, for his purposes, he defines as 'the relative freedom of economic activity from social controls and its theoretical bulwark in the idea of economic life as the operation of natural law rather than a system developed by men'. It corresponds to a phase, if an ill-defined one, in history; a phase in which 'social and economic relations became determined almost entirely by free play of the market in the buying and selling of things, labour and services'. The genesis of this phase is described judiciously. Canon Demant does not fall into the error of treating the emergence of modern economic society as a sudden birth. He notes the evidence that certain features of what is popularly called capitalism existed in the Middle Ages; that the Early Reformers inherited much of the medieval prejudice against usury (to which it might be added that it was not only

[1] This paper was first published in *The Cambridge Journal*, vol. vi, No. 5 (1953), pp. 281–90.

the early Reformers: at the height of Dutch economic predominance the *doyen* of the Dutch Calvinists excommunicated a god-fearing woman because her husband was a pawnbroker). It took, he admits, from the sixteenth to the nineteenth century for this conception to become embodied as 'the formative factor in the workings of modern industrial society' (p. 35); and it was, apparently, in sharp contrast to the medieval conception of economic life as 'a normative activity responsible to ethics and religion for its means and ends . . .' (p. 15). About the character of this medieval society he is less explicit; but since the contrast with what followed is clearly implied, it may be useful to pursue the point further before examining the later conception.

How sharp is the contrast? If we were solely concerned with economic *ideas*, it would not be difficult to acquiesce in the notion of contrast. If the question were simply a broad comparison of a primarily agrarian society with an increasingly industrialized society, likewise. But Canon Demant is concerned with more than these things: as a sociologist he is (or surely should be) concerned with economic behaviour as well as with economic ideas: with the relation between economic behaviour and the quality of the civilization itself. And here comes the first snag: the discussion must be removed at once from the forum of ideas, with its relatively clear because artificial distinctions of schoolmen and economists into the infinitely confused world of human conduct: the world in which Coulton and Gasquet carried on their long battle. There would be little profit in renewing it. It is, on the other hand, surely dangerous to regard the medieval economy as if it were solely or even principally moulded by religious idealism. Medieval people faced certain economic problems, amongst them the ever present one of scarcity and the recurrent one – in Europe anyway – of starvation. They faced these problems with a very limited economic apparatus: expansion of their resources was slow and painful. Their strategy was necessarily a defensive one of conserving prudently and distributing fairly. To interpret medieval economic thought and policy on a purely material basis would be folly: but to leave out the element of rationality and expediency in it is to invite misunderstanding. Even so, its results did not satisfy everybody: certainly not, for example, the disillusioned fourteenth-century author of the complaint 'Syr Peny':

In erth there ys a lityll thyng,
That reynes as a grete Kyng
There he is knowen in lande;
Peny is hys name callydde,
Ffor he makyth both yong and olde
To bowe into hys hande.
Pope, Kyng, and emperoure,

Byschope, abbot and prioure,
Parson, preste and Knygt,
Duke, erle and baron,
To serve Syr Peny are they boen
Both be day and nyght.

. . . . . .

Peny may buy both hevyn and helle,
And alle thyng that is to selle,
In erth hath he that grace:

And so on for fifteen stanzas. This may not be an accurate description of economic life as an 'autonomous activity': but it does not sound as if it were 'socially' any more satisfactory for that. And at the same time as he was drawing distinctions between lawful and unlawful interest, Aquinas was defending servitude as economically expedient. One is left wondering whether the study of the abstraction we call the history of economic ideas is any very reliable guide to the student trying to assess the moral condition of society. He should take note not only of the so-called 'integrated' character of medieval society but also of the wars, the vagrancy, the servitude, the continual litigation, petty and otherwise, by which it was disturbed. 'Everyone', said Macaulay, 'ought to read Froissart.' He might have added, 'especially economic historians'.

If closer examination raises doubts as to the suggested state of grace of medieval society, what light does it throw on what followed? When did society fall, and how far? Canon Demant does not, as we have seen, make the mistake of placing the event at the conventional point usually chosen for the birth of modern politics and sometimes appropriated by economic historians. It was not before the age of Franklin and Adam Smith, 'who did as much as any man to give a rational foundation for the emancipation of economics from religious or ethical control' (p. 79). He recognizes, too, that even Adam Smith's economic man was to act within the limits of justice and self-command, restrained by that quality of 'sympathy' with others which was an integral element of man's nature. He goes further: he quotes with approval E. H. Carr's observation that 'the ingrained and irrational habits of personal abstinence and public service ... played a more important part in building up the liberal and *laissez-faire* society of the nineteenth century than the rational morality of the harmony of interests' (p. 136). Elsewhere, the birth of economic liberalism as 'a crusading passion ... a militant creed' is put as late as 1830. Though in yet another place Canon Demant recognizes that by this time 'more and more movements' were growing up 'to intervene and interfere with the free play of the market economy' (p. 27). Thus to one's growing doubt as to how this 'autonomous economic activity' (which apparently ended before it began) can have existed in time, is added a query as to whether it ever existed at all. For the argument that it only managed to exist at all because it grew upon a basis of ingrained ethics comes perilously near admitting that economic thought was one thing and economic behaviour another. Did the capitalist invariably (or often, or even ever) behave as his text book told him he should? Was Mrs Crossley, the wife of the founder of Crossleys of Halifax, merely the relic of an earlier age when she made her daily vow entering the works at 4 a.m.: 'If the Lord does bless us at this place, the poor shall taste of it'? And was it because she was too ignorant to understand the *Wealth of Nations*, or because she understood it better than others, that she advised her sons in bad times: 'If you can go on giving employment during the winter, do so, for it is a bad thing for a working man to go home and hear his children cry for bread when he has none to give them.' Where in fact does 'the market economy' end and 'sympathy' begin? The working classes of Oldham were not so sure when they presented an address to John Platt, the great machine maker of Oldham, in 1871. His efforts, they thought, had 'provided employment and wages for thousands of our industrious people ... bringing and diffusing amongst us a stream of wealth ...' By his public work and generosity he had built up the institutions of the town and nurtured educational schemes irrespective of sect or party; these things, they concluded, 'have shown to us the true catholicity of your mind, and the universal charity of your heart'. There are several chapters of Victorian working-class opinion which do not appear in our orthodox histories of the working class which are drawn from the pages of *The Pioneer* and *The Clarion.*

Examples such as these could be multiplied indefinitely. Yet the rejoinder might still be that these are the swallows that do not make a summer: or that to bring this argument into the market place of economic behaviour is to risk another prolonged and unprofitable quarrel about what really happened, which can have no end and reach no conclusion. Canon Demant senses the difficulty: his final chapter oscillates between measured approval for a system which made possible 'a standard of living for millions which before had only been enjoyed by the more sheltered classes' (p. 188), and less sober aspersions on the wickedness of a way of life that 'violated the natural order of man's inner structure', was apparently partially responsible for the British failure to oppose aggression (this needs rather more explanation), provoked 'colossal social dislocations', prostituted and doped the consumer, promoted the itch to have more and more, and ended in a worship of money-lending. The best that can be said of this is that where it is not obscure it is exaggerated. Even the dangerous tendency to equate the economic thought of the few (preferably philosophers whose administrative talents would have been stretched by the necessity of organizing a jumble sale) with the economic behaviour of the many, does not wholly invalidate it.

What is more serious is that it persists in treating economic behaviour as a wilful and voluntary running after false gods. There must be something profoundly unsatisfactory to an economic historian about a study of the history of economic change which fails to notice the material pressures under which such change took place. In his little book on *The Industrial Revolution*, Professor Ashton has a half-page of conclusion which throws more light on the problem than a hundred pages of lamentation. Replying to an historian who has written of 'the disasters of the industrial revolution', he condemns as perverse the view that technical and economic changes were themselves the source of calamity. 'The central problem of the age was how to feed and clothe and employ generations of children outnumbering by far those of any earlier time.' If England had remained 'a nation of cultivators and craftsmen' she would have shared the fate of Ireland – starvation or emigration. England was delivered (Professor Ashton continues) 'not by her rulers, but by those who, seeking no doubt their own narrow ends, had the wit and resource to devise new instruments of production and new methods of administering industry'. When Macaulay compared his own day with the past, it was inevitably to rejoice in the change. Since popular economic history was appropriated by the Fabians, any similar contemporary comparison would equally inevitably be an occasion for lamentation. The structure of left-wing history (the political purpose of which was largely hidden from subsequent generations nurtured in the bosom of popular education) depended for its emotional appeal on forgetting Malthus and his discoveries as resolutely as possible.

It is into this heresy of regarding the operations of 'capitalism' as a voluntary process that Canon Demant has fallen. To him the growth of population was merely a consequence of industrialism. This is to neglect the research of the last thirty years which has upset the simple thesis that industrialism 'created' the population problem. That is a remediable error. The other problem – to know how far capitalists did in fact conform to the instructions of their philosophic pedagogues – is more difficult. We are still very ignorant of the history of capitalism as a productive mechanism and of the entrepreneur as a directing force. For the Fabians and Liberals were preoccupied with the shortcomings of capitalism as a means of distributing wealth: its virtues as a productive system they either took for granted or forgot. Our economic history has been written from every conceivable source except the records of business itself: and these records might put a rather different complexion on things. Let us not be in too much of a hurry to reach for the black cap: there is more evidence to come. Merely to survey the often sordid physical consequences and social dislocations of the age of industrialism is not enough: they may be the evidence of the failure or limited success of capitalism, the impact of the attempt on the problem: they are no adequate guide to the intentions or social morality of the capitalists. The tidy-minded military planners and bureaucrats of 1940 did not intend to leave England littered with squalid rural slums scattered over a hundred airfields and encampments. The Ecclesiastical Commission did not create the Paddington jungle of which it finds itself the embarrassed owner. But the world changes disconcertingly: men in a fit of fright (or optimism) act quickly: today's panacea is tomorrow's poison. It is all very confusing: but if we neglect to notice the problems to which these economic 'systems' were really improvised answers, we shall fail wholly to understand the relationship of economic thought and economic fact.

Economic change means a change of institutions, habits, ideas: it takes place, partially at any rate, because the old institutions, habits and ideas have become ossified, or purposeless or obstructive, or merely inconvenient. Behind the change from the defensive, 'social' economic policies of the Middle Ages to the offensive, 'individualist' economic policies of the nineteenth century is one major factor: the consciousness of man's increased power over nature. The age of Malthus was in some respects as short of indispensable necessities as the age of Aquinas, but it was equipped with better tools and blessed with a few men whose vision pierced the contemporary gloom to glimpse an age of plenty beyond. It may be that the cultural side of life 'has a precedence over politics and economic activities', that 'a society in which the cultural life has not a certain priority in this sense violates the natural order of man's inner structure': but our history will assume some odd appearances if we assume that men with empty bellies will in general think about culture first and food afterwards. There is no particular reason, except unhistorical prejudice, why the doctrine of the Hidden Hand should 'seem to us today so odd'. It worked abundantly in its day and it is still not clear that its material benefits are everywhere exhausted. The economic primacy of Victorian England cannot be explained entirely in terms of natural resources, James Watt and a fortunate absence of foreign competition. Somewhere those much neglected men of wit and resource ought to be in the picture.

If doubts arise as to the historical reality of Canon Demant's conception of economic life, other doubts arise as to the logic which lies behind his definition of capitalism – the conception of 'economic life as an autonomous activity'. During the broadcast of these lectures, their author received a Shavian postcard which scouted the suggestion that capitalism was in a decline. 'Capitalism', it ran, 'far from decaying, has been carried to unprecedented magnitudes in the Tennessee Valley and elsewhere, and is culminating in state capitalism, *alias* communism, socialism, Fabianism, all requiring Capitals beyond the means of private enterprise. Capitalism is an entirely uncontroversial term, like magnetism: civilization is impossible without it. There is no such alternative as capitalism versus socialism: the issue is between plutocracy and democracy. . . .' The first half, at any rate, of the Shavian dictum goes to the heart of the matter, and so far as can be seen, has not been adequately answered in these lectures. But there is a mixture of hesitancy and rhetoric in the closing lecture which suggests that it has not gone unheeded. Thus we read that 'economic life lost its proper autonomy and became the slave of one of its own activities, namely the market relation; and today the total human reality is seeking to redress this aberration by depriving economic life of its freedom which has had such great productive success'. Now this seems to turn the whole argument upside down. Either 'autonomy' is of the essence of capitalism or it is not, and it does not close the gap in the logic to say that the 'collectivism' which has replaced the former 'individualism' is the wrong kind of collectivism exercising the wrong kind of control. It merely means that we are apparently debarred from considering any kind of economic system except *sub specie aeternitatis*. This is not in itself unreasonable, but it shortens (or should have shortened) a discussion of the kind Canon Demant has conducted at some length.

There is an added piquancy in Shaw's reference to the TVA in that the late Chairman of that authority, Mr David Lilienthal (more recently the Chairman of the US Atomic Energy Commission) has just published a striking *apologia* for modern American capitalism. It is a more thoughtful study than its title *Big Business for a Big Country* would suggest. The three most significant points in our immediate context are: first, his complete confidence in capitalism as a productive and distributive mechanism: there is nothing to suggest that Mr Lilienthal – nor for that matter many other millions of Americans – has yet been attracted or alarmed by the idea that capitalism is in decline. Secondly, it has not occurred to him that the disappearance of the old 'autonomy' has fundamentally weakened or vitiated capitalism as an economic way of life. 'Government', he writes, 'now is an active, and frequently the dominant factor' in economic affairs, which is to say that few important decisions of businessmen are made in which the influence (or direction) of government does not play a significant role.' Thirdly, he reflects the enlightenment that has been slowly but surely changing the whole field of human relationships in industry. '. . . the individual human being has become the very centre of management and labour's concern in some of our more progressive huge business undertakings . . . How can the relations between men, working together, be improved? Most important of all, how can men find in their work in large organizations and with huge machines the quality of satisfaction and joy in their work which craftsmen of old found in theirs? In the creative effort to find the answers to such questions, modern management and unions are laying the foundation of a new individualism.' The process is perhaps not so novel as it seems: enlightened capitalism has an organized history of nearly a century in the 'lighter' industries of this country.

The reply to this is no doubt again that we are thinking of different things: the 'control' is the wrong kind of control. True, it is not the medieval method of making economic life responsible to ethics and religion clothed in institutional form. But it is a very long way removed from that 'autonomy' which is the target elsewhere in the lectures. Are we or are we not to deny such a system the title of 'capitalism'? If not, are we prepared to argue that a way of life still pursued with vigour, intelligence and hope is in decay? Is Canon Demant after all thinking of America or only of Europe? Or perhaps only of Britain (as much of his dating of historical phases would suggest)? The questions are not wilful: they arise inevitably from the complexity of the task which Canon Demant has set himself. It is easy enough to feel a sentiment for an agrarian society, to dislike industrialism while recognizing its contribution to material wealth, to share William Morris's nostalgia for the town that was 'small and white and clean'. It is easy to discern and tempting to condemn the human selfishness that seems to lie at the root of the social evils that accompany industrialism. The real problem is to convert the moral platitude into positive teaching, and it is no less true than it was when Cunningham pointed it out seventy years ago that moralists are apt to 'waver between principles of Christian duty and judgements of political expediency . . .' It is this very perception of the weakness of moral denunciation which leads the modern commentator to the study of sociology, economics and economic history, in the hope that they will provide objective conclusions capable of being combined in a new synthesis with religious principle. There will be those who will beg leave to doubt whether the synthesis has been achieved. The traditional foundations of Christian teaching on social matters were the duty of work and the evil of greed. The second is here in full force: it is the *pleonexia* which receives its full share of attention. The duty of work seems to have disappeared, one suspects because the secular economics on which Canon Demant relies pushed it into the background. Nor is this the only instance where the synthesis is frustrated by the inadequacy of the apparatus of 'modern' thinking used in these lectures. Canon Demant seems to have fallen into what in others he deems the 'inexcusable' error (though as he says 'it is the most frequent error of the human mind when it is seeking to find a meaning to history') of regarding what is relative and contingent as absolute: for neither his conspectus of economic development, nor his equation of economic thought and economic behaviour, nor his round condemnation of certain features which he associates with modern industrialism can be regarded with certainty as anything more than a series of subjective impressions.

Let us return to the original imagery, the foundations and the superstructure. We can know a little about both. Given the necessary evidence and skill we can compare, within certain limits and in certain respects, the economic condition of a political society at different periods. We can say that numbers, total wealth, wealth *per capita* . . . were x in such a year and 2X or $\frac{x}{2}$ in another year. This sort of national balance sheet introduces some element of precision into economic history: it will tell us about as much and as little as a company balance sheet does about the abstraction to which it refers. It does not tell us how to convert these economic facts into terms of human contentment or moral health. We can only guess at that if we think it worth while to do so. Equally we can know some facts about the civilization that rises upon the foundations. But our opinion of the condition of our abstraction in each case will remain a subjective impression. Even more so our view of the relationship which the parts of our structure bear to one another; especially if our approach to the problem is made in a spirit of reformation. Any simple view of the relationship will lead us into the position of the Marxist solemnly trying to find the link between the qualities of Shakespearian prosody and the disappearance of the small freeholder; or trying to decide how far the genius of Degas can be explained in terms of a delayed industrial revolution. The nineteenth-century discovery that you could explain everything in terms of everything else was a very mixed blessing: for it has led us to assume that these links are readily apprehensible, an assumption which is apt to leave the inquirer facing intellectual opportunities about as promising as those which faced the proverbial monkey with the typewriter.

It is sometimes difficult to avoid the impression that the new sociology is but the old allegory writ large (though not necessarily more clear). The characters have changed. Fellowship, goods, knowledge, discretion, good deeds – have gone: in their place is a set of new abstractions which people Canon Demant's stage – collectivism, individualism, activistic socialism, commodity Hedonism, urbanization, capitalism. And instead of ailing *Everyman* is a hollow-eyed abstraction, *Society*. The new characters, like the old, have their exits and their entrances and in between play their many parts. Yet some will feel that the new form of moral entertainment is less convincing than the old. Their doubts will centre on the character of the leading actor. 'Society', writes Canon Demant, 'is always sick, but it is not always mortally sick' (p. 15). The doubters will not necessarily be doubters for either of the reasons Canon Demant suggests; not because they subscribe to an inane belief that human perfectibility can be achieved through the latest quack politico-economic remedy, nor because they are resigned to the equally inane conclusion that nothing can be done for the patient at all. It may be simply that they doubt whether the sociologist is yet (or ever will be) in a position to decide when to administer extreme unction. In particular, one or two will continue to suspect the efficiency of that historical thermometer. Do those alarming fluctuations really represent the patient's temperature? Or can it be that the probationer nurses have been holding it by the wrong end?

9

Government Policy and Private Interest in Modern English History[1]

The title of my paper may have misled you into thinking I am about to be philosophical. I beg you not to be alarmed. I am no philosopher and I am not so rash as to immerse myself or you in that great dispute that divides Rousseau or Burke or Coleridge from Bentham; in the conflict between, on the one hand, the belief that the public interest is different from the sum of private satisfactions and, on the other, the belief that the public interest consists in securing to each individual or social group the greatest degree of satisfaction consistent with social harmony. My task is rather to inquire into some of the assumptions that have been made by *historians* about the ways in which, in practice, a particular aspect of the public interest – national economic policy – has come to be formulated, and to see whether their assumptions hold water in the light of some recently acquired knowledge. The general and the special problems are connected. The second is an aspect of the first. But my approach will be largely analytical and empirical. I am concerned with a branch of the history of government and of economic history and only indirectly with problems of political philosophy. And I shall restrain myself roughly to a period of two and a half centuries before the repeal of the corn laws – a period which witnessed the rise and decline of two contrasting systems of political economy in Britain.

One of the fathers of English economic history, William Cunningham, was dedicated to the belief that government

[1] This paper was presented to the Irish Conference of Historians at Trinity College, Dublin, in June 1965.

economic policy had been of decisive and, on the whole, benevolent importance in English history. It represented a 'conscious effort', 'a deliberate endeavour' to expand the economy through laws and political institutions. The thing called 'the mercantile system' was a reality. Yet it would be difficult to point to any other scholars of comparable stature save the Germans who have shared this view. George Unwin, R. H. Tawney, the Swedish historian Eli Heckscher and many of their pupils have shared in some degree Unwin's liberal-Mancunian suspicions of state power and the 'evil' part it had in general played. Unwin used to say that government policy had attracted students because it had the merit of looking like a convenient chain of causation in history. But in reality (he thought) it was too easy an answer. The chain was an illusion. Policy was a sham. Hence his attacks, echoed by Tawney, on Seeley, on the German school of historical economists, but above all on Archdeacon Cunningham, that renegade Scot who denied his philosopher-ancestors, and proclaimed Germanic doctrines learnt in his student days in Berlin from an archdeacon's pulpit. Oh the heresy of it all! And him not even a professor! Since Unwin the English historical tradition has rarely been kind to government economic policy in the past. Indeed, the common view became not so much that it was a monster but that it was an illusion. For Mr Christopher Hill it was not only local government which in the course of the seventeenth century came to be controlled by the rich and propertied in their own interests but central government and taxation too. Parliament and government itself are reduced to mere puppets of the governing classes.[1] Here the Marxist and liberal interpretations come very close to each other. It became virtually an orthodoxy that 'policy' must be either a mischief or an illusion. It became 'a commonplace' (Professor Fisher tells us) of undergraduate essays that 'the Tudor state was more forced than forceful and that the origins of its actions are to be found less in any theories held by its rulers than in the pressure to which it was subject from vested interests and urgent social and financial problems'.[2] On this I will for the moment restrict myself to noting a more recent

[1] C. Hill, *Century of Revolution* (1961), pp. 307–8.

[2] 'Commercial Trends and Policy in 16th century England' in *Essays in Economic History*, ed. E. Carus Wilson, pp. 152–3 (1954).

comment by Dr Elton: 'We simply do not know', he has concluded, how the majority of Tudor economic planning laws originated, though he has unearthed evidence that *some* of them at any rate represented attempts at conscious control, not mere money-raising devices, and he has seen round Thomas Cromwell the (admittedly shadowy) administration of a planning group.

We are left nevertheless for this, as for later periods, with the impression that policy was formulated during these two and a half centuries by methods which superficially resemble those which Professor Finer has discovered in modern policy-making. The interested parties stake their claim through a series of 'lobbies'. Authority then makes the awards to the successful candidates.[1] There is, however, an important difference. Professor Finer is willing to allow a high degree of responsibility and social value to most of those who lobby in the twentieth century, as well as a considerable degree of independence to authority in reaching its decisions. Few historians who have commented on the problem in the past have been prepared to do so. Most have worked on assumptions short, sharp and simple. They have worked on a 'lobby' theory of policy-making in which the palm always goes to those who could shout loudest or pull hardest. Government, whether by Henry VIII, Oliver Cromwell or George IV, becomes a reflex of dominant contemporary business interests. Such an interpretation has many merits: it satisfies both liberals and Marxists, and ministers generally to that general distaste for tradesmen that has long activated most cultivated, even academic, Englishmen. Yet how well do these assumptions stand up to inquiry? How, in real life, *were* the decisions made on which rested such fundamental and long-term decisions as those to regulate shipping, the flow of raw materials like wool, to protect some home manufactures but not others? For such policies as those, even if we cannot prove that they made Britain the leading economic power of the eighteenth- and nineteenth-century world, certainly did not hinder her from becoming it. Did they rule the English economy for two centuries or more simply because money talked? Or were there other reasons, and if so what were they?

Let me say straightaway that I am not in the least going to

[1] *Anonymous Empire: A Study of the Lobby in Great Britain* (1958), p. 103.

argue that important private individuals and social groups, including rich companies, did not bring powerful pressure to bear on governments, did not try to persuade government to do what they wanted. They certainly did. In doing so they were exercising that ancient privilege of all subjects to petition the king which was confirmed by the Bill of Rights of 1689. It was likewise a function of Parliament to receive via the individual members, the subjects' petitions to Parliament. It always strikes me as curious that such privileges, so highly valued by us in our capacity as historians of law or politics, should be at once transmuted into strange and sinister 'pressures' when we look at them in our capacity as economic historians. The second, and more important point, however, is this. The stream of petitions from clothiers, merchants, poor weavers, gilds and companies and the like did not only represent an exercise of constitutional rights; they also represented the best and often the only source of information the government could obtain on complex economic problems. The chorus of tut-tuts that instinctively arises from historians the moment they sense what they call a lobby or 'pressure-group' is natural but seems to me misplaced. It derives from a well-meant assumption that government servants ought to live in a kind of vacuum, prepared to take their decisions uncontaminated by contact with the corrupting world of business, money and even subject citizens outside. This may be laudably high-minded, but it rests on an academic ignorance of, or unconcern with, how government really works. It is not true, or even possible, in the highly bureaucratized world of well-organized communications of our own day. Civil servants and even government experts have to rely on constant advice and help from private individuals on both sides of industry, from employers and unions. It is ludicrous to suppose that in an age unequipped with any kind of public economic service, government could have done anything or even known anything except with the help of those who were themselves interested parties. But now let me make my third point: advice, guidance, help – all were offered, sought and given. Bribes and gifts passed freely: sometimes they were effective; more often, one suspects, not. Mistakes were made equally freely. Scandals proliferated. Yet when the final balance is struck we are left – at the very least – unable to prove that policy was *merely* the residual product of pressure-groups. Equally, it would be foolish to deny that there were occasions when such pressures were the force that stirred to action what might otherwise have been lethargic authority.

Let us take those laws which were shaped between 1600 and the 1660s to control the two most important elements in the economy outside agriculture – the wool and cloth industry and the shipping industry. Cloth represented 80–90 per cent of exports by value, and employed many thousands of workers all over the country. Dozens of acts were put on the statute book in the seventeenth century, all aiming to prohibit the export of wool, to reserve it (and other raw materials) for the benefit of the cloth manufacturers at prices that reflected the lower demand as diminished by the former needs of foreign industries, especially Dutch. The objectives seem to have been achieved. Prices levelled off and fell after about 1610–20. The Dutch complained bitterly that their interests were damaged. Land-owners and farmers got worse prices. It is often argued that all this came about because rich clothiers had longer pockets than graziers, and were better organized politically than the gentry. Yet the evidence is quite indecisive on the point and it is *prima facie* improbable that a ruling class would allow itself to be over-priced in an auction of this kind, assuming it was simply an auction. Especially as in another industry also affecting farm rents and landlords' incomes – the leather industry – the government took precisely the opposite view. Over-ruling the attempts of the manufacturing industry to get the export of raw leather stopped, it allowed leather producers to export freely. In yet another long quarrel between the various sections of the tobacco-*growing* and tobacco-*manufacturing* interests, the government also came down on the side of the growers – the Virginia planters also wanted to export their leaf tobacco freely, as distinct from the British manufacturers who wanted to export their treated, rolled and packaged products and therefore wished to get their hands on the leaf tobacco as cheaply as possible. The debates, representations and lobbying made it clear that the board of trade were not prepared here to sacrifice the large trade in the raw product for the sake of a small industry with dubious export prospects.[1]

[1] Jacob Price, 'The Tobacco Adventure to Russia', *Transactions of the American Philosophical Society*. (March 1961.)

Again, we ask, why did tobacco and leather manufacturers lose and cloth manufacturers win? The historian of this episode, Dr Jacob Price, of Illinois, falls into line with tradition. He explains the government's action as mere 'fiscalism'. I am less sure. Could the outcome of these tournaments, one wonders, have been influenced by the memory of the earlier disastrous decision when James I chose to support another demand from a manufacturing interest and had brought everybody a fearful cropper? About that episode – the Cokayne project – much is still obscure; but, briefly, it was an ambitious plan to widen the scope and raise the economic value of the English cloth industry. A great deal of the cloth exported at this stage was only a semi-finished article and was dyed and finished abroad, most often in Holland, and in those finishing processes at least half the final value lay. Cokayne, a tycoon whose finger was in every contemporary pie, was very close to James. James proved willing to do down the current export monopolists, the Merchant Adventurers in order to hand their monopoly to Cokayne's new company. His proclaimed ambition was to build up a dyeing and finishing industry in England to replace the Dutch. The plan failed, the Dutch took severe reprisals, all was chaos. To the question, why was this done, several historians have returned the answer: obviously because James was thus repaying his known debts to Cokayne. Here they see another sample of the notorious weakness and gullibility of government before pressure groups. The king was suborned by the Cokayne lobby. I will return to this in a moment.

Let us look at shipping. This was regulated from 1651 by the first navigation act and from 1660 by a revised act or set of acts. Yet for centuries there had been legislation attempting to achieve at any rate part of the objects of these acts. Who was behind the new acts? Here the argument has raged ever since Adam Smith's day. And I must tread carefully, for the last writer on the subject has credited me with the belief that the trading companies were primarily responsible for securing the act.[1] Which shows how difficult it is to make one's position clear. Now it is true that this *is* the general opinion of most historians. The best and most exact account of the companies' influence, however, is given in M. P. Ashley's *Economic and financial policy*

[1] J. E. Farnell, 'The Navigation Act of 1651', in *Economic History Review*, 1964.

under the commonwealth and protectorate. This makes it clear (which not all accounts do) that the merchants' part in bringing about these acts was to present their *varied* and often *conflicting* claims for specially favoured treatment. It also makes clear that in the event nobody got the whole of what he asked for. The ship-builders, the exporting companies, the importing companies were all treading on each other's toes. Historians following the 'lobby' tradition invariably fail to identify the problem here: somebody had to sort out these fairly evenly matched contestants; somebody had to decide, in our judicious current jargon, priorities. Who did this? The government; to be more precise, their agent. In 1651 he was probably Oliver St John, a lawyer by trade; in 1660 it was probably Sir George Downing, by trade a bureaucrat, conspirator, turncoat. Neither was a merchant.

In each of these cases, you will notice, there are always two elements. There is a lobby, usually a number of lobbies. And there is the arbiter, the government, the decision-taker. Until very recently, any suggestions that the decision was *not* reached quite simply in terms of the buying power of the lobbies would have raised a sceptical smile. No doubt it still will in many quarters. But another view has appeared. Another view is tenable. In a strongish form, it is put by Dr R. W. K. Hinton in regard to the relations between the government and the Eastland Company which he has investigated: these (he believes) 'were based on ancient and conventional ideas about the commonwealth which the subjects abundantly shared and which easily transcended the interests of particular groups.' The government, Dr Hinton says, 'had a will of its own'.[1] Dr Hinton would accordingly see the landed nobility, the traditional governors, and their servants as the repository of these guiding principles of legislation. Government, even in the early seventeenth century, was a reality, with independent views. It was not merely pushed from pillar to post by vested interests. In the cases I have cited, it can be argued with some force that the decision reached was either correct and beneficial or at any rate could be plausibly defended. The Dutch, who suffered by it and should have known what they were talking about, thought that the acts aimed against wool export *were* effective and that they

[1] *The Eastland Trade and the Commonwealth in the Seventeenth Century*, p. 164.

conferred advantages on England and inflicted damage on themselves. They were equally sure that they were injured by the navigation acts. The two most recent expert investigators of the navigation code (Professor A. Harper and Professor Ralph Davis) have spoken decisively in its favour. Even for the Cokayne plan it may be argued that it purported to put into action principles which were both popular and, in a sense, cogent. *If* it had worked, it would have increased national wealth, employment, exports, customs yields and profits and done down the Dutch rivals into the bargain. Of course, it failed, and historians have no more patience with failed economic planners than with unsuccessful admirals. No doubt critics were entitled to lament the scandalous folly and greed of the king, who was duped. He was. It is worth noticing, however, that the privy council was not. They come with reasonable credit out of the imbroglio. For if they were not strong enough to resist the king at this particular juncture, they showed a sense of responsibility, they kept their heads when MPs lost theirs, they were judicious and honest and methodical in a matter where information was scanty, emotional pressures were strong and prognostications weak. In retrospect, the affair seems doomed in advance: in prospect it must have seemed a bright and beckoning vision, a plan that logically extended the ban on exporting valuable raw materials into one on exporting semi-manufactured articles. It is possible to see through these confusions a glimpse of that system-of-ideas-transcending-private-interests which Dr Hinton describes. The government (and plenty of others) might be divided about how to achieve national ends, but what they were after was maximum employment and minimum public disorders, maximum exports, minimum loss of native raw materials, maximum shipping tonnage. These were, in turn, compendiously contained within a formula which they read as a sort of shorthand for a dynamic economic model: the favourable balance of trade. In short, the public interest, the 'general economic will' here was *thought* to be coterminous with what later came to be described as 'the mercantile system'. It could claim, in my view, to be at any rate a more coherent set of rules and regulations than existed in most other countries; most of its central features were based on decisions that could be defended as sensible and reasonable, and I do not think the superiority or efficiency of the system can be explained simply as what was left behind after a dog-fight of vested interests. I can see no reason to suppose that here as elsewhere *ideas* were not a powerful element in shaping history. The balance of trade, rightly or wrongly, was as powerful and influential an obsession to the seventeenth century as free-trade was to the nineteenth. Here it approached closely the central body of ideas which Dr Hinton has described in the governors of the commonwealth.

And when we look at those governors, how probable is this underlying assumption that they would come to heel at the sound of a tradesman's whistle? Let us look at them engaged in their business of policy-making. Hear Samuel Pepys on the lords commissioners of the treasury in 1667. 'I do like the way of these great lords that they admit nobody to use many words nor do they spend many words themselves, but in great state do hear what they see necessary and say little themselves but bid withdraw.' How well one can imagine them – Albemarle, Ashley, Clifford, Coventry! It would be interesting to hear what they thought of the phrase 'pressure-group', or of the suggestion that the power of decision lay with anybody but themselves, subject only to the king. It was indeed in men such as these that the contemporary general will resided.

We may pass on conveniently to consider the relationship of the monied men themselves to the affairs of government in the next century – in fact, to those alleged bankers' ramps which seemed to some contemporaries (and not less to some twentieth-century historians) a satisfying explanation of some obstinate conundrums. How far *did* financiers guide or dictate government economic policy in the eighteenth century? On the face of it such a suggestion seems plausible enough. Certainly, some of the largest fortunes in the City were made out of supplying money to the state. From time to time the monied interest exercised considerable power. It helped to prevent Walpole from reducing interest rates on the national debt in 1737. It influenced the conversion scheme in 1749–50. Yet Miss Sutherland, who has investigated the problem most thoroughly, concludes that neither of the occasions when the ministry was said to have 'lost the City' to opponents (1710 and 1746) is substantiated by the facts. The City (she has written) was a broken reed for purposes of party politics because the prosperity of its members depended on being on good terms with the government of the day. There was too much gang warfare among the financiers for any one man or group to dare take on as opponent the universal provider of so many good things. Defoe was right when he argued that it was not that 'they that have the money must have the management': it was 'they that have the management will have the money'.[1] Recent scrutiny of voting in the eighteenth-century House of Commons has borne him out fully. The merchant-contractors in the Commons received contracts because they sided with the government; they did not vote with the government because they had been awarded contracts. Even on economic policy, business influence was negligible.[2]

This was the essence of the system of influence. I suspect it applied already to the seventeenth century. It was still strong in George III's time. There is a letter from Clive to a friend in 1762 describing the reception of the governor of the East India Company by Lord Egremont's secretary. 'At last poor Rous [the governor] was sent for and after having been scolded and sworn at by Mr Wood and then by his lordship himself, the articles were consented to be altered.' Obviously things had not changed much since Pepys's day. Even the Duke of Newcastle, hardly a by-word for physical or moral courage, treated Sir Joshua Vanneck, the leading City financier to whom the government owed debts of both gratitude and money, hardly less casually. It was his fate (Sir Joshua used to lament at regular intervals) to be kept waiting in his grace's ante-room for hours, only to be told at last that 'the duke had gone away' or 'was unable to see him'.

Things had not altered when the younger Pitt came to power. Pitt's economic policies were, as Mr Ehrman has shown, more pragmatic than dogmatic; but any idea of mercantile dictation can be ruled out. When great economic issues were at stake a few great merchants might be *invited* to give evidence – Boulton and Wedgwood, for example. But they played no part in the negotiations. Like the treasury commissioners a century and a quarter earlier, the government was brief and to the point even with these great tycoons. It was long-established custom that merchants, and companies, were entitled to submit their views

[1] L. Sutherland, in *Essays Presented to Sir L. Namier* (1956).
[2] Sir L. Namier and J. Brooke, *History of Parliament*, i, 135.

on points that specifically concerned them. But affairs of state were the affairs of statesmen and of nobody else. Everybody in business recognized the limits within which the merchant community must operate. To quote Mr Ehrman: 'So, certainly, did the polite world. The suspicion of mercantile or industrial self-interest was strong in an aristocratic society.'[1] If this is (as I believe it is) a fair and accurate picture of the relations between government and trade in the eighteenth century, it would seem wise to pause before accepting at its face value the proposal that government economic policy was guided and exclusively decided by lobbies and pressure groups.[2] The men who ruled England were for the most part arrogant, quick to anger, highly-strung, bred to the habit of command and jealous of their prerogatives. Between themselves no quarter was asked and little was given. They extended the same treatment to inferiors as a matter of course, and the inferiors included all those commercial and business interests who came to seek favours. Without the pressure they tried to exert and without the information they brought, economic policies would have been different, and certainly worse than they were. Merchants might influence government; but they did not manage it. The decisions taken were those of government itself, composed as it was of men who believed that the business of government was to govern. They acknowledged the relevance and importance of the views of the subjects but they retained their independence of judgement in decision to a far greater degree than is often recognized.

With Pitt's Anglo-French negotiations we began to feel a new breeze blowing through British economic policy. But the breeze had to blow for a long time before it blew the old ideas and institutions away. It had taken three-quarters of a century to lay the foundations of the mercantile system; it was to take as long before Pitt, Huskisson, Peel and Gladstone could dismantle

[1] John Ehrman, *The British Government and Commercial Negotiations with Europe 1783–1793*, p. 184.

[2] In an article in the *Economic History Review* (Aug. 1965), published after this paper was delivered, Mr. G. C. Bolton argues that the resistance of the woollen manufacturers to the commercial clauses of the act of union with Ireland illustrates the 'influence of business pressure groups even on the unreformed parliament'. ('Some British reactions to the act of Union'). But if, as Mr Bolton admits, the lobbyers 'failed to find allies' and collected only twenty votes for 'reconsideration' of the commercial clauses, the incident seems to illustrate the manifest weakness of the lobby rather than its effectiveness.

them. What brought the walls of this old Jericho tumbling down? Was it the single blast of the priestly trumpets of the Anti-Corn Law League? Was it a hundred insidious whisperings from Manchester and elsewhere that persuaded authority that more and cheaper coffee *from* Brazil meant millions more yards of cotton *for* Brazil? Or was it the work of a fifth column inside? How, in practice, *were* the fundamental mercantilist beliefs and their practical legislative corollaries, the whole apparatus of economic interference and control, switched over to the new belief in increasing economic freedom?

Any lingering notion that the Manchester temple was early crowded with eager disciples of the new faith is easily disposed of.[1] Until the middle of the nineteenth century it was still possible for a man piously to believe in the merits of freely importing more tea, or coffee, or corn without seeing equal virtue in freedom to export machinery or skilled artisans. Empirically, they picked and they chose. This is not, perhaps, an inappropriate occasion to remind ourselves how late was the general fusion of convenience and principle and how specific the fuse.

Now I do not suppose that even the most fervent disciple of the 'lobby' school of historians would claim that the representatives of private interest would have had much impact on government before 1832 if government had not been in a receptive frame of mind. The powerful influence that the new doctrines had already had on Pitt, Huskisson, Peel and Gladstone meant that the door was already ajar; it did not need to be pushed very hard. What has more recently become clear[2] is the power these doctrines exercised *behind* the governmental scenes through a lower but very powerful echelon of public servants. In 1830 the board of trade fell under the guidance of Poulett Thomson, later Lord Sydenham, 'the greatest coxcomb [said Greville] I ever saw, and the vainest dog – though his vanity is not offensive or arrogant'. With him came a dependent tribe of devout Benthamites, for Thomson was nothing if not doctrinaire. So for his lieutenants: Deacon Hume, an earnest, clerkly zealot; McGregor, of whose excursions into authorship the *DNB* tartly remarks that 'he was as unfit to write history as to make it';

[1] A. Redford, *Manchester Merchants and Foreign Trade 1793–1858* (1934), ch. X, XI.

[2] Lucy Brown, *The Board of Trade and the Free Trade Movement, 1830–1842* (1958).

Bowring, tireless traveller and self-styled polymath, endless chatterbox and universal busybody; Porter, assiduous collector of figures on anything and everything, and husband of Ricardo's sister. They shared strong connections with the homeland of the new faith; they were all zealots to put the economy right. They shared one other common characteristic: everyone was a hopeless failure in practical affairs, everyone lost his patrimony by injudicious investment. This in no way impaired their confidence that they were just the men to manage everybody else's business. For years they rigged select committees, managed witnesses, trimmed evidence as they steered England steadily towards free trade. They were helped by a fact of great importance. Just as in the formative period of mercantilism, so now business opinion was hopelessly and characteristically split on the tariff issue. The cotton and woollen manufacturers were fairly solid for free trade; but (in spite of the board of trade's attempts to give a different impression) hardly anybody else was. Some sections of industry, like shipping, were protectionist, and so, of course, was the agricultural industry.

In such circumstances, when nobody could easily define the state of public opinion, it was not difficult for the bureaucrats to make hay. Their task became, not to initiate changes demanded by public opinion, for opinion was hopelessly divided, but to persuade the public why change – change to free trade – was desirable and necessary. To ease the task, however, they did not hesitate to improve the shining hour by exaggerating the degree of support they enjoyed. They spoke (as Miss Brown says) 'over the heads of parliament to the general public'. Indeed, one of the most characteristic features of this rather unattractive caucus was that they invariably spoke over the heads of any masters they were supposed to serve. Nevertheless, the efficacy of their campaign is undeniable. It was not only their hatred of old *ideas* that put fire into their bellies; it was hatred of old *men*. Deacon Hume, said a contemporary, was not in favour of Godwinism or Owenism – quite; but his 'abhorrence of the aristocracy and landlords and monopolizers of property often brings him on the confines of those wild regions'.[1] This gritty, statistical, utilitarian fanaticism was the steam in the boiler. As Miss Brown concludes, the foundations of Peel's policy on corn were laid in the board of

[1] Brown, *op. cit.*, p. 25, quoting J. L. Mallett.

trade. The old mercantile system was destroyed in large part from within.[1]

Let me emphasize again that I am not concerned with the economic virtues or vices of these various policies, mercantilist or anti-mercantilist, nor with their morality, nor how far they could claim in practice to be a kind of economic general will. I am concerned with their origins, with the mechanism by which they became an effective system governing economic life through deliberate controls, or influencing it through freedom. The theory that the mechanism always resulted from the irresistible pressure of private interests on a supine or ineffective government seems to me historically casual and logically inadequate. With all its imperfections there was an element of system, of coherence and rationality in the mercantilist economy which distinguished it markedly from the chaos of Spain or the Italian states and rendered it superior to that of France, or Sweden, or even Holland. If only moneybags, or the momentum of inertia, or the self-interest of the *status quo* had been the deciding factor, there could hardly have been so much of that encouragement of innovation, of change, of struggling minorities which is so remarkable a feature of even the seventeenth-century economy. One would have expected the entry to trade and industry to have become more difficult; yet it became more easy. The vitality of the system never quite died. It is, after all, something to say for it that it contained the germs of its own decay; for even those bacteria, so dear to every historical student, flourish in live bodies, not in dead ones.

No, I believe it is plain that the livelier the lobbying, the more numerous the pressure-groups, the more obviously necessary became that power of decision, of choosing between alternatives, which resided only in the government – in the crown, the privy council, the ministry. Decisions were taken on the basis of established conventions which might and often did transcend private interests, sometimes very powerful ones. Especially when the alternative choices were neatly balanced, the deciding factor might well be those economic, political, social and strategic desiderata which seemed commonplaces to the governors of the time. For the mercantilist period there was no single exponent who articulated these central ideas as Adam Smith was to do

[1] *Ibid.*, p. 230.

for the second phase of our national economic policy. But writers like Mun, Child, Downing and many others did give coherent expression to them in a way unequalled in any other country, even in France. These classical formulations of doctrine, whether by Thomas Mun or Adam Smith, had a special function in policy making. They were neither merely short-sightedly commercial nor merely remotely academic. They seemed to reflect the current situation, to meet current needs so appropriately and so perfectly that they acquired a kind of controlling dynamism of their own, taking hold of men as a spirit is supposed to take hold of a human medium. There is a remarkable passage at the end of Keynes's last book where he touched on this persuasive force exercised by ideas:

. . . the ideas of economists and political philosophers, both when they are right and when they are wrong, are more powerful than is commonly understood. Indeed the world is ruled by little else. Practical men, who believe themselves to be quite exempt from any intellectual influences, are usually the slaves of some defunct economist. Madmen in authority, who hear voices in the air, are distilling their frenzy from some academic scribbler of a few years back. I am sure that the power of vested interests is vastly exaggerated compared with the gradual encroachment of ideas.[1]

People often talk nowadays as if such academic thought simply reflects current material interests. Alfred Marshall used to say that free trade was really a projection of British national interests. Mrs Joan Robinson has pushed this a step farther in her stimulating little book on *Economic Philosophy*:

The hard-headed classicals made no bones about it. They were arguing against the narrow nationalism of mercantilists in favour of a more far-sighted policy, but they were in favour of free trade because it was good for Great Britain, not because it was good for the world.[2]

There is a confusion here. As an economic *system*, British free trade was, of course, manifestly in British interests: it was designed to be. But Mrs Robinson is speaking of the economists, and if she refers to Adam Smith or to David Hume I believe she is wrong. They made quite a few bones about precisely this. At the time they were laying and even inscribing the foundation tables of the new system, there were relatively few businessmen

[1] J. M. Keynes, *The General Theory of Employment, Interest and Money* (1936), p. 383.
[2] *Pelican edition* (1964), p. 117.

with the foresight to understand the case they were expounding. Like their predecessors, the physiocrats, they were universalists. They drew their strength from the antithesis they portrayed between the weaknesses of the actual economy and the virtues of the ideal economy. The *Wealth of Nations* might to a later generation become conveniently justificatory; when it was written it was prophetic, decades ahead of its time, and in this lay much of its attractive, persuasive force. By penny numbers, and gradually, some of England's businessmen grasped, half a century after it was published, that the general doctrine of the *Wealth of Nations* might suit their book. The encroaching power of its prophecies makes it the perfect proof of Keynes's contention. In this first instance, however, the 'practical men' who were most influenced by Adam Smith were not for the most part tradesmen or industrialists; they were statesmen and politicians, bureaucrats and statisticians. So, just as Cromwell, Charles II, Downing, Coventry, Locke, Newton and Walpole had set to work to build the concept of the balance of trade into the economic laws of the nation, so Huskisson, Peel, Gladstone, Poulett Thomson, McGregor, Deacon Hume and the rest set to work to dismantle the whole mercantile apparatus. For all their differences, mercantilism and *laissez-faire* had some things in common. They both claimed to represent the public interest as much as the private. Even *laissez-faire* claimed to be a kind of economic general will, though its doctrine was older than Rousseau. It went back to Pope's belief, proclaimed in the *Essay on Man*, that true self-love and social were the same. And, if my arguments are correct, both economic systems derived as much from government authority and the 'encroachment of ideas' as they did from the ambiguous, often mutually destructive pressures exercised by private interest. The 'lobby' theory of economic legislation, at any rate in its simpler formulations, remains non-proven.

10

The Entrepreneur in the Industrial Revolution in Britain[1]

Refuting the errors of those who have written of the 'disasters of the industrial revolution' Professor Ashton has pointed out that 'the central problem of the age was how to feed and clothe and employ generations of children outnumbering by far those of any other time'.[2] If England had remained a nation of cultivators and craftsmen she must have shared the fate of Ireland and submitted to the remedies of emigration or starvation. 'She was delivered', he writes, 'not by her rulers, but by those who, seeking no doubt their own narrow ends, had the wit and resource to devise new instruments of production and new methods of administering industry.'[3]

Here is a starting point for further inquiry. Professor Ashton has himself suggested some of the diverse considerations which led employers to reorganize industry on new lines. In the iron and cotton industries technology suggested large-scale production and the application of power in the factory. Elsewhere, economic rather than technological considerations prevailed. In the chemical and engineering industries, supervision was necessary to ensure quality of workmanship. In textiles, too, oversight was necessary and Benjamin Gott, the great woollen manufacturer at Leeds, saw the factory system as a preventive against the waste and embezzlement of materials. Wedgwood's *Etruria* was devised partly to exploit the economies to be derived

[1] This is a revised and shortened version of a paper given at a conference at Harvard on the Entrepreneur and Economic Growth in November 1954 under the auspices of the Harvard Research Centre on Entrepreneurial History, later published in *History*, Vol. XLII (1957) pp. 101–17.

[2] Ashton, *The Industrial Revolution*, p. 161. [3] *Ibid.*

from the division and subdivision of labour. And so on.[1] The inquiry remains, nevertheless, in an early stage. What were the 'ends' which the entrepreneur of that age had before his eye? How 'narrow' were they? Why was he moved to devise new instruments of production and new types of industrial organization? And what was the social background against which this great increment of wealth was created?

First, however, let us remind ourselves that the economic historian who deals with the industrial revolution without reservation in terms of period will do so at his peril. Each industry had its own rate of progress. He will do well to remember too that he is dealing with a society which, though growing, was still relatively small and compact, and in which a more abstract and generalized system of economic relationships was only just beginning to encroach on one based largely on local and often family relations. The intimate connections between the growth of industry and the several kinds of religious dissent – especially the older sects – have been fairly fully investigated and proven. It was not only the better (and more practical) education that dissenters provided for themselves but the necessary solidarity they felt between themselves that helps to explain the phenomenon. The meeting house or the chapel extended the ties of the family, and you lent and borrowed within your known community with a confidence hardly yet to be extended beyond such limits. The parochial character of industry persisted much longer than is usually supposed: perhaps it still persists. A knowledgeable businessman could write in 1903 as if the spread in industry of limited liability was a recent thing, and about the same time a soap maker could write to a Bristol rival: 'personal knowledge of each other is a great factor in the cohesion of the soap trade. . . .' He was only repeating what earlier makers had said: that 'good fellowship' in the trade was worth ten shillings a ton.[2]

The entrepreneur was not, that is to say, operating in an anonymous world. Nor, on the whole, for all its difficulties, was it an unfriendly world. An observer trying to explain the rapid growth of the British economy in 1800 ascribed it to the improvements in public utilities and cost-reducing inventions applied in industry. To greater output and better quality was due 'the

[1] *Ibid.* p. 109. [2] Charles Wilson, *History of Unilever*, 1954, i. 70.

universally increasing demand' for British goods. But, he added significantly, 'All these advantages she owes to her social system, which gives equal respectability to trade and equal security to the capital invested in it.'[1] The tradition had deep roots. Thomas Deloney, the Elizabethan writer, remarked 'the younger sons of knights and gentlemen, to whom their fathers would leave no lands, were most commonly preferred to learn this trade [cloth making] to the end that thereby they might live in good estate and drive forth their days in prosperity'.[2] But in the early eighteenth century Defoe noted that the social stream ran in both directions and 'many of the great families who now pass for gentry in the Western counties have been originally raised from and built up by this truly noble manufacture'.[3]

Such was the background to what Dr Johnson called 'an age of innovation', and such are a few of the limits and circumstances, local and special, which must be borne in mind as the particular context within which the entrepreneur of the industrial revolution worked. The nature of the entrepreneur's function has been defined shortly by Professor Cole[4] as 'the utilization by one productive factor of the other productive factors for the creation of economic goods': the motive or result being an increase of profit or efficiency, or an accession or shift of personal power, or the growth or survival of the business as a unit. Enough evidence is readily available to suggest that this definition may well suggest new modes of inquiry into the industrial revolution. As Mantoux pointed out in his classic study, the great figures of the movement made their reputations as *organizers*.[5] Their distinctive characteristic was that they fulfilled in one person the functions of capitalist, financier, works manager, merchant and salesman. Here was 'a new pattern of the complete businessman'.[6] So much is common knowledge: we usually assume that such men, though far from common, were responsible for changing the climate of opinion amongst the manufacturing class as a whole. Yet, oddly enough, there has been relatively little attempt to bond their total function into

[1] Henry Beeke, *Observations on the Produce of the Income Tax . . . including important facts respecting the extent, wealth, and population of this kingdom*, 1799.

[2] Eileen Power, *Medieval People*, 1937, p. 155. [3] *Ibid.*, p. 147.

[4] Lane and Riemersma, *Enterprise and Secular Change*, 1953, pp. 183–4.

[5] Mantoux, *The Industrial Revolution in the 18th Century*, 1928, p. 382.

[6] *Ibid.*

the economic context. A dozen biographers from Samuel Smiles onward have rendered tribute to Wedgwood, Boulton and many others. Yet Wedgwood's fame rests largely on his application of the principle of division of labour. Boulton is famous for his association with and promotion of Watt and his invention. So with the others. Yet further survey of the field of their labours prompts the question whether here, as so often in history, we are not allowing our eye to be attracted by the spectacular difference, while ignoring the common quality shared by all these great entrepreneurs and not for that reason of less significance but perhaps more. If too rigid a pattern is not to be imposed on the bewildering variety of circumstances, our sense of this common characteristic must be kept as general as possible. I should define it thus: *a sense of market opportunity combined with the capacity needed to exploit it.* The conventional accounts of change have in reality concentrated so much on the exploitation of opportunity as to obscure the nature of the opportunity itself. The fact that Wilkinson was the best and most reliable borer of cylinders in England is no doubt a technical fact of some importance, as is the fact that Hargreaves' jenny could spin eighty threads at once. Yet economically such facts are quite useless unless it is explained why the accurate boring of cylinders or the greater output of yarn was not only necessary but seen by some men 'of wit and resource' to be necessary and potentially profitable.

Before entering on a more detailed inquiry into the function of the later entrepreneur it is necessary to consider how far research in recent years may have modified Mantoux's conception of him as 'a new man'. Professor Carus Wilson has shown how wide were the ramifications of commercial capital in medieval industry and how strong the ties by which the artisans were bound to the masters, not only in England but in Flanders and Italy.[1] Jean Boine Broke, the great *drapier* of Douai, Henry Houhil of Leicester, or the *lanaiuoli* of Florence all in a greater or lesser degree intervened in the various phases of woollen manufacture, from the purchase of raw material to the sale of the finished product, exercising a varying degree of control. How 'typical' this type of centrally controlled (but geographically dispersed) organization was, it is difficult to say. What is clear is that in the urban industries of Continental Europe

[1] *Cambridge Economic History of Europe*, Vol. II, Ch. VI, *passim*.

entrepreneurial control was nowhere complete: and it was everywhere supplemented (and in another sense limited) by *corporate* regulation through the gilds. Matters of quality in particular were supervised to a very large extent by gild ordinance – a necessity which suggests that the physical control exercised by the entrepreneur may not have been adequate to achieve the desired ends. And it is worth noting that in the textile industries of Leiden in the sixteenth and seventeenth centuries, a very considerable degree of entrepreneurial supervision had to be supplemented by corporate regulation.[1]

In these respects the later medieval English cloth industry presented some unique features. Developing as it did away from the old cities, in the small market towns and countryside, it demonstrated a degree of experiment not found elsewhere, and notably a greater degree of mechanization. Normally the function of the big clothier entrepreneur was restricted to a general managerial supervision of an organization partially concentrated – as regards dyeing and finishing – and partially spread – spinning and weaving. But again, supervision was the fundamental problem. In both the west country and East Anglia therefore there are to be found clothiers who closely resemble the later entrepreneurs of the industrial revolution. The figure of the famous Jack of Newbury who was alleged to have put over a thousand artisans to work on his own premises remains shrouded in legend. Stumpe, who converted Malmesbury after the Dissolution into a cloth factory, is better attested. Likewise, at the Essex village of Coggeshall, where the Paycocke family established 'the truly noble manufacture' of cloth, Thomas may well have gathered some of his weavers and other workers under his own roof. That the practice was on the increase may be seen from the petitions of the independent weavers against clothiers who kept weavers and fullers in their own houses and agreed on a single price for the same job.[2]

These seem to be phenomena of a rural industry, freed from the restraints and controls of urban corporate bodies, by which quality had been achieved and maintained. In the absence of such regulations, the tendency for the entrepreneur to secure the needs of his market through a greater degree of centralized

[1] N. W. Posthumus, *De Geschiedenis van de Leidsche Lakenindustrie*, Vol. III, Ch. 1.
[2] Power, *Medieval People*, p. 157.

control and even physical concentration of industry would be strong. Yet we must ask with Clapham the fundamental questions: how large? how long? how often? how representative? And the answer must be that these were swallows that did not make a summer. The typical system everywhere remained the dispersed outwork system, in which entrepreneurial intervention and control was partial and uneven. The reason may well lie in the nature of the product and the market. Until well into the eighteenth century a considerable proportion of woollen manufacture consisted of semi-finished or unfinished cloth, exported in the white. The point at which supervision was most vital – the finishing processes – was beyond the purview of many clothiers and it is significant that those who included it in their operations often owned the necessary plant and operated it under their own control. As for the market, it is perhaps reasonable to suppose that a predominantly rural society would probably remain content with a fairly stable type of commodity.[1] Manufacturing industry, up to the industrial revolution, was rarely more than half-way between the peasant industry that catered for its own needs, and the commercial manufacture that must take heed for the discerning customer.

It seems not unreasonable to assume therefore that the problems of manufacture, both as regards quantity production and quality production, though by no means negligible, were a good deal less formidable than they were to become with the growth of more sophisticated urban markets in a later age. In so far as pressing problems existed in these respects, the solution was provided by varying types of organization within which the individual entrepreneur, corporate industrial bodies, and municipal and national governments shared responsibility for the control of production and sale. Viewing the bewildering range of processes and what later observers came to regard as the waste of effort, time and money involved in the carriage of materials and supervision, one is inclined to wonder whether, as a system catering for a market, this can have been anything but a gamble in respect of quality, quantity or price. Yet, given the relatively slow movements of population, taste and demand it

[1] Such notable innovations as did occur (e.g. the New Draperies) were invariably introduced from more advanced economies, such as that of the Low Countries, and operated initially by immigrants from those areas.

seems somehow to have functioned. And the entrepreneur whose ingenuities were exercised by its problems represents no less an advance on the earlier wool merchant (whose function was that of buying and selling an unchanged commodity, and arranging its transport and economic time of sale) than the complex cloth industry represents over the earlier wool trade.

'To study the entrepreneur', Professor Cole has written, 'is to study the central figure in modern economic history and to my way of thinking, the central figure in economics.'[1] Certainly a legitimate approach to modern economic history might be to trace the development from Paycocke to Horrockses: from the slow gathering of control over the different processes within a single industry to that outward seeking after control not merely of one industry but of the ancillary industries and processes on which the so-called 'central' manufacture depends – in short to the vertical combine in which modern industrial development has reached (some might say, passed) its peak of self-fulfilment.

If we narrow our focus, for the moment, to the textile industries of Britain in the period of revolution, certain general features of change will be seen to emerge. First, for nearly a century before industry itself was revolutionized by the new technology, there had proceeded an expansion of markets which, though small in relation to what was to follow, was very large indeed by comparison with what had gone before. The 'official' value of British exports in 1760 was twice that of 1700 and nearly eight times that of 1660, and though the proportionate importance of cloth declined steadily, its actual value rose rapidly. It remained till 1802 the most valuable single export: this moreover in a period when the price revolution is no longer available as a convenient *deus ex machina* in the historian's apparatus of analysis and explanation. The falling rate of interest was certainly an important factor in expansion: but it seems to me to have been rather in the nature of an enabling condition for those prepared to take advantage of it. It did not prevent the decline and virtual extinction of well-established industries in some areas. It is, however, not merely an expansion of production, linked no doubt to an increase of population, fundamental developments in public finance, and better facilities for transport, that is significant. There is besides

[1] Lane and Riemersma, *Enterprise and Secular Change*, p. 187.

a marked shift of emphasis in the nature of the articles produced, and a new phase of interregional competition for market supremacy. In this battle – and especially in the battle for exports – the East Anglian industry slowly overcame the weakening resistance of the West, only to be overwhelmed in turn by the ingenuity and assiduity of the Yorkshire industry.[1]

The movement away from the older heavier woollens to lighter and brighter worsteds (extended later in the growth of demand for printed calicoes and cottons) clearly represents a phase of social and economic change: in this the development of an urban middle-class demand and the growth of tropical and semi-tropical exports were to combine. Sir John Elwill, a great Exeter cloth merchant, wrote in 1714 to a Dutch client that the manufacture of 'mixt Serges' was declining and would 'never flourish as heretofore'. The reason was that they were 'not worn by Many Sort of People as formerly': but 'Some new sorts of Drapery were invented ... which are used by many that formerly used Serge'.[2] Yet the West was to fail utterly in the struggle for the market in the new cloths and it is not altogether fanciful to seek part of the explanation of her failure in the relative weakness of the link between manufacturer and merchant. In Devonshire, the two functions were often separate: in Norwich and Yorkshire they were often combined. After a brief glory, Norwich gave way to Yorkshire, where the link was most strong. There, by the end of the eighteenth century, as Professor Heaton has shown, 'many merchants had gained absolute control over production by becoming manufacturers themselves'.[3] Merchant and manufacturer were united in one person and a term was put to the friction between the former, who alone knew what the customer would buy, and the latter, who was often more interested in persuading the merchant to take what he had always made. Equally there is evidence here of the commercial sense of the industrialists which is less evident elsewhere.

[1] The reputation of the Gloucestershire industry under the leadership of the famous 'gentleman-clothiers' remained high until the nineteenth century and was in some ways a model from which Yorkshire learned much. But though it seems to have been more responsive and flexible than the Devonshire industry, evidence is not lacking of unusual difficulties by the late eighteenth century.

[2] Charles Wilson, *Anglo-Dutch Commerce and Finance in the Eighteenth Century*, p. 37. For the West Country industry, see also W. G. Hoskins, *Industry, Trade and People in Exeter 1688–1800*, 1935.

[3] H. Heaton, *Yorkshire Woollen and Worsted Industry*, p. 388.

Professor Heaton has shown us the indefatigable Sam Hill, toiling and sweating to imitate the latest worsteds from Norwich and ending triumphantly on a note of pushful confidence that defied contemporary depression and becomes enterprise personified. 'I think it now evident these manufactories . . . will come in spite of fate into these northern Countries.'[1]

It is difficult not to see a relationship between the growth of the worsted market (which by the 1770s was on the point of overtaking the older production of woollens) and the change in industrial organization which brought carding, slubbing, spinning, and in some cases finishing and dyeing – but not yet weaving – into the factory between 1790 and 1825. These developments in technology and industrial organization fill in the framework sketched by Mantoux: it was the continental demand for English worsted which enabled the enterprising clothier to profit from circumstances.[2] A petition from the weavers presented to the House of Commons in 1794 spoke of the large numbers of merchants who were turning clothiers, especially in and near Leeds and Halifax, setting up large factories for making woollen cloth.[3]

It must be evident that the most progressive of these men who were to set the pattern for future development owed as much to their grasp of commercial opportunity as they did to their capacity to apply and develop the new inventions. Benjamin Gott, the first of the great Leeds spinners, was a merchant whose mind turned first to the nature of demand and secondly to the means of satisfying it. His most important innovations were the application of new chemical techniques to the vital finishing and dyeing sections of the cloth-making process. Here thousands of pounds and infinite patience were expended in developing an industrial process scientifically controlled throughout.[4] In the early nineteenth century the process of concentration can be taken a step further in the worsted business of William Foster at Queensbury, then a small village half-way between Bradford and Halifax. In his own lifetime the founder saw his industry change from a domestic affair into one where all the numerous processes were comprised and controlled within Foster's own factories. The special feature of Foster's, however, was their

[1] *Ibid.*, p. 270. [2] Mantoux, p. 106. [3] *Ibid.*, p. 272.
[4] A. and N. Clow, *The Chemical Revolution*, pp. 220–1.

development of high-grade fabrics for dresses from mohair and alpaca. These, his Victorian biographer tells us, 'were dispersed over all the countries of the world, lending new charms to female loveliness wherever they are seen, whether it be to form a chastely flowing garment for an Eastern beauty, or to adorn the figure of the most fashionably attired Parisian belle'.[1] And at this point we may watch the vital transition from market sense to advertisement proper. For faced by the wiles of the Paris fashion-dictators Foster decided to invoke the aid of an aristocratic beauty, the Countess of Bective, in support of a patriotic movement in female fashions. What became known as the Bective movement was in fact the first essay in what was later to become a regular feature of advertising: the ingenious exploitation of snob appeal.[2] The Countess of Bective must go into the history of industrial change as clearly as the spinning jenny. For the charms of aristocratic beauty were to be no less an instrument to the hand of the entrepreneur than the steam loom itself.

That invention and organization were intimately related to possibilities and changes in demand is no less clear from the history of cotton than from that of wool. The eighteenth century yielded nothing to the twentieth in the extravagance and caprice of its tastes and fashions in clothing. Within a matter of months a fad would take hold which called for immediate response, which was not possible without the most flexible commercial and industrial organization. It was presumably through such a series of changes that the great markets for Lancashire goods were built up. The general trend in Europe at any rate was an extension of the demand for lighter, finer fabrics and in particular for fabrics which imitated the qualities of those previously imported from the East. The ingenuity of the entrepreneurs who seized this opportunity to develop a local imitative industry has been traced by Wadsworth and Mann,[3] and their application

[1] *Fortunes Made in Business* (by various writers), 1884, Vol. II, p. 32. This is a relatively unused work. No indication of the authorship is given but many of the biographies are written with shrewdness and perception. The collection was apparently well known to Alfred Marshall, who drew on it for evidence to support a number of conclusions in his *Principles*. Mantoux likewise knew of it, but otherwise it has been much neglected.

[2] *Ibid.*, ii. 49–50.

[3] *The Cotton Trade and Industrial Lancashire*, Book 2.

of chemical knowledge to their production problems by Mr and Mrs Clow.[1] Thus behind the staggering increase in Lancashire exports to Europe – from practically nothing in 1750 to £218,000 by 1770 – lies the story of the experiments in dyeing by John Wilson of Ainsworth (near Manchester) and others. Most of the increase was accounted for by cotton velvets and checks. The correspondence of Samuel Oldknow with his London agents about this time brings out clearly the relationship between markets and manufacturer. The manufacturers were advised which types of fabric were a poor sale and should be dropped, which sold well and should be developed. 'We want as many spotted muslins and fancy muslins as you can make, the finer the better. . . . You must give a look to Invention, industry you have in abundance. We expect to hear from you as often as possible and as the sun shines let us make the Hay.' And later: 'We rather wish you to drop the Sattinets, they are not new here and only fit for 2 months sale. The Buff stripes are liked best but still do not pursue it, turn the loom to something else. They are not fine enough for People of Fashion, for which they are only calculated for . . . try your skill at Table Linen. . . . Arkwright must lower his Twist and he must spin finer, tell him the reputation of our Country against Scotland is at stake'.[2] The pressures of the market and competition were bearing in on the industrialist from every direction. What came to be a widespread muslin industry in Lancashire and Scotland depended on the ability of the mule to produce a thread even finer than the best hand-spun yarn from India. Only with the water-frame could English calico weavers compete with Indian calicoes. Only the water-frames of Arkwright's mill at Derby could produce the strong thread for Strutt's speciality – the ribbed stocking.[3] And so on.

It is evident that if manufacturers were to be able to rise to these exacting occasions their control of the productive process must be firm and flexible. Herein lies, it seems to me, one of the most important facts behind the movement to include all the several processes of manufacture – spinning, weaving, dyeing, finishing – under the control of a single entrepreneur, which

[1] *The Chemical Revolution.*

[2] G. Unwin, *S. Oldknow and the Arkwrights*, pp. 62–5.

[3] Mantoux, pp. 228 and 243.

according to Professor Ashton was developing by 1820.[1] It was illustrated most strikingly in the development of Horrockses of Preston where the whole process from sorting out American and Egyptian cotton bales down to dispatching their special finished cotton products – sheetings, shirtings and long cloths – to merchants at home and abroad was gathered into one organization by the 1830s.[2]

It was as true of other industries producing consumer goods as of wool and cotton that the entrepreneur's first effort had to be concentrated on innovation and organization designed not merely for quantity production but for quality appropriate to the existing or potential demand. What an observer said of Crossleys, the great carpet makers of Halifax, might have been said of many others. 'No amount of cheapening of production would have availed them anything if they had not also been able to take the lead in the beauty and originality of their designs.'[3] The best-known achievement of Josiah Wedgwood, one of the classical entrepreneurs of English industrial history, was to found his factory *Etruria* on the principle of division of labour. But mass production *in vacuo* might well have been a failure, even given the growing demand for crockery from which to drink coffee and tea, had it not been combined with a shrewd perception of the contemporary appeal of pseudo-classical designs. Having provided all Europe with table china his commercial imagination was by no means exhausted and in the late 1770s he wrote of his intention to develop a new line of manufacture – 'earthen water pipes, for London first, and then for all the world'.[4] His later rival, Herbert Minton at Stoke-on-Trent, had no less sharp an eye for a profitable line. He regularly embarked on long tours of Europe in search of new technical ideas and the famous 'English Majolica' sprang from a chance observation at Rouen of 'some common flower pots, with a green opaque glaze' which, he guessed, might sell well if improved.[5]

Perception of a small but important need in an expanding commercial society – the steel pen – led Josiah Mason to establish a factory at Birmingham which became the largest of its kind in the world. Mason was not himself an inventor but

[1] Ashton, *The Industrial Revolution*, p. 75.
[2] *Fortunes Made in Business*, iii. 1–31. [3] *Ibid.*, iii. 304–5.
[4] Mantoux, p. 395. [5] *Fortunes Made in Business*, iii. 78–9.

he had (as his biographer observed) a 'quickness in seizing a new idea, sagacity in realizing its possibilities of development and courage in bringing it within range of practical application'. It was these qualities which later attracted his attention to the invention of electro-plating and its usefulness in the manufacture of cheap table ornaments and spoons and forks, '. . . knowing, as he shrewdly said, that the reputation as well as the solid profit of the enterprise must rest upon articles capable of being made by the hundred thousand and requisite for common household use'.[1] Much later, in the 1880s, a similar perception that a new type of customer, the working-class housewife, 'clean, saving and thrifty', was available, led William Lever to launch a patent 'washer' soap with qualities which had a special appeal to this type of use. Backed by every kind of advertising – mostly borrowed from North America – he built up in less than twenty years a business which surpassed in scope and size all other British competitors.[2]

The qualities and capacities which have been stressed in the entrepreneur are most clearly discernible in those industries and trades producing goods for a wide range of consumers. Yet it would be rash to assume that they were less important in industries like the iron industry, an important part of which – and that most swiftly revolutionized – manufactured capital goods or munitions. In the course of the eighteenth century an industry which was splintered into a vast number of small separate enterprises – furnaces, forges and slitting mills – became increasingly concentrated in large 'integrated' establishments in which all those processes from the mining of the ore down to the delivery of cannon mortars, bombs, cannonades, boilers, mill-gear and the like were carried out. The great ironmasters like Richard Crawshaw, Anthony Bacon and John Roebuck, though their market may have been less capricious in some ways than those for which the textile makers catered, had their own problems of quality which could only be mastered by trial and error, in a concern where (as a French visitor to the Carron works noted) 'everything is arranged and carried on with exact precision and nothing is left to mere routine or chance'.[3] The quality of iron used in making an iron railing

[1] *Ibid.*, iii. 151. [2] Wilson, *History of Unilever*, vol. I, Ch. III.
[3] B. F. de St. Fond, *Travels in England and Scotland*, 1784, p. 187.

would be different from that suitable for making a horse-shoe or a cart-wheel. Not the least of the problems of an industry in which vast amounts of capital had to be sunk was the uncertain character of its wartime market. It needed the passionate, single-minded, almost ludicrous faith of a John Wilkinson in his product, to transfer the new material to peacetime use, not only in bridges, ships, and cast-iron pipes for public water supply but in numerous more or less suitable architectural uses. The story of the partnership between the ironmasters and those architects of the Gothic Revival who sent clustering columns and high traceried windows soaring up in cast-iron in hundreds of fashionable buildings has yet to be told. But it could hardly fail to record remarkable enterprise.

Similarly, if a point had to be chosen from which Bessemer's later invention sprang it might well be the day in France when he, knowing little at the time of iron metallurgy, saw that the type of iron used in gun-making left much to be desired. Likewise John Brown of Sheffield, to whose faith in steel Bessemer owed an incalculable debt, owed his own fame to his vision of the railway system. 'He saw boundless demand in this new adjunct of civilization.' And he thrust his invention of the conical spring buffer (1848) on the railway companies, bullied the doubting Admiralty into adopting iron plates and cajoled the railways into adopting steel rails by distributing free samples.

The drift of these detailed inquiries seems to me to be clear: it is the tendency, powerful, yet in the period of industrial revolution far from ubiquitous, for the entrepreneur's intervention in certain important fields of industry to widen into an all-embracing function. This was necessary, it seems to me, if stability of costs, assured production in point of quantity or quality, and the requisite flexibility with regard to markets was to be achieved. A detailed examination of those markets suggests that it is misleading to consider the industrial revolution (as many textbooks do) merely in terms of undifferentiated commodities called cotton or woollens or iron. Such a treatment obscures the fundamental fact that the need to be met was for highly specific versions of such general categories of commodities and the relation between this fact and the consequential changes in industrial organization. It might be argued that in the last analysis it was a commercial flair that was basic. 'The tradesman', as an eighteenth-century writer put it, 'stands at the head of the manufacturer.'[1] Or as a later German historian wrote: 'Every commercial capitalist, whether he understands the technical side of his business or not, is always a trader. It is trade which decides what commodities shall be produced, where they shall be produced and how they shall be produced.'[2] And perhaps the classic instance of the captain of industry who owed his success to his commercial gifts as much as anything was Boulton, who dared to risk financing Watt because, as Mantoux has said: 'He was a bold and clever trader versed in the needs and possibilities of the market.'[3] The fact that the lineage of many of the new entrepreneurs may be traced through generations of yeomen or artisans does not necessarily damage the claims such a theory may have to our consideration.

Much ink has been spilt in attempts to identify the sources from whence came the entrepreneurs and the capital they disposed of. Yet the evidence remains too flimsy and incomplete to conclude with confidence more than this: that they came from every social source and every area. A great land-owner like the Duke of Bridgewater created new forms of transport; merchants came to make the things they had previously only sold, scientists turned into industrialists, parsons into inventors, small farmers and weavers became captains of industry. Arkwright was a barber, Samuel Walker of Rotherham turned from schoolmastering to become a great ironmaster. The capital required likewise came from a variety of sources. In many enterprises, from those of the early entrepreneurs down to those of the last of the line, personal saving played a great part. The great iron business of Walkers at Rotherham rose in the 1740s largely on capital amassed from ploughed back profits.[4] And in the 1890s William Lever was making £50,000 a year, living modestly on £400 a year and with the remainder creating and purchasing his own ordinary shares.[5] In yet other instances, capital was raised by means of partnership deeds and mortgages while short-term funds came from the banks. Only great public enterprises – turnpikes, canals, docks and the like – were public

[1] W. Hutton, *History of Birmingham*, 1795, p. 98
[2] A. Held, *Zwei Bücher zur sozialen Geschichte Englands*, 1881, p. 566.
[3] Mantoux, pp. 106–7.
[4] Ashton, *The Industrial Revolution*, p. 97.
[5] Wilson, *History of Unilever*, i. 48.

companies drawing on a national capital market. For the rest, investment was, and often long remained, local and even sectarian.

The brakes which early centuries had placed on the economic freedom of the entrepreneur – the restrictive and paternal legislation of gilds, municipalities and states – had largely disappeared from the world of Boulton and Watt. Even in the 1730s the poet's theme was already a philosophy which seemed eminently suitable to the entrepreneur:

> That REASON, PASSION, answer one great aim;
> That true SELF-LOVE and SOCIAL are the same. . . .[1]

Thus long before economic freedom became rationalized and systematized into a doctrine, the climate of opinion was becoming favourable to its practical development. An attempt in 1690 to set up an *omnibus* 'Guild or Fraternity' under the control of the Leeds Corporation for controlling cloth-working was recognized by 1720 to be a dead letter 'by long disuse and failure'.[2] Companies of this type – and they were tried in many places – could not exercise effective supervision over materials, workmanship, hours, wages and quality, which in the Middle Ages had been partially controlled by specialized gilds, partially by the entrepreneurs. Apprenticeship and supervision of wage rates by the Justices of the Peace were likewise falling into desuetude in the century before the industrial revolution proper began. The idea of regulation persisted very much longer in regard to external trade. The cotton industry grew up behind the shelter of the Calico Act (1721), designed to protect the woollen industries from India silks, and it was not until a century or more after the nominal date usually assigned to the beginning of industrial revolution (1760) that all the remains of the old mercantilist system were finally swept away. At Manchester, where ideas of economic freedom were most strongly developed, sectional opposition, obstinate and prolonged, was still evoked by proposals to export textile machinery. Even here, however, there are signs in the eighteenth century that the demand of entrepreneurs for adequate supplies of cheap materials was raising up a strong body of opposition to the monopolies of the

[1] Pope, *Essay on Man.*
[2] Clapham, *A Concise Economic History of Britain*, p. 254.

great importing companies which had long formed an integral part of the old system.

On the whole, the entrepreneur was empirical in his economic views. The nearest thing to a general economic philosophy evolved in the transitional stage from the mercantile system to the full doctrine of *laissez-faire* was probably enshrined in the sub-title to Mandeville's *Fable of the Bees* (1714). It ran 'Private Vices, Public Benefits'. This economic application of Pope's equation of self-love and social welfare was frequently elaborated by popular philosophers like Dr Johnson and others. The 'evil of luxury', said Johnson, was one of those false things 'transmitted from book to book'. The truth was that luxury produced much good: the expense went to the industrious poor and the demand gave rise to 'so much general productive exertion' that it could not fail to be beneficial. In short, here is the beginning of a philosophical divorce between ethics and economic doctrine. It remained, nevertheless, far from complete so far as the entrepreneur was concerned.[1] It may be, as some have attempted to show, that the new capitalism was relatively free from social controls and rested on a theoretical basis of the operation of natural law rather than on a system voluntarily developed by men.[2] Yet those who saw much virtue in the operations of the Hidden Hand, and no doubt with good reason, often acted in practice in ways which denied its claim to be the sole regulator of human affairs. As E.H. Carr has observed: '. . . the ingrained and irrational habits of personal abstinence and public service . . . played a more important part in building up the *laissez-faire* and liberal society of the nineteenth century than the rational morality of the harmony of interests'.[3] Even Adam Smith's economic man was to act within the limits of justice and self-command, restrained by the quality of 'sympathy' which was an integral part of man's nature.

When Mrs Crossley entered her works at 4 a.m. she made a daily vow: 'If the Lord does bless us at this place, the poor shall taste of it.' And she left this advice with her sons on the conduct of business

[1] Johnson himself could not follow Mandeville in accepting the divorce: the *happiness* of society 'depended on virtue'.

[2] See, for example, V. A. Demant, *Religion and the Decline of Capitalism*, 1952.

[3] E. H. Carr, *The Conditions of Peace*, 1942, Ch. V. The point is discussed at length in Essay 8 above.

in bad times: 'If you can go on giving employment in the winter, do so, for it is a bad thing for a working man to go home and hear his children cry for bread when he has none to give them.'

Humanitarian and Fabian preconceptions in our writing of economic and social history have tended to obscure the existence of an older tradition of philanthropy and welfare that runs like a continuous thread through the operations of the greatest of the entrepreneurs. Plans for the welfare of adult workers and the care and education of child labour were not a monopoly of Robert Owen. Boulton and Wedgwood were not only cultivated men but just employers who regarded a humane code of labour relations as an efficient system of production and gave a lead to others in such matters as the provision of schemes of social welfare and education. They were imitated by scores of others; so that even in the 1850s, when elementary education was a recognized public charge, Price's Patent Candleworks were still running an elaborate and expensive set of schools for their boy and girl employees at Battersea. Early Victorian England was for many a hard and cheerless world: but there seems at the moment to be less danger of exaggerating the sense of responsibility that the best entrepreneurs possessed than of assuming that their outlook was typified by the worst. The age of domestic industry was not the Golden Age it once seemed, nor was the factory town exclusively a society of juvenile chimney sweeps and cadaverous spinning elves.

The leading entrepreneurs may well turn out to have a just claim to rank high amongst those who not only swept and garnished their own houses but initiated a national process of social amelioration in an age facing insuperable problems of social adjustment. Some of the most vigorous social reformers, like Robert Peel, Samuel Whitbread, and Harriet Martineau came from this class and the tradition lasted down to the enlightened capitalists of the late nineteenth and early twentieth centuries like the Levers and the Cadburys with their new housing schemes. It was not merely their own success but their palpable contribution to material national well-being and their consciousness of social responsibility which drew to them popular esteem and social prestige. They were associated by partnerships and friendships with the nobility.[1] Wedgwood and Boulton

[1] See Mantoux, *op. cit.*, p. 406, n. 1.

joined in business enterprises with Lord Stamford, Lord Grey, Lord Gower, the Duke of Bridgewater, Lord Anson, Lord Cathcart and Lord Talbot. In Scotland Lord Dundas and Lord Dundonald were far from negligible figures in the movement to apply chemical knowledge to industry. In South Wales Lady Charlotte Guest, the daughter of the eighth Earl of Lindsey, played no small part in managing the great Dowlais ironworks of her husband. Royalty itself made a point of conferring its patronage and interest. George III and his Queen several times received Boulton and in 1787 the Royal visitors were received at Whitbread's great brewery at Chiswell Street, where half an hour out of a two-hour visit was spent examining the steam engine recently supplied by Boulton: '. . . in which it was apparent this was not the first half-hour thus usefully employed on economic arts, for His Majesty, with becoming science, explained to the Queen and the Princesses the leading movements in the machinery'.[1] The entrepreneurs and their new industries had become a matter for high favour and national pride.

The generally favourable conditions thus described did not, however, prevent the innovators from running into problems and rigidities in the contemporary economy. Of serious shortage of capital we hear strangely little: presumably the traditions of thrift and mutual confidence deep rooted in a commercial and often dissenting society worked to the advantage of the entrepreneur, leaving him only the lesser though not unimportant problems of temporary shortages of working capital and a defective coinage. This latter led many employers to issue token coins or 'shopnotes' convertible (theoretically) into cash by shopkeepers, or to resort to truck payments. To obtain a factory labour supply was more difficult. Dr Ure noted that it was 'nearly impossible to convert persons past the age of puberty, whether drawn from rural or handicraft occupations, into useful factory hands'.[2] The need was supplied by the new millions of children who quickly acquired the new manual skills. It was longer before the problems of skilled supervision were solved, but slowly a code of discipline and organization was shaped to match the productive process itself. Managers and foremen

[1] London *Chronicle*, May 1787.
[2] Quoted in Ashton, *The Industrial Revolution*, p. 116.

emerged, schemes for piece rates and bonuses were devised, with fines for drunkenness, carelessness and idling.

Such problems have received less attention than those posed by the attacks made on the new industrial system. Those who employed physical violence in machine-breaking and the like – the Luddites who smashed stocking frames and power looms and the unemployed handloom weavers who met at Peterloo – have had their story told many times. Their ranks were filled from the workers whom the new technology left on the scrap-heap. But scarcely less important, and continuous rather than spasmodic, was the growing power of organized labour. Trade clubs and unions in the guise of friendly societies are found everywhere in the eighteenth century. By 1800 when an Act made it generally illegal for any person to join with another to obtain increased wages or reduced hours of work, there were already many Acts on the Statute Book forbidding such practices in individual industries. But the new Act, like its predecessors, seems to have had little effect. Employers, then as now, had to reckon with much organized interest and natural conservatism; so that when William Fairbairn, the founder of the great Fairbairn engineering business of Manchester and Leeds, first came to London in 1811 as an almost penniless lad seeking work with Rennie, then building Waterloo Bridge, he found the trade unions were masters of the situation. 'I had no difficulty in finding employment; but before I could begin work I had to run the gauntlet of the trade societies; and after dancing attendance for nearly six weeks, with very little money in my pocket . . . I was ultimately declared illegitimate and sent adrift to seek my fortune elsewhere.'[1]

Scarcely less obstructive were the activities of those who saw their own interests being affected by the innovators. The small manufacturers threatened by Arkwright's improved production invoked doubtful legislation against him, but when he had won this battle there ensued a series of others, against rival inventors and producers who challenged the validity of his patents. All in all Arkwright, a litigious customer admittedly, spent a not inconsiderable part of his time, energies and capital in Parliamentary and Court actions on such accounts. Boulton likewise had to petition Parliament to extend the rights for his

[1] *Fortunes Made in Business*, ii. 243.

engine in face of Burke, who protested in the name of liberty against this new monopoly. And like Arkwright, he and Watt were engaged in interminable law suits against users of the engine (like the Cornish copper mine owners) and rival Soho manufacturers to protect their rights.[1]

The way of the innovator though theoretically cleared for him at many points was thus far from smooth; yet so strongly was the tide running with him and so remarkable was the combination of qualities which, at his best, he evinced, that opposition of the kind adumbrated – partial, sectional, but on the whole ill-organized – did little to check the swift growth of his enterprise. He did not yet control, nor was he ever to control, the whole of the economic process. Yet where he did, his grasp was hard to shake. Men of this kind came to speak with a new tone of authority – new because they were exercising a new and comprehensive kind of economic control, capable of indefinite extension. Lifted on to the plane of philosophy, his voice became what Victorian England recognized, rightly or wrongly, as the voice of progress. '... he knew', the historian of early Victorian England has written, 'that in the essential business of humanity, the mastery of brute nature by intelligence, he had outstripped the world, and the Machine was the emblem and instrument of his triumph. The patriotism of early Victorian England ... was at heart a pride in human capacity, which time had led to fruition in England. ...'[2] It is difficult – impossible I would say – to understand the momentum behind the process unless it is realized that Arkwright, Boulton, Wedgwood and the rest shared with the ferocity of enthusiasm in a faith which they managed to raise to the status of a sort of *Zeitgeist*; a faith which was finally enshrined in the historical philosophy of the most honoured child of the age, Macaulay. The opportunity to direct such a large part of the economic and social process brought forth both good and evil. On the whole the best among them rose to their responsibilities. Their motives swiftly came to outrun the mere desire for profit. At worst their passion might degenerate into a desire for personal power: but it often remained a genuine delight in quality for those who bought from them – perhaps even for its own sake – and a better life for their

[1] See Mantoux, chs. II and IV.

[2] G. M. Young, *Portrait of An Age*, p. 8.

work-people. 'I don't work at business,' a later one cast in the same mould wrote, 'only for the sake of money. I am not a lover of money as money and never have been. I work at business because business is life. It enables me to do things.'[1] It was the enlarged scope which the new type of business organization offered for 'doing things' which perhaps helps to explain the character of those who did them.

[1] Wilson, *History of Unilever*, i. 187.

II

Economy and Society in Late Victorian Britain[1]

Some ages are born to controversy. Others have controversy thrust upon them by historians. The debate on the economic situation of late Victorian Britain was begun in the 'seventies by the Victorians themselves. The historians have continued it. Whether the period deserved the name of 'the Great Depression' or not, it was a time 'when people *said* there was a Great Depression'.[2] At any rate *some* people said there was, and the pessimists were vocal in the House of Commons, in the Political Economy Club, and in many other places and journals. Their pressure was enough to secure the appointment of two Royal Commissions (in the '70s and the '90s) on agriculture, two (in the '80s) on trade and industry, another on the monetary system (in 1887) and (incidentally) to dominate later thought. With the twentieth century, and the passing of what had first been felt as an acute phase of competition, the fury of controversy abated. But it never quite disappeared. Economists like Marshall continued to echo the disquiet at some of the characteristics of British industry which seemed to them to help to explain the troubles of the preceding decades. And in the 1930s the controversy broke out again in earnest with H. L. Beales's classic article in which he challenged the legend of the Great Depression.[3] There was, he agreed, a *unity* about the period 1873 to 1896. It saw prices and profits

[1] This paper was first published in the *Economic History Review*, Second Series, Vol. XVIII, No. 1 (1965), pp. 183–98.

[2] H. L. Beales, 'The Great Depression in Industry and Trade', *Economic History Review* V (1934), 65–75.

[3] *Ibid.*

fall. There was some demand for protection. There was 'a slight falling off in the rate of material progress but the *outstanding* fact was the rapid industrialization of other countries and the continued industrialization of this'. For such a phase, 'Great Depression' was not, he suggested, an appropriate description.

Professor Rostow's inquiries followed a year or two later.[1] They did not seriously challenge Mr Beales's judgement but, starting from Keynesian assumptions they provided a new analysis and shifted the emphasis to the ending of the railway building boom and to the effects of the previous half century on consumer prices. Rising real wages were as much a feature of the period as falling prices and profits – 2 per cent a year if unemployment is ignored, 1·85 per cent if it is not. Over 90 per cent of the population was employed at wages which bought a little bit more each year than they had bought the year before. Professor Rostow agreed that the *rate* of growth slackened; yet he was impressed by the evidence for a 'net shift' towards intensive investment at home.[2]

Before these points had been resolved, the discussion took a new turn with the article on 'The Climacteric of the 1890s' by Professor E. H. Phelps Brown and Mr S. J. Handfield-Jones in 1952.[3] The authors were concerned to explain the check to productivity which they discerned in the 1890s. They did not dispute the general criticisms of failing enterprise amongst managers and growing restrictive practices amongst unions. But the special and immediate cause of the check seemed to them to lie in the declining rate of application of power, transport and machinery 'comprised beneath the names of Steam and Steel'. This hypothesis was in turn swiftly challenged by Mr Coppock on the grounds that the decline of steel use in the 1890s did not seem to produce 'any significant decline in the growth of

[1] W. W. Rostow 'Investment and the Great Depression', 'Investment and Real Wages, 1877–86', 'Explanations of the Great Depression, 1873–96' (*Economic History Review* VIII (1938), 136–58; *Economic History Review* IX (1939), 144–159; *Economic History*, supplement to *Economic Journal* IV, 1940, 356–70. *The British Economy of the Nineteenth Century* (1948).

[2] Prof. Rostow's thesis was later criticized by Sir D. Robertson ('New Light on an Old Story' reprinted in *Utility and All That* (1960) and by John Saville, 'A Comment on Prof. Rostow's *British Economy*', *Past and Present*, VI, 1954, 66–84.

[3] *Oxford Economic Papers*, New Series, IV, 3 (October, 1952).

productivity'.[1] Mr Coppock thereupon removed his climacteric to the 1870s, where it rested on 'the end of the general application of steam and iron machinery to the staple industries of Britain'. Hence a decline in productivity after the 1870s. Declining entrepreneurial talent in heavy industry contributed, too, and so did export difficulties in world markets.

In his turn, Mr Musson was not long in joining battle with Mr Coppock. Mr Coppock, he thought, exaggerated the deceleration of growth in the Great Depression. Was not this part of a longer-run process? Mr Coppock cannot agree. And Mr Musson sticks to his contention: economic growth goes not steadily but by 'great leaps and bounds which depend on technological innovation.[2] It is hardly seemly for a third party to enter upon a debate whose echoes have scarcely died away. Enough to remark that both writers seem to agree that these years *did* see a deceleration of growth though they do not agree on its exact dimensions. They seem to agree, too, on the observation commonly made and mostly accepted by everybody who writes on the subject, that entrepreneurial talent declined also. On this last aspect, the most recent contributor of all, Mr Aldcroft, has concluded that 'the British entrepreneur had lost much of the drive and dynamism possessed by his predecessors of the classical industrial revolution'.[3]

Certain conclusions seem to emerge from the history of the controversy thus briefly summarized. In general, while the gloomiest versions of the 'depression' have been modified, the pessimists seem so far to have achieved a qualified victory. For 'absolute decline' most analysts would now substitute 'decelerated growth', and place some emphasis on rising real wages and rising *per capita* income down to 1896. Decelerated growth has been bracketed with intensified home investment, though the latter concept suffers from lack of detailed substantiation. The tale of declining enterprise seems almost universally accepted. Yet, in retrospect, one cannot but feel some uneasiness at the apparent obliteration of elements in the argument to which

[1] D. J. Coppock 'The Climacteric of the 1870s' in *The Manchester School of Economic and Social Studies* XXIV, 1 (January, 1956).

[2] A. E. Musson, 'British Industrial Growth 1873–96: a Balanced View', *Economic History Review* 2nd series, XVIII (1964), 397–403.

[3] D. H. Aldcroft, 'The Entrepreneur and the British Economy, 1870–1914' *Economic History Review* 2nd ser. XVII (1964), 113–34.

contemporaries attached great importance. Apparently greater precision of analysis and measurement (in some respects at any rate) seems to have led to a narrowing of focus. Some evidence has been treated with a reverence it scarcely deserves. Some assumptions have been made which (it will be suggested) need to be reviewed in the light of broader evidence. Most of the recent controversialists freely admit that much of their evidence is dubious, yet some of them reach conclusions of dogmatic rigidity. In the all-important question of 'enterprise', there has been little attempt at systematic *social* analysis, little to distinguish between the effects of indigenous or exogenous factors on new businesses and old businesses respectively. Above all there has been little recognition that the business of a national 'economy' is to serve the needs of society as society sees them and not to perform statistical feats unrelated to what men at any rate *thought* they wanted.

Let us go back to the centre of the period itself – in fact to 1887, the year when Giffen read an address to the British Association at Manchester in his capacity as President of the Economic Science and Statistical Section. Summarizing the arguments of the pessimists, Giffen said this: '. . . many contend that not only are we not progressing but that we are absolutely going back in the world . . .' The signs of undoubted growth were, he admitted, less easy to read than before 1870, but the 'Fair Traders' could easily be proved wrong in their extreme pessimism. There was evidence to suggest that the production and consumption of 'staple articles' was increasing less fast in the years 1875–85 than it had done earlier. But was this as serious as it seemed? Giffen thought not, because:

> . . . industry by a natural law is becoming more miscellaneous and as populations develop, the disproportionate growth of the numbers employed in such miscellaneous industries, and in what may be called incorporeal functions, that is as teachers, artists and the like, prevents the increase of staple products continuing at the former rate.

The 'new' (or 'revived') industries where the export figures of the previous decade showed substantial increases he quoted as: candles, cordage, plate glass, jute, iron pieces, sheets, tinned plates, oil and floor cloth, paper, skins and furs, soaps and spirits. In spite of the fall in prices since 1870, the value of this group of exports had grown from £9·7 millions to £10·6 millions. The increase of imports similarly pointed to a 'growth of miscellaneous wants amongst the consumers'. The census of occupations gave added support to his view. Persons engaged in transport, commerce, art and amusement, literary, scientific and educational functions had risen between 1871 and 1881 from 947,000 to 1,387,000, or from 8·8 per cent to 11·7 per cent of the self-supporting population.

Giffen's argument is not invulnerable, and it is presented in terms that to modern econometricians may seem unsophisticated. Yet where our statistics of growth are themselves highly vulnerable, indeed often fanciful, (see below, p. 184–5) his proposition, which gains cogency from the contemporary socio-economic context, deserves more attention that it has received. Of course, his main point has not been wholly neglected. Mr Musson has pointed to the growth of 'service' trades.[1] Professor Rostow has, as we have noticed, pointed to this period as one when investment shifted on to the home ground. Yet Professor Rostow remains puzzled by what he regards a 'lag' between Britain's age of economic 'maturity' (achieved by the time of the Crystal Palace Exhibition) and her arrival in the next stage of 'high mass-consumption' (only achieved by the 1930s).[2]

In this, Mr Coppock follows in Professor Rostow's footsteps. His hypothesis is one which suggests a dynamic relationship between basic, dominant industries producing iron, steel and coal and the rest of the economy. We shall look at this relationship later. Let us note here only that Mr Coppock's statistics refer mainly to these dominant industries, except where Hoffman's figures are used, as they are extensively by both Mr Coppock and Mr Musson. In his latest article Mr Coppock supplements his arguments by referring to the incidence of

[1] A. E. Musson 'British Industrial Growth 1873–96; A Balanced View' *Economic History Review* 2nd series, XVII (1964), 397–403.

[2] W. W. Rostow, *The Stages of Economic Growth* (1960), pp. 68–70. The problem is surely of his own making? There is something, it seems, in the doctrine of 'high mass-consumption' which makes it doctrinally necessary to excommunicate from the ritual such commodities as ready-made clothes and corsets, boots and shoes, newspapers, cheap jam and patent medicines. The bicycle passes muster but a motor car is better. Most of these products came from relatively small plants. No single plant represented an essay in *massive* investment or even technological innovation of a radical kind. Hence perhaps the economist is apt to be unimpressed by them.

unemployment, which he believes was more serious than is often allowed.[1] Taking the unemployment figures for 'All Unions' he finds that unemployment was 'significantly higher' from 1875 to 1889 and 'abnormally high' from 1885 to 1889. Yet how broad a base are we using here? In 1871 Britain had an estimated labour force (male) of 9·3 millions. Thirty years later the equivalent figure was 13·8 millions. Yet even at this last date the total membership of the trade unions was only 1·9 millions. The percentage of females in industry who belonged to unions was tiny.[2] 'All Unions', in fact, on whose returns his unemployment figures are based, probably comprised not much more than a tenth of the total working population, male and female. It is, moreover, perfectly evident that the high averages Mr Coppock quotes derive in large measure from exceptionally high unemployment in *heavy* industries in one or two particular years – 1879, 1885 and 1886 especially. It is equally noticeable that the unions with a sizeable or complete stake in 'consumption' industries – wood workers and (especially) printers and binders – contributed little or nothing to the swollen unemployment averages of the years of the Great Depression.[3] The same was to be true in later recessions e.g. the 1920s. Once again we seem merely to be back with a proposition that nobody disputes i.e. that heavy industry and export industries were badly hit in particular years.

It will, however, be objected that as well as such evidence relating to a specific and possibly untypical group of industries, historians have also made use of W. Hoffmann's much wider series of industrial studies.[4] Does not this also point, and perhaps with more justification, to 'a steady decline in the rate of increase of British industrial output after 1870'?[5] – even, in some instances, an 'absolute decline of output'? What is the basis of

[1] D. J. Coppock, 'British Industrial Growth during the "Great Depression" (1873–96); a Pessimist's View' *Economic History Review* 2nd series XVII (1964), 389–96.

[2] B. R. Mitchell and P. Deane, *Abstract of British Historical Statistics* (1962), Chapter II.

[3] *Ibid.*, p. 64.

[4] W. G. Hoffmann, *British Industry 1700–1950* trs. by W. O. Henderson and W. H. Chaloner (1955).

[5] *Ibid.*, p. 213. Sixteen lines farther down, Dr Hoffmann refers to the '*rapidly* declining' rate of growth (my italics). From these alternatives I have chosen the more judicious version.

these calculations and how reliable are they as a means of calculating economic growth or decline?

The Hoffmann method (except for those industries like coal and iron whose direct figures of output exist) is to use figures or estimates of raw material consumption or import and assume (in general) a fixed relationship between that and the resulting manufactured product. The result is a highly ingenious survey of great value. Yet the author recognizes not once but many times in the course of his inquiry that his indices based on this conversion process cannot all lay claim to the same degree of accuracy. It is, unfortunately, in Giffen's 'miscellaneous industries' that the largest possibilities of error reside. Hoffman's calculations for output in the soap industry, for example, show a virtually static industry between 1860 and 1890 subject only to odd annual fluctuations. My own calculations suggest a very different story: a doubling of *per capita* consumption supplied almost entirely from a home industry that more than doubled its output. (To digress from our immediate topic: the assumption of rapid increase thereafter until 1910, followed by 'absolute decline', seems equally erroneous. From 1890 to 1910 was a period of difficulty and consolidation. Between 1910 and 1938, however, production rose from 366,000 tons per annum to 510,000 tons.) How have these discrepancies arisen? Possibly from mistakes over the soap-making formula? Hoffmann assumes that only tallow, palm oil, coconut oil were used before 1914. In fact cotton seed oil was used certainly from the 1880s and probably earlier. Most soaps contained a 'filling' of 'silicate' of soda. Resin was another ingredient. And of course here as everywhere there was a steady improvement in technology which gave more soap for less material.[1]

Another error of a similar kind seems to have been made over the confectionery industry. Hoffmann here uses the consumption of cocoa beans as a representative figure for calculating his production index 'because they are the most important raw material of the industry'. Even this assumption achieves a very high rate of expansion. Whether it would have been higher or lower had other assumptions been made about raw materials it is difficult to say. The fact is, however, that until the fourth

[1] Hoffmann, *op. cit.*, pp. 286–7, 314, Diagram J in C. Wilson, *The History of Unilever* (1954), Vol. I p. 9; Vol. II Appendix 10.

quarter of the nineteenth century, the trade was almost entirely confined to sugar confectionery – candies, toffee, drops, boiled sweets, etc. Chocolate was a relatively rare luxury. Even in 1900 eating chocolate only accounted for a third of total output by weight. Its main growth came after 1900.[1]

Other indices follow similar lines. Cloth output derives from the consumption of wool, based on estimates of the home sheep population and estimates of wool imports. Leather goods output is calculated from estimated cattle numbers on an assumption that a fixed percentage was slaughtered each year and that each hide weighed on an average the same. The result is a relatively static picture for the years 1870–1900 which seems incredible when placed against a background of rising population, rising real wages, the growth of the industry as we know it and a reorganized and expanding retail trade. (See below, p. 186). The precarious character of such calculations needs no further demonstration. Building output is similarly estimated from brick and softwood consumption on houses. It can (as Hoffmann admits) 'be estimated only in a very rough and ready manner if the number of new dwelling houses built in a particular period are regarded as representative of all building'.[2] But can it? Can we assume that in the 1880s (any less than in the 1960s) there was no competition for productive capacity between house-building and other types of building? These were years when contemporaries pointed proudly to the new buildings rising on all sides – town halls, churches, chapels, schools, colleges, universities, art galleries, banks, libraries, to say nothing of shops, shop extensions (witness thousands of older residential houses in London and scores of other cities and towns converted as to the ground floor) and, of course, factories and offices. How then do the Hoffmann estimates of *output* come to agree with estimates based on dwelling-house construction which ignore these other constructions?[3] Evidently there are large margins of error here also.

There are also strange omissions, sometimes explained, sometimes not. The decline and extinction of the candle industry is duly noted.[4] But it is not mentioned that this was the

[1] J. B. Jefferys, *Retail Trading in Britain 1850–1950* (1954), p. 254.
[2] Hoffman *op. cit.*, p. 292.
[3] *Ibid.*, p. 293. [4] *Ibid.*, p. 194.

consequence of a change in technology and social habit which just as surely proved the occasion of the rise of another industry – the mineral oil industry that supplied the domestic lamp. The shale oil industry was for a time of considerable importance. So, it might be thought, was the fact that this was the time when Marcus Samuel turned his knowledge of mother-of-pearl trade with the East to sell oil to Japanese fishermen and thereby laid the foundations of one of Britain's largest industries – Shell.[1] The decline of sugar refining in face of foreign competition is noted. There is nothing on the rise of margarine production. Glass and pottery are excluded from the production index on the grounds of size. The clothing industry is excluded because its statistics contain umbrellas. This would hardly seem an adequate reason for neglecting an industry which in 1891 occupied one quarter of the entire labour force in manufacturing industry and in this regard ranked second only to 'textiles' as the largest employing industry.[2] By 1871 there were already 129 hosiery and knitwear factories. In the years 1881–91, clothing factories at Leeds increased from 7 to 54. Everywhere co-ops, retail clothiers and multiples were distributing a growing volume of factory-made clothing, largely to the working classes. These were the years when the Randalls, Bostocks and Manfields were gathering the still dispersed rural boot and shoe industry of the Midland countryside into their Northampton factories. And they were good years, sandwiched as they were between the end of the craft age and the twentieth century invasion of the North American cheap imported shoe.

The Hoffmann indices, ingenious and valuable as they are, need to be used with discrimination. They hardly warrant the uncritical reverence which they have sometimes been accorded. Moreover, though Hoffmann's study recognizes *en passant* the impact on certain consumer industries of rising real incomes, it fails to notice (what some contemporaries and others since have noticed) the very special characteristics which price-income relationships gave to economic development in the age of the so-called 'Great Depression'.[3] On the contrary, its long-term comparisons of coefficients of growth in producer and consumer

[1] See Robert Henriques, *Marcus Samuel* (1960), chs 1–3 *passim*.
[2] Deane and Cole, *op. cit.*, p. 146. Table 32.
[3] *Ibid.*, pp. 92–3.

sectors tend to obscure what seem to be changes of major importance.[1]

It is not necessary to rely on the impressions or calculations of the Victorians themselves, though this would not of itself risk accepting optimism at its face value. If Giffen was an optimist, he found plenty of critics to give him pause for thought. The generally congratulatory descriptions of a brilliant journalist like T. H. S. Escott pointed towards economic expansion and widespread social improvement.[2] There were plenty of other sober social surveys that offset undue complacency. A recent authority on the age finally concludes that the 1880s were indeed 'a time of great and many-sided advances in the nation's general standard of living', while warning his readers of the darker side of the economic picture.[3] Plainly, as many observers have remarked, the question is one of balance. There has been more danger in recent years that economists interested in statistical trends will forget what most Victorians agreed were the social achievements of the age than that historians will be seduced by the delights of Victoriana into ignoring its shortcomings. It was the instinct of that master of Victorian studies, G. M. Young, that change of a 'social' kind was transforming the late Victorian economy. No one has divined better than he how '... the lead of the great industries was shortening: and, in compensation, capital, labour and intelligence were flowing away to light industry, distribution and salesmanship'.[4] Economically as well as socially, this is the heart of the matter: that the Armstrongs, Whitworths and Brasseys were giving way to (or being joined by) the Levers, the Boots, the Harrods, Whiteleys and Lewises. The full implications of this revolution of the domestic economy (for it was nothing less) escaped the attention even of Giffen, whose thoughts were still preoccupied with *export* figures. Until the last few years, they have escaped the notice of historians as they still escape the attention of economists; for they rested on little that could be regarded as

[1] *Ibid.*, e.g. pp. 74–5. For a general critique of Hoffmann, see W. A. Cole 'The Measurement of Economic Growth' in *Economic History Review* second series, XI (1958) 309–15.

[2] *England; its People, Politics and Pursuits* (1885). *Social Transformations of the Victorian Age* (1897).

[3] R. C. K. Ensor, *England 1870–1914*. Chapters IX and X.

[4] G. M. Young, *Portrait of an Age* (1949), p. 159.

spectacular innovations of science or technology. Machine-made boots, ready-made trousers or corsets, ladies' hats at 3*s* 11*d*. each (Lewis's sold quarter of a million in 1886) or the distribution of jam, corned beef and margarine are not the most obvious stuff from which to fashion either weighty economic theory or even significant history. Yet significant history, at any rate, is beginning to emerge. Mr Jefferys's study of the retail trade has outlined the dimensions of a revolution which was not merely of commercial (or social) importance but was vitally connected with profound industrial change.

The Britain of the Crystal Palace Exhibition may have been (as Professor Rostow has argued) economically mature. It was, nevertheless, still a world of haberdashers, chandlers, mercers, bakers, butchers and candlestickmakers, of market stalls, packmen and pedlars. It was precisely in the years of the Great Depression that the distributive trades were revolutionized by changes whose importance Mr Jefferys had compared to the earlier changes we call the Industrial Revolution. The 1,500 odd multiple stores of 1880 became the 11,645 such stores of 1900. Specialized multiple grocers like Liptons or Home and Colonial, shoe shops like Freeman Hardy & Willis, chemists like Boots (with 150 shops by 1900), tailors like Hepworths, newspaper and book stores like W. H. Smith and scores of others transformed the retail scene. Co-op sales rose from £15 millions in 1881 to £50 millions in 1900.[1]

The importance of the retail stores was not simply as a commercial improvement. They were in many instances unavoidably necessary if the industries whose products they were designed to sell were to work economically. Perishable goods like margarine, imported meat, milk, eggs needed the swift put-through of the multiple. Hence one reason for the tie between producers and retailers in the grocery trades.[2] Joseph Lyons's new mechanical bakery and its rivals demanded the turnover only a multiple shop system could provide. The manufacturers of machine-made boots and shoes also needed swift mass distribution of their output at the lowest cost. Hence the 500 specialized retailers of 1875 became the 5,000 of 1900. Behind

[1] For an admirable study of one large retail store group see Asa Briggs, *Friends of the People* (1956), a study of Lewis's stores.

[2] See C. Wilson, *The History of Unilever* (1954) Vol. II.

the new multiple tailors was a new industrial organization replacing the bespoke tailor sitting cross-legged on his board with needle and thread in the back room of a cottage. The emergence of the retail stores of manufacturing chemists (like Boots) likewise marked a new division of trade and industry in drugs. Sewing machines, bicycles, pneumatic tyres all needed specialized sales and repair arrangements. Newspapers, by day and night, needed a highly efficient system of distribution and sale. Thus at every point the retailing changes were closely connected with new or reorganized systems of mass manufacture; each indeed was a function of the other. Each called for capital, labour, enterprise, ingenuity to supply the needs of an urban people living at standards which most believed were higher and all agreed were different.

Increasingly, therefore, in a more diversified and variegated economy, the industrial-commercial revolution rolled on. The years of the Great Depression saw great volumes of goods previously supplied (if supplied at all) from the craftsmen of village or town move into the factory stage of production. From machine to shop there flowed the branded, packaged, standardized, advertised products newly characteristic of this urbanized, industrialized society that was setting itself new patterns and standards of social life. Bulk supplies of soap, margarine, confectionery, tobacco, shoes, hats, clothes and patent medicines now replaced the products that formerly came from village grocer, chandler, shoemaker, weaver and witch. To compare the amenities it provided with those of a past Golden Age of rural peasant England is to waste time. How does it compare with the contemporary amenities of industrialized Germany (where Mr Coppock sees the entrepreneurs not waiting for the second industrial revolution but producing it)? Once again, one is really comparing two societies at different stages of socio-economic development. But they are not so totally dissimilar that one cannot say something in favour of the increasingly balanced and diversified economy of Britain. The slum populations of Liverpool and London were a blot on its surface. But so were the depressed ex-peasant immigrants of the German industrial towns. They lived on far lower wages and their black bread and margarine diet was more typical of German proletarian life than was any similar diet of English conditions. No social revolution of the kind we have discerned in late Victorian Britain had yet happened in Germany, because no comparable mass market had yet arisen to attract capital and enterprise into this type of investment as it had in Britain. No popular press had yet aimed at the literate artisan as did such journals as *Tit-Bits* (1880) and *Answers* (1888). To scan the advertisements in such magazines (themselves part of the new economic exploitation of better working class demand) is to find oneself in a world palpably nearer our own. The competition prize winners, with a large element of Lancashire working men, suggest the pattern of their readership. To them the advertisement columns of the '80s and '90s offered a variety of novel satisfactions – Coventry bicycles, including (a trifle oddly) the *Godiva* for men[1]; sewing machines, home printing dies, cheap watches, concertinas and melodeons; household goods still familiar – Hovis bread, Cadburys[2] and Rowntrees cocoa, Brown and Polson's corn flour, Players Navy Cut tobacco, Reckitts Blue, Sunlight soap, Cherry Blossom Boot Polish, Bovril, extracts of beef, Robertsons jams, Lipton's tea, Birds Custard and scores of others. Patent medicines bulk large – from Beechams Pills, Scotts Emulsion, Owbridges Lung Tonic, Eno's Fruit Salts down to the dubious claims of curative syrups and 'electric' belts to disperse all human ills from heart disease to indigestion. The appeal to superstition and hypochondria remained as strong in city as it had ever been in countryside. We must add to such advertising industries the important investment represented by organized sport and entertainment.

Altogether, these ventures represented a massive new response to a demand situation revolutionized by a combination of factors The population increased *faster* in the thirty years of the Great Depression than in the previous Golden Age. Ten million mouths were added as against five million. Real wages were rising faster, partly because wealth had grown faster, perhaps because labour was better organized to increase and hold its share, but above all because Britain's earlier investment over-

[1] See below, p. 194 for the connection between Coventry engineering and the growth of the Midland printing and publishing industry.

[2] On the eve of their removal to Bournville in 1879, Cadburys employed 230 workpeople. Ten years later the number was 1,200; ten years later still, 2,685. The factory space trebled between 1879 and 1899. See I. A. Williams, *The Firm of Cadbury 1831–1931*, pp. 68–9.

seas now fructified abundantly, creating both crisis and prosperity simultaneously. In one of Mr Fay's most characteristic phrases: 'The bogy of the seventies was a real bogy from across the ocean. Its feet were ships of British steel, its arms railroads stretching across the prairies and its belly was Chicago wheat.'[1] A bogy? For some farmers, yes; but not for the workers of Britain and their families. Here, in falling raw material prices, lay a main source of the new mass purchasing power that called new kinds of enterprise and investment into being.

Two scholarly preoccupations in particular have bedevilled the study of these new areas of growth. First, the obsessive concentration of economists on the importance of spectacular technological innovation and massive investment as the indispensable condition of economic growth. Few of these industries could boast any such thing. Most of them grew by marginal adaptations of well-established technologies undertaken with a keen eye to market opportunity. This has been the path to growth more often than we usually admit. Economists who live under the persistent illusion that technology has a monopoly in growth might ponder Keynes's dictum: 'It is enterprise which builds and improves the world's possessions.' Second, and no less misleading, has been the belief that certain key industries 'normally determine the tempo of industrial expansion for other industries'.[2] Such assumptions can be misleading if they are taken to suggest that industries responded uniformly to boom or depression under the guidance of 'key industries'. Obviously the supplies of basic materials, iron, steel, coal, are in various degrees and at various times indispensable to industry. But the *prosperity* of basic and consumer industries were by no means the same thing. During the 'two decades . . . heavy with gloom' when the laments of iron masters, bankers and investors were grievous, the soapmakers were never happier.[3] Conversely, in the late '60s, before the fog descended, they were sufficiently perturbed to seek comfort in association; and between 1887 and 1890 when the older industries were enjoying better times, the

[1] C. R. Fay, *Great Britain from Adam Smith to the Present Day* (1932), p. 68.

[2] Hoffmann *op. cit.*, p. 13. Mr Coppock similarly assumes that the experience of 'unionized' labour in these years is a safe guide to the general incidence of unemployment. (*Economic History Review* 1964).

[3] H. Heaton *Economic History of Europe* (1948), p. 666.

soapmakers were less happy.[1] In general, where raw material prices represented such a large element in costs, the depression in the markets combined with rising working class (and other) purchasing power gave the green light to expansion. '... the very influences which, by producing low wholesale prices, worked against the capital goods industries, worked in favour of consumer goods by raising retail customers' purchasing power.' Economists' fears did not prevent David Lewis from setting up his great Manchester store in 1879 nor his even bigger Birmingham store in 1885. Lever was undeterred at Warrington in 1885 and at Port Sunlight in 1889. He was always perfectly conscious – and he was not the only one – that he owed his own opportunities to the combination of the falling price of necessities and the rising demand for better conditions of life among the working classes.[2] Many other 'new' industries, especially food manufacture, must have been similarly influenced, though the element in costs represented by raw materials obviously varied widely from one industry to another. Cheap iron, coal and steel were certainly an important element in the rising output and exports of the engineering industry in these years. There seems, in fact, to be some analogy here with the agricultural situation described by Mr Fletcher in a recent and arresting analysis.[3] The depression here was not, as he shows, uniform. Corn farmers in the south and east and livestock and dairy farmers in north and west experienced very different fortunes. The latter were sustained on rising demand and 'every fall in the price of cereals, so damaging to corn growers, was to them ... clear gain because it meant a reduction in the price of their most important input ... feed'.[4] The 'inputs' of many of the industries mentioned above were likewise the products of the depressed industries or of buyers' markets in raw materials. In these new areas, where marketing skills were paramount, lay many of the blue chips of the future. If it be true that such growth has been seriously underestimated, we can make an adjustment which will also help to close the gap between the

[1] W. J. Reader, 'The United Kingdom Soapmakers' Association and the English Soap Trade 1867–1896'. *Business History*, Vol. I (1959), 77–83.

[2] *Ibid.*, p. 83.

[3] T. W. Fletcher 'The Great Depression of English Agriculture 1873–1896, *Economic History Review*, 2nd series, XIII (1961), 417–32.

[4] *Ibid.*

apparent slackening of economic growth and the better substantiated estimates of rising aggregate national income, a conundrum to which no really satisfactory answer has yet been given.[1]

Was this suggested renewal and growth, especially in the new and miscellaneous industries on which Giffen specially remarked enough to offset slackening and decline in the older industries? It is impossible to say. All that can be said is that the manufacturing industries we have had in mind represented a substantial proportion of the productive capacity of the nation. Even if we exclude textiles and engineering, and, of course, all the capital goods industries, we are left with a large group of industries which seems to account for about a third of the gross output (or 'selling value') of all the manufacturing industry covered by the 1907 Census of Production. It had occupied likewise perhaps a quarter of all employed labour, male and female, in the previous quarter of a century. The value of its output was probably about equal to the total value of British exports (not, of course, coincidental with them).[2] It was therefore no trivial or trumpery thing.

Finally, we come to that indispensable *ignis fatuus* of modern economic history, the entrepreneur. Mr Aldcroft stood in a long and honourable critical tradition when he wrote recently of British entrepreneurs from 1870 to 1900 as 'weighted down by complacency, conservatism, and antiquated methods ...', deficient in that 'drive and dynamism' that had characterized their forefathers. True, a last moment reprieve is suggested by his reference to 'progressive types such as Lever and Beecham', but this hardly alters his general tone of excoriation. For some of his comment there is, of course, ample warrant; but his qualification is too little and too late. The new industries, where factory was encroaching on old craft, and the multiple on Mr Jefferys' obscure 'centre of mystery', the village shop, were all the product of vigorous and ingenious entrepreneurs as dynamic as any of their predecessors, and with an equally shrewd eye for profitable long-term investment. There is no evidence that the growth of *new* industries or the development of new territories

[1] See P. Deane and W. A. Cole, *British Economic Growth 1688–1959* (1962) pp. 296–99.

[2] *Census of Production 1907*. *Cd.* 4896. c. ii. 655 (1909). *Cd.* 6320 c. ix. 1 *et seq.* (1912–13).

was inhibited by lack of entrepreneurial talent. From all walks of life (but perhaps especially from the ranks of the small shopkeeper) they emerged – not only Lever and Beecham but many others, within and without Britain. These were the years of the epic rough and tumble in South Africa which ended with Cecil Rhodes's establishment of De Beers Consolidated in 1888. The following year came the British South Africa Company. While Rhodes, Alfred Beit and Barney Barnato were active in the south, George Taubman Goldie was busy creating the commercial empire in the Niger Basin which in 1886 received its royal charter as the Royal Niger Company. The year 1889 saw Ludwig Mond, founder of the future ICI, delivering his presidential address to the Society of the Chemical Industry on the inventor as the creator of 'new wants in society'. If Lever's strongest suit was salesmanship, Mond's was science and technology. Yet their utterances showed that each was keenly aware of the importance of the gift that was the special genius of the other. The story of the giants of the publishing world who seized the opportunities provided by Forster's Education Act of 1870 – the rise of George Newnes and Alfred Harmsworth especially – has been often told. The newspaper revolution resulted from many factors. Newspapers were closely connected with progress in engineering and communications. The future Northcliffe served his apprenticeship at Coventry. There in the midst of the Great Depression he edited *The Bicycling News* for Messrs Iliffe and Sons. The Iliffes were themselves outstanding entrepreneurs. A Coventry family of local yeoman stock, they had been drawn into printing *via* ribbon making. By the 1880s they had already built up a sizeable empire in technical journals for the Midland engineering industry. Then came the *Birmingham Post* and *Mail*. By the 90s Iliffe's Publications were on a national scale. The son of Northcliffe's master (later the first Lord Iliffe) was probably the most brilliant business brain amongst the Press Lords of the twentieth century. Other famous names were mainly connected with light industry of one sort or another. Their activities have already been touched on – Lipton, Cadbury, Rowntree, Guinness, Boot, Courtauld, etc. But though the expansion of light industry was most characteristic of these years, it did not entirely monopolize the scene. In 1884 Charles Parsons, ex-Cambridge, ex-Armstrongs, ex-Kitsons, registered his first turbine patents that were to revolutionize industrial and marine power technology. Five years later Parsons founded his own firm which still stands in the first rank of the engineering industry. From 1889 the public utilities of Mexico during the economically dynamic Diaz régime were largely provided by W. D. Pearson, later the first Viscount Cowdray. It was not only in Mexico that Pearson held sway. In face of ferocious local competition he also won contracts for tunnels under the Hudson River. By the 1890s, Pearson was 'indisputably the largest contractor in the world'.[1] These and scores of others extended the scope of entrepreneurship far beyond those frontiers of pig iron and cotton stockings which still seem to bar its understanding to some who write about it.

There seems here to be a fairly clear (though by no means perfect) contrast between new industry and old; and it is partly explained not only by the physical, internal problems of ageing industries, though these were serious, but by the changing context of social attitudes through which England moved between the early and late nineteenth century. The faith in progress, in human mastery of nature through the machine, had waxed and waned. For nearly a century after the inauguration of industrial revolution, industry and trade floated on a tide of social, even intellectual, approval. It reached its peak round about the mid-century and the Crystal Palace Exhibition. Tennyson's *Ode* to that occasion was not his only salute to industry. There was also *Mechanophilus*, a *Paeon* to railways and seaside piers:

> Dash back that ocean with a pier,
> Strow yonder mountain flat,
> A railway there, a tunnel here,
> Mix me this zone with that.

There was his own disastrous investment in a mysterious enterprise for mechanical wood-carving known as *Pyroglyphs*. Brougham said it was a miracle of which all the world should know, but it cost Tennyson his patrimony. The authentic voice of the age was Macaulay's but down remoter corridors reverberated the tones of lesser prophets like Samuel Smiles, whose improving manuals were still being distributed by William

[1] Keith Middlemas, *The Master Builders* (1963).

Lever to promising young recipients in the early twentieth century. By the '70s however there had been a profound change. Enthusiasm had given way to doubt and disenchantment. The new voice was that of Matthew Arnold who held views on economic and social progress very different from those of his father. 'I rejoice to see it', wrote Dr Arnold of the railway train, 'and think that feudality is gone for ever.' This was no longer the aspect of mechanical transport that impressed his son. 'Your Middle Class man', wrote Matthew Arnold, 'thinks it the highest pitch of the development of civilization when his letters are carried twelve times a day from Islington to Camberwell and from Camberwell to Islington, and if railway trains run to and fro between them every quarter of an hour. He thinks it is nothing that the trains only carry him from an illiberal, dismal life at Islington to an illiberal, dismal life at Camberwell.' No wonder the Americans failed utterly to understand what he was talking about when he visited them in 1883. How different from Herbert Spencer's triumphal progress in the United States ten years earlier! Arnold's analysis was not only a condemnation of the poverty and anarchy of contemporary society in Britain; it struck at the very roots of all materialist societies. In Britain, at any rate, the (to Arnold) disastrous coalition of Dissent, middle-class philistinism and the obsession with 'machinery' had some social-cultural counterpoise elsewhere. 'Feudality' had, after all, not entirely disappeared and English social life was still a fabric made up of the tangled skeins of established religion, ancient civility, and social idealism. By the later years of the century, the secular adventism common to Arnold, Mill and Marx had combined with the Christian socialism of Kingsley, the nostalgic vision of Morris, the social egalitarianism of the Fabians, the philanthropic bent of Green, and Ruskin's vision of the 'good society' to blunt the edge of materialist, progressive enthusiasm of earlier years. All represented in varying degrees a characteristically English mixture of upper middle-class moral or religious criticism of materialism and upper middle-class snobbery towards trade and manufactures.

Contingent all this might be. Nevertheless it could not fail to affect attitudes within industry, exacerbating the physical problems into which firms now in the third generation since the Industrial Revolution were running. It cannot have affected the supply or quality of entrepreneurial talent for *new* industries nearly as much as it did the supply for the older ones. The new entrepreneurs were recruited from humbler walks of life untroubled by what they no doubt saw as the curious moral caperings and contortions of their social betters. Again, the economy was affected in different degrees by the same phenomena, and this time the criterion was simply one of age. Never far below the surface of industry, and coming nearer to the surface with time, were strong currents of idealism, philanthropy, sometimes of a kind of neo-feudalism. They emerged in many different ways. Model villages, free libraries, industrial schools were of eighteenth and early nineteenth century origin, but the movement reached a new peak during the Great Depression. Beatrice Webb noticed that Charles Booth, the greatest social investigator of the age, looked more like 'an ascetic priest' than a businessman.[1] His social work of the 80s and 90s was financed from his business earnings and carried on simultaneously with his direction of his great Liverpool company. Vigour and interest in business families did not always evaporate with wealth and time. The story of Pilkington's glass is one of a family concern that survived both with conspicuous success.[2] Many others were less successful. In the Napier engineering business, a kind of aristocratic pride inhibited the owners from any vulgar truck with advertising or expanding markets. Their ambition remained that of dealing with a few large and prestigious customers – the Bank of England, the Mint, etc. The end was desolation.[3] The decline of Marshalls, flax-spinners of Leeds, was rooted in the owners' 'growing dissatisfaction with business as a full-time occupation'.[4] Politics, social life on an elegant scale, philanthropy, careers in the professions became their aim. The business expired, appropriate for by our purposes, in 1886.

The old family firms that survived the rigours of the Great Depression years were those favoured by Providence with a more than ordinary fertility and continuity of family talent. Given that – and a reasonably promising market like Pilkington's in glass or an unreasonably promising one like Guinness's

[1] A. H. John, *A Liverpool Merchant House* (1959) pp. 71–2.
[2] T. C. Barker, *Pilkington Brothers and the Glass Industry* (1960).
[3] C. Wilson and W. J. Reader, *Men and Machines* (1958).
[4] W. G. Rimmer, *Marshalls of Leeds* (1960) p. 277.

in stout – all could be well. Likewise, relatively new firms could prosper even in those industries that were generally facing difficult times in overseas markets and elsewhere. For Albright and Wilsons, the chemical manufacturers, these were years of strong management, important technological advances and innovations, and of general business expansion.[1] The accounts of the 'decline' of the iron and steel industry usually mask the fact that alongside falling prices and decelerating progress, another of those recurrent migrations of an entire industry was in progress. The new steel industry in the north-east meant Bolckow, Vaughan and Dorman Long – this last a new firm established in 1875. Here, or at Frodingham in Lincolnshire, and in Sheffield, there was still plenty of entrepreneurial talent. It was here that progress, especially in the new steel, was able to offset decline in iron in the older areas. The north-eastern steel masters were as far ahead of the Stafford ironmasters as Ludwig Mond was ahead of the old Le Blanc alkali manufacturers.

The fact was that in these years the older basic industries had to withstand the impact of export difficulties as well as the accumulating problems of obsolescent plant and obsolescent management. Primitive systems of accounting that made little provision for depreciation and replacement combined with Victorian principles of thrift to make survival, let alone innovation, a problem. Yet behind all this lay the problem of management, and it is still with us, even in the day of the public company and the managerial revolution. No family business could expect that after several generations it would still automatically be capable of producing from family talent a flow of competent managers: it could only hope and pray that it might do so, or more modestly still, that the family might have the sense to choose a professional manager acceptable to everybody concerned. It might: it might not. How a *public* company was to select and train a continuity of managers was largely a problem for the future. Here, much depended on the capital structure that emerged. Some entrepreneur-owners when converting their private company to a public one had the sense to keep control of the entire equity and, with it, retain control of policy. In others, all control was hopelessly divided and chaos followed. Company structure is frequently the key to the success or failure

[1] R. E. Threlfall, *100 Years of Phosphorus Making 1851–1951* (1951), Chs. VI–X.

of the business. In the years under discussion external problems frequently coincided with internal crises of management for old firms in a way that was not to bother the generally younger American or German business firm for some time to come. It was precisely the families of these older businesses, their sons at school at Eton, Winchester or Rugby, then later at college at Christchurch or Trinity, that were most vulnerable to that social mobility long characteristic of English life. If their interests ran in more intellectual channels they were likely to fall victim to the scarcely less serious moral seduction of late Victorian idealism. Either way, their attendance on business was likely to suffer.

Thus, in a variety of ways, the new urban and industrialized society that was Britain moved towards a new and different economy. It was in large measure the economy men wanted, an economy that supplied their needs abundantly and on the whole efficiently. It was able to do this because capital and enterprise themselves responded in these years to the prospects offered by the mass demand for consumer (and other) goods in a context of rising real incomes.

To their armchair critics who demanded to know why the old exporting industries did not introduce technological improvements to reduce costs and raise productivity, the industrialist might not unreasonably have replied with a counter-question. What good would it have done when tariff walls were everywhere rising to keep his products out, however they were priced? Even the most vigorous of the new men in consumer industries (like soap) found that exporting was doomed.[1] The only way was to go 'over the garden wall'. Heavy industry was not so agile or mobile.

Recent discussions of the economic problems of these years have tended to concentrate on attempts at aggregate measurements with a view to single answers – up or down? more or less? faster or slower? better than *x* or worse than *y*? Yet on examination the 'statistics' of production often prove to be little more than speculations or extrapolations, and certainly a precarious

[1] The relatively poor showing of the electrical industries in Britain cannot be explained thus, for other exporters (e.g. Philips of Eindhoven) were to develop a large export trade to Germany, Russia and France. This was an industry with a relatively weak home demand, due in turn to the presence of widespread sources of steam power and gas lighting and heating of an earlier date.

base for ambitious attempts at precision. It does not seem unreasonable in such conditions of uncertainty to use evidence derived less from dubious or partial statistics than from well-authenticated historical impressions. The historian also has a duty to be concerned not only with quantities large enough to be capable of significant measurement but also with things immediately too small for such measurement but known to be significant for the future: in fact to remember the truth, *Ex Glande Quercus*. The Great Depression years were in fact years not only of crisis but of new growth, sometimes actual, sometimes potential. A balanced appraisal of the industrial economy seems likely to conclude (as Mr Fletcher has concluded for the agricultural sector) that it was demonstrating in these years not a uniform tendency to move in one direction but a marked proclivity to move in several different directions at once. The division can be made – though very roughly and with exceptions – into old industries and new industries, basic industries and light industries, industries largely based on home markets and others on export markets. The problems of the entrepreneur were likewise not uniform: they varied according to the age and prospects of his industry. Averages and aggregates obscure such realities that derive from historic, social development. In short, the British economy in these years was neither a stale egg nor a fresh egg. It was a curate's egg.

12

History in Special and in General[1]

It is now almost seventy years since the most ambitious historical enterprise of this University, the *Cambridge Modern History*, was conceived. Half a century separates it from its successor which is appearing in our own day. Between the two, the conception of what history is has been transformed by a revolution of ideas, comparable to that revolution of the seventeenth century which is one of those many aspects of history revealed and illuminated for us by my predecessor in this Chair.

Like the earlier revolution, this of our own time is bound up with a radical process of material change experienced by society at large. It is certainly no less of an upheaval than those transformations experienced by science, or economics or philosophy, with which it is connected. To measure its effects we have only to glance back at the letter which Acton wrote to his collaborators in the *Cambridge Modern History* in 1898. Here was a vision of an approaching 'final stage in the conditions of historical learning'. By a 'judicious division of labour' among scholars, the accumulated mountains of material would be removed and digested. Older histories, calculated only to retard and mislead the honest student, would make way for a definitive universal history in which all local differences, errors and egotisms would be sunk.

This vision rested on a belief in the nature of history similar to that which Creighton had formulated a decade or so earlier in his editorial preface to the first issue of the *English Historical Review*. This was the first periodical in Britain dedicated to the study of history, and significantly it opened with one of Acton's

[1] This paper was presented as an Inaugural Lecture in Cambridge on 12 March 1964, and published by Cambridge University Press in 1964.

most brilliant articles on the German School of History. Its definition of the function of history – 'to discover and set forth facts' – was to exercise a powerful influence on historiography for many years. Yet, in the long run, few things have done more to thwart Acton's vision of definitive history than the flood of historical journals which he helped to unleash. Today the classified catalogue of our own University Library lists well over one thousand such journals under the heading of 'History'. This does not include any of the considerable number devoted to economic history which, by lapse into an error otherwise avoided by this University, is included with the study of economics. Little did those eminent Victorians realize that they were turning academic gun-runners; that the function of the learned journals of the future would be less that of establishing historical certainty than of destroying it. For here was the perfect sniper's weapon. With a dispatch that commends itself to overworked schoolmasters, scholarship candidates and, not least, history dons, a handful of sharp-pointed monographs was to be plunged into the heart of Victorian scholarship. With the aid of a few well-contrived pages it could be suggested that it was not merely not necessary but positively harmful to plough through Stubbs and Maitland and Cunningham and Ashley.

From the ensuing battles the definitive conception of history emerged both bloody and bowed. It is no longer seen as permanent, unshakable upon its immovable foundation of fact: too often, perhaps, it is seen as something relative and subjective which the minds of historians push this way or that, as children at play puff a balloon backwards and forwards between them. Philosophers sometimes divide the history of history into phases. We have now passed, we are told, through the phase of scientific achievement into the phase of critical reflection. Now the element of relativism, of subjectivity, in the process of creating history, is undeniable. But neither the activity of reflecting, nor the activity of behaving in a scientific manner, mean what they would have meant fifty years ago. Nor can they be satisfactorily separated. The scientist no longer views his function as merely to observe and reveal facts. Neither does the historian. Both in practice work by testing hypotheses, and the quality of any history depends in large measure on the imagination and intuition which the historian brings to the creation of his hypotheses; to the skill and judgement with which he seeks out and selects his evidence. All this we recognize. Yet no one trained in the Cambridge school of economic history would easily subscribe to the doctrines of those who see history as merely the toy of current opinion. If we manage to avoid repeating the historical errors of our forefathers it will not be simply because we live in a different context and therefore fall into different errors. It will also be because in the last half century scholars have established certain *facts* which nobody would at present dispute. To the relativist I would reply by paraphrasing Johnson's rebuttal of Berkeley, striking my foot against one of those massive volumes of Clapham, and crying: 'I refute it *thus*.' The historian's boat does not float rudderless at the mercy of wind and tide. We should not allow our new consciousness of the limitations of historical judgement to blind us to the vast advances of systematic inquiry in the last hundred years.

But I will skate lightly on the frozen surface of this deep, dark pool called the philosophy of history. For here the ice is thin, the casualties numerous and often distinguished. Let me hasten on to what concerns me more; the practice of history. Out of the mixed shower of praise and abuse with which the *New Cambridge Modern History* has been greeted, I detect general agreement on one point: that it marks the end of a phase of historical writing that was largely political, diplomatic and biographical. One reviewer trained in that older school of history, Sir Harold Nicolson, remarked of the volume edited by Mr Hinsley on the late nineteenth century, that it represented this new trend. In the old days, he wrote, a little nostalgically, we should have been provided with a narrative of facts concentrated on the personalities of Napoleon III or Alexander II. But now Marx and Darwin claim as much attention as Bismarck or Mr Gladstone. Personalities are less important than social and economic trends. 'Thus [he concluded bravely] we are given here many bright pages about pig-iron.' As one whose academic business has so far often been with pig-iron and other useful commodities, I want to pursue this theme a little further. Not, let me add, because I think that many people nowadays dispute the general truth of Sir Harold Nicolson's remark. On the contrary, the clamour for what is sometimes called 'history in depth', social analysis and the like, is to be heard on all sides. Indeed, the need to place individuals in their social context (which is one half of the permanent historical equation) is probably more readily accepted amongst practising historians today than the need to measure the mark of individuals upon their surroundings (which in a true orthodoxy is the other half of the equation). The older generation of tripos examiner would ask candidates to explain the influence of Adam Smith on his times. The present generation is more likely to ask them to explain the influence of his times on Adam Smith. I recently heard a teacher of history in another university describing with approval the progress of the recently developed tutorial system there. More specialized and sophisticated studies had been made possible – but at some cost. Ten years ago, he said, when an undergraduate was asked to write of Marie Antoinette, the *Philosophes*, Robespierre, Danton and so on. Now all this is changed. Apparently the standard essay revolves round the price of bread, the declining wage-rates of shoemenders and the falling profits of Paris wig-makers in 1789. The economic historian and historical sociologist have, it seems, never had things so much their own way. This is to risk over-correcting for error. To reduce great historic dramas to graphs and curves, to purge them of human values, is merely to substitute one kind of myopia for another. It is to deny the basic principle that history is a true counterpoint between man and his circumstances. Worst of all, it is to make history not only dull but silly.

Yet, however naïve and misguided, the fashion is common enough to suggest that there *is* a deeply felt need to 'explain' historical phenomena in new ways and by new evidence. Political and constitutional history no longer satisfies. We demand more definition and more explanation of the social origins of politics. The problem posed by such attempts is that of fashioning more refined techniques for handling economic and sociological evidence hitherto neglected; techniques that will not simply substitute crude and often unscientific economic interpretations of a Victorian kind for the older political interpretations, but techniques that will help us to bond our total knowledge of a situation into a new pattern of understanding. It is not enough simply to let the different types of analysis march in parallel and never meet, nor to encourage novel facts to drive out the old. The web of history must be re-knit, so that the new strands of knowledge become part of its warp and weft, and not merely frills round its edge.

It is remarkable but not altogether surprising that we have progressed slowly with this problem during the seventy or eighty years when economic history and historical sociology have been flourishing branches of historical study. Marxists, it is true, have attempted massive frontal onslaughts, using the concept of the class struggle, but history has been as obstinate in yielding up its secrets before them as a modern fortress attacked by peasants armed with pitchforks. Nor is it self-evident that the new schools of sociological historians are necessarily more scientific than their predecessors. *They* were no doubt too ready to accept the conventional categories of political history with too little inquiry. But have we shown ourselves to be more critical of the clichés of Victorian sociology? The uncritical application of Victorian conceptions of 'class' to pre-industrial history has caused at least as much confusion as the failure of earlier historians to define what they meant by 'liberty'. Likewise the currently popular fashion for treating 'thought', economic or political, as merely a derivative of its own material context, a progeny without progeny, deserves as much critical scrutiny as assumptions of the autonomous character of intellectual influences on social development. The scientific posture and the scientific achievement are different things.

Our local tradition of economic history has been modest in its claims to explain the larger phenomena outside its own boundary. 'Economic history', Sir John Clapham wrote, 'is the most fundamental branch of history – not the most important. Foundations exist to carry better things. . . .' Yet even this sensible definition, with its suggestion of architectural, static relationships between politics, culture and economics, does not help us much with the problem of exploring their dynamic relationships. Cunningham, who absorbed much from the German historical economists, would have said that the solution, so far from being the interpretation of politics in economic terms, lay in the interpretation of economics in political terms. It is not a suggestion that has found much acceptance since his time. Yet it is at least arguable that the decline of once flourishing economies like those of Spain or Holland may still be best understood in terms of political error or political nemesis.

Equally, that economic progress in England would have been unthinkable without the relative political stability of our society. It is only very recently that historians have begun to analyse thoroughly the complex sources and nature of 'power' as it is reflected in the policies of governments over the centuries. But plainly the pressure of economically interested groups is not the whole or even the major part of the explanation. For reasons sometimes good, sometimes bad, governments in this country have often governed without regard to such pressures.

There are of course many situations in which a knowledge of some basic economic facts can easily and immediately illuminate and explain what would otherwise be obscure. The historian of primitive societies will often have little difficulty in assigning a primary place to the simple economic urge. We should not progress far in understanding the evolution of Kenya without taking account of the land-hunger of the Kikuyu. In modern European history, the diplomatic historians' picture of what they used to lump together as 'first-class powers' – France, England and Holland – battling in a political vacuum is a thing of the past. Even a rudimentary knowledge of the character of their respective economies immediately deepens and illuminates our understanding of the reasons why they fought and the course of their political and military struggles in the seventeenth and eighteenth centuries. We shall fail to grasp the politics of Imperial Germany if we overlook that this was a society of medieval rusticity plunged suddenly into the problems of urban industrialization. The really intractable problems emerge when we come to the great explosions that have marked the history of advancing societies and which have engaged the energies of the greatest historians. In entering into the great classical controversies – the origins of the revolutions of the sixteen-forties, or 1789 or 1848, the revolt of American colonies against England or the American Civil War itself, historians are, I think, increasingly conscious of the dangers of snap judgements, of those *nostrums* that appeal to investigators from more recently founded schools of social science. All social sciences pass through a phase of belief in universal laws. It usually disintegrates as they become established disciplines, rather as the confident panaceas dear to the politician in opposition make way for more judicious improvisations as he becomes minister in office.

The historian's discipline is a little too old to leave him unaware of the complexity of the problems that face him. His 'models' do not have to be artificially contrived. They are real. What then, faced with all the multiple increases in material and problems, does the historian do? Has he a simple choice between pausing to ponder and synthesize, and cutting his coat to suit his cloth? Is it still possible for the historian to 'cut a colossus from a rock'? Or is he condemned 'to carve heads on cherry stones' in those thousand historical journals? Or in despair, to limit history to narrative, placing the problems of explanation in the office tray marked 'too difficult'? Surely not. I have no ready formula by which these problems of causation can be untangled. My conviction, however, is that the historian must, if he is to be a historian at all, preserve at all times an acute awareness of what John Stuart Mill called a century ago 'the state of society'. By that he meant the totality of knowledge of a civilization – economic, cultural, political, social.

> What is called the state of society [he wrote] is the simultaneous state of all the greater social parts or phenomena. Such are the degree of knowledge, and of intellectual and moral culture, existing in the community, and of every class of it; the state of industry, of wealth and its distribution; the habitual occupations of the community; their division into classes, and the relation of those classes to one another; the common beliefs which they entertain on all the subjects most important to mankind, and the degree of assurance with which those beliefs are held; their tastes, and the character and degree of their aesthetic development; their form of government, and the more important of their laws and customs.

This need not mean now, any more than it did then, that every historian is required to have a detailed and specialized knowledge of all these related aspects of a society's history. On the contrary, it means that we must never imagine that we can understand the particular aspect which we have isolated in order to analyse, without retaining this sense that it is part of the whole, temporarily separated for analysis only to be unified ultimately with the rest. This sense of totality in the historian must be visceral as well as cerebral: a desire and pursuit of the whole. In our own day we have watched an epic of this kind take shape before our eyes in Mr Carr's great *History of the Russian Revolution*, where all the varied themes and subjects are woven in precisely this tautly controlled counterpoint. Of course, the pattern of each historical situation is different. It is suggested in a kind of dialogue between the historian, his problems and his materials. But the personal sense of the whole must be there in each case. People listen to an historian because he has a personal vision of the past. Herbert Butterfield has ranged over a wide diversity of subjects – Renascence Italy, George III's England, Napoleonic France, contemporary Europe, historiography, science, and religion. Yet in the last analysis it is not so much the range of his knowledge but the intensity of his *vision* of history, expressed in the uniquely individual turn of thought and phrase, that has caught and delighted our minds and imaginations and made him a powerful force in our time, in Cambridge and outside it.

I do not know who coined the phrase 'history in depth' which is so often used to describe the modern technique of treating history. It was Herbert Butterfield who wisely counselled us that these explorations in 'depth' (by which we often mean economic and sociological analysis) must not cause us to lose contact with the traditional techniques of historical narrative. This is profoundly important. Chronological narrative is often despised by modern historians of the analytical kind. Yet often almost the only thing we know about the past with certainty is its order in time, that some things happened before other things. This sense of the time order and the unalterability of history remains basic. If we lose it we shall be swallowed up in a dream world of meaningless contingencies. It was the present Professor of Economic History in this University who warned us that the contribution of historians to the advance of knowledge must be 'small and uncertain'. The business of the economic historian is (as he said) to go on studying the individual problems of societies or units of societies like manors, industries, business firms. So with the other specialists. There is, I think, no great harm done if they go on talking their latest professional jargon to each other in private: if economic historians prattle of liquidity, variables or backward sloping curves, or sociologists of motivations, élites and social roles. Provided always that we return to some common plain language which recovers this specialized shorthand for purposes of civilized intercourse and ultimate history. For practical purposes – for the use of Ministers of the Crown, for instance, or those of them who have the sense to insist on it – specialists have always proved themselves able to oblige. We can do the same for ourselves. The principle of the division of labour need not mean the division of mankind.

The disappearance of ideas of definitive history had at least one good result. It has made historians less arrogant about the past. We do not now see society in the past merely as stupid or wrong. Few historians nowadays regard themselves as capable of 'explaining' historical phenomena as a scientist can explain the workings of the dynamo or the internal combustion engine. Unlike earlier schools of historians they see their task not as judging or condemning but of understanding. In this change lies also the continuing and indeed increased claim of historical study to be a vital part of modern education. For if we have lost the assurance of certainty, we have gained by the emerging conception of history as both a humane study and an experimental science. The curious conceit that one man should set countless past generations to rights has given way to the more modest conception that he should try to understand *why* they did *what* they did. The peculiar value of studying history is not that we can achieve total explanation but that we cannot. The causes that produce individual genius or great outbursts of national culture remain, as Trevelyan said half a century ago, mysteries. The origins of this very Western European dominance that is now passing, what an Indian writer has called 'the age of Vasco da Gama', remain obscure. We are not likely ever fully to understand how small and peripheral peoples like the Portuguese, the Dutch or for that matter the English, managed to conquer half the world. But this does not reduce the value of continuing to study the problem. Any age of material progress creates as well as solves problems. In our age, when the efficiency of communications often seems to outrun our capacity to use them properly, when the benefits of scientific knowledge are accompanied by the risks and confusions of pseudo-scientific charlatanism, the perspective which a disciplined historical training can bring has never been more necessary.

We are often told we are living in an age of unbelief. On the contrary, we can be persuaded to believe in almost anything, even the theology of the Bishop of Woolwich. Constant exposure to novelty is as likely to induce gullibility as scepticism. In our post-Keynesian age of affluence, where it often seems to matter less what a man does than how much he is paid to do it, the most urgent task of higher education is not to instruct or to entertain, not even merely to convey knowledge, but to develop independent critical judgement. The effective threat that the study of history presents to totalitarianism is that it breeds variety and nonconformity. It is almost impossible for historians not to disagree, as any attempt to reshape the history tripos always proves. My old Tutor, Bernard Manning, a great and dedicated medievalist, to whom I owe much, wrote to me early in the war from Cambridge:

> Yesterday, I met X [a colleague]. He tells me we must change the tripos again and I expect he is right. Nothing is more curious to me than the way a curriculum *apparently* so ill-organized regularly produces such good men, unless it be the way *apparently* better organized courses produce men so much worse.

The Cambridge history school has a deserved reputation in the world. Can its arrangements be improved? Obviously yes. The discussions designed to do this have now been going on for two years. If the present proposals come into force they will embody several principles, but behind all of them is the permanent dualism of the historian's problem; specialization and generalization. No man who reads the history tripos will be able to retreat from the specialization which is the key to knowledge in our time. General courses, such as find favour with those professional educationists who are never tired of telling us our business, have no place in the proposed scheme of things. Undergraduates do not, I believe, either deserve or like the kind of pre-digested pap which seems to be what some of our reformers have in mind. This is quite a different conception from what we do propose as a counter-weight to the rigours of specialized courses. There is obviously a need for courses which stimulate the student to cultivate his interests in historical problems far beyond the boundaries of his special studies. But these explorations in breadth should in their way be as intellectually exigent as the explorations in depth. And the two types of course will be complementary one to the other. The only way in which history can be studied in present conditions seems to be to preserve this distinction between a man's historical interests and his specialized knowledge. The first is where his imagination and curiosity can range widely over comparative problems of time and place. The second enables him to pursue a very different intellectual exercise, developing those techniques of exact study which give history its claim to be a science. As the student moves forward he will be given greater freedom of choice amongst the different options, and be required to study each in ever-increasing depth, until as the climax of his undergraduate curriculum he reaches the semi-research of a 'special subject'.

Finally, the tripos of the future will embody more opportunities for the close study of extra-European societies than it has hitherto done. This seems a development particularly appropriate to the Cambridge history school. The charge that our teaching is Anglocentric is a difficult one to take seriously. Of course, so long as we remain a uni-lingual people, English history must remain basic to our tripos, not for reasons of sentiment but simply because it alone can give us the experience of the closest and most rigorous type of study. But few departments anywhere can claim as ours can to have selected and encouraged so many scholars who have enlarged and are still enlarging our historical knowledge, not only of Europe and the Commonwealth, but of North and Latin America, Russia, India, Africa and the East. And the pressure for these new studies has not had to wait for the stimulus of government committees. It was generated here in our history school itself. A more assured place in the tripos will certainly stimulate further research in these extra-European fields.

Such a curriculum will be rigorous. The history tripos has always been rigorous. I do not believe the Cambridge history faculty intends to abate its rigours now. The prize that a real historical training should offer is a sense of proportion that comes from studying man and society in time. This sense of man in relation to time is the dimension that only the historian can add to the thought of the social sciences. And it becomes more vital as our capacity to remember seems to be fading in an age when good journalism is being swamped by trivial and spurious, and when, with the death of the habit of letter-writing, literacy has to be taught to adults as a special discipline (called 'communication').

The modes of study commonly followed by the historian often

seem to logicians to lack system. We do not construct artificial models and maybe we are too apt to amuse ourselves deriding the abstract constructions of our fellow social scientists. But those who doubt the claim of history to be a discipline should ponder the historical ventures of those who have not been through a historical mill. Few survive close scrutiny. Keynes, an economic genius, wrote historical essays which were illuminating and provocative. Yet his writings are defective in that feeling for historical change which fused Clapham's statistics into an organic, historic whole. The historical sense is something besides historical econometrics. The historian's hypotheses are chosen from inside history not from outside it. Somehow he learns to watch the swing of the pendulum, to separate what is transient from what is enduring, what is trivial from what is essential. It may be objected that the rigours of the historical education we are shaping here are designed only to create professional historians. Far from it. To train the new generation of university teachers is certainly a vital function for Cambridge, perhaps the most vital in the immediate future; but at tripos level it is far from being our only concern. A true curriculum is precisely the same for all comers. Only if our Historical Tripos is rigorous can it claim to perform a critical educational function in modern conditions. In my experience, undergraduates do not mind hard work provided they are shown how to go about it. If the tripos is to be rigorous, our methods of teaching need to be examined.

How are we to achieve the ends we desire? We are certainly not short of advice from the outside world. From reformers, politicians and government committees, comes a steady stream of exhortations, threats and sermons on our duties. The impressions they create are diverse: curricula, especially of the older universities, are depicted as dull and arid, our teaching antiquated and sterile; conversely we are too clever by half. This conflict is resolved by the Hibernian argument that at any rate we are an insult to egalitarian principles and an obstacle to social progress. It is apparently preferable to abolish individual tuition and cut clever boys down to size, rather than admit that some boys are cleverer than other boys, or risk one don earning a few more pounds than another. The future that opens up is a future in which larger and more splendid lecture halls arise in ever greater numbers. A future where professors more numerous and pontifical than ever lecture at growing thousands of inanimate students doomed to a life of passive obedience. One is reminded of the poet's nightmare where

> Society is now one polished Horde
> Formed of two equal tribes, the *Bores* and *Bored.*

No wonder that the victims of this kind of academic tyranny band themselves together in students' unions against their masters. The older universities are fortunate and wealthy enough to have avoided this disastrous system so far. Obviously, lecturing is a part, and an important part, of any balanced scheme of teaching, but if higher education is to mean training in critical judgement, the business of learning how to learn, it must not be the whole or even the dominant part. 'Reading', said Bacon, 'maketh a full man, conference a ready man, and writing an exact man.' He passed over in merciful silence what kind of man a sole diet of lecturing would make. At the moment, our supervision system is under fire. Reformers among us are much for seminars. The seminar can undoubtedly be a useful aid to the teaching system. Its twin dangers are the passive witness and the fluent chatterbox – Bacon's 'ready man'. A lecture demands much from the lecturer, and a good one something from the listener. Individual supervision demands much from both pupil and teacher. Seminars too often demand nothing from either. Likewise, that never-ending flow of witty, topical, entertaining lectures envisaged by some of our reformers as the centre of a university system, is a mirage and a misconception. Nowhere does the law of diminishing returns set in so rapidly as in the lecturing system. Here, 'more' invariably means 'worse'. It would be unnecessary to repeat old commonplaces such as that 'all higher education is self-education', but for the growing number of educational reformers to whom they are apparently both novel and incomprehensible. The teacher's task is to attract undergraduates into that degree of personal involvement and participation in the learning process which alone can remove the need for stick or carrot. The question of methods still stands in urgent need of systematic inquiry.

According to the Robbins Committee, our supervision system (or what they prefer to describe as 'the old-fashioned tutorial') is outmoded. It is, they believe, too exacting for the average student. I must confess I find it hard to retain my composure when faced with such frightening ignorance of one of the central functions and institutions of the older universities. I can only charitably suppose that it is some years since any member of the Robbins Committee took part in a tutorial, even an old-fashioned one. If we are to treat individuals as permanently classified before their university education even begins, then we may as well close our universities down. In real life, the naturally α-candidate is most likely to look after himself. It is precisely in helping the γ-man to become a β-man, or a β-man to achieve an α, that one great satisfaction of the supervisor lies. The uniquely valuable relationship between the academic and non-academic world in this country rests not least (I believe) on the unpatronizing care and attention that the older universities have always given to their academically less than brilliant pupils who comprise two thirds of the total.

Whatever may be true of other branches of learning, my own experience has convinced me that, for at least his first year, every history student needs individual, solitary attention. The transition from the habits of school instruction to the methods of independent inquiry appropriate to a university course can best be accomplished in this way. Our supervision system will become more, not less, necessary as the number of candidates from less well-endowed schools increases. A distinguished American historian and former Pitt Professor in this University, Professor Richard Hofstadter, has recently examined the origins of anti-intellectualism in the United States. He concludes that one important source has been what he calls 'evangelical egalitarianism' and the distrust of the clever boy. The English are by long tradition a race of successful cultural plagiarists. So far from being insular, the élite with whom cultural decisions have in the past rested, ransacked the world for their models. This process of cribbing was redeemed by the taste of the imitators and a sure sense of adaptation. But the élite has gone. Our culture is again in the melting pot. The current model is transatlantic and it is unlikely that education will be unaffected by the tide that has already swept over advertising, technology, popular music and what we are still permitted for the time being to call the English language. It would be ironic if in our higher education we were passively to copy examples of mass production which are dubiously relevant to our situation, just when they are being questioned and abandoned by their original promoters. If the study of history is to achieve that dual function which Mr Carr sees as its object – to understand the society of the past and increase man's mastery over the society of the present – we must build our historical education organically and upon the best tried models. By all means let us expand and reform but let us protect what we know to be best in our system from attacks based on political expediency, prejudice and plain ignorance.

M. Raymond Aron has likened history to a dialogue between past and present in which 'the present takes and keeps the initiative'. Even this may be too static a conception of history's role. For amongst those forces which shape our idea of the present is our personal experience and conception of history. We may have discarded the idea of definitive history, but the potential influence of history as an educational and intellectual process that is not merely subjective or relative in its values remains. The play between past and present is fully mutual, as it is between man and his circumstances. Nor does the process stop with the present. We may no longer share Buckle's confidence in the uniformity of human conduct, social responses and the sequence of events. Yet it was no steady Victorian rationalist but the great and wayward Byron who wrote that 'the best Prophet of the Future is the Past'. Is there any shadow of doubt that the future of civilized human relations, whether social or international, must rest on that historical understanding which it is the business of any history school to cultivate?

Index

Index

Abingdon, 8
Acton, Lord, 92, 93, 101, 202
advertising, 165, 168, 189, 190, 197
Africa, 29, 107
Agriculture, 24, 28, 43, 46, 51, 63, 98, 122, 126, 129, 136, 144, 152, 178, 192, 200
Albright and Wilson, 198
Aldcroft, D. H., 180, 193
America, 24, 39, 50, 52, 53, 115, 135, 136, 167, 168, 186, 196, 199
American Civil War, the, 206
American War of Independence, 27, 38, 115, 206
Amsterdam, 23, 25, 28, 30, 32, 33, 34, 35, 36, 37, 38, 39, 41, 45, 50, 59, 60, 100, 111
Anglicanism, 18
Anson, Lord, 90
Aquinas, 130, 134
aristocracy, the, 1, 17, 18, 64, 86, 141, 144, 146, 150, 152, 173, 174
Arkwright, 166, 170, 175, 176
Armstrong, 187
army, 4, 5, 7, 9, 10, 28, 30, 31
Arnold, Dr, 196
Arnold, Matthew, 196
Aron, M. Raymond, 215
Ashburnham, Lord, 8, 9
Ashley, M. P., 65, 145, 202
Ashton, Professor, T. S., 132, 133, 156, 167
Atlantic, the, 15, 29, 30
Austria, 76
Austrian Succession, war of, 31

Bacon, Anthony, 168
Baltic, the, 23, 24, 25, 28, 34, 50, 51, 52, 53, 54, 55, 59, 60
Banbury, 7
banking, 34, 35, 36, 37, 38, 39, 44, 59, 148, 170, 191
Barnato, Barney, 194
Bavaria, 36
Beales, H. L., 178, 179
Becher, J. J., 90
Beers Consolidated, De, 194
Beecham, 190, 193, 194
Beit, Alfred, 194
Bellers, John, 75, 79, 83
Beloff, M., 74
Bentham, J., 140, 151
Berkeley, 203
Berlin, 141
Bergen, 23
Bessemer, 169
Bill of Rights (1689), 143
Biscay, 24, 50
Birmingham, 66, 167, 192
Bismarck, 203
Blathwayte, 14
Bolckow, 198
Boot, 187, 188, 189, 194
Booth, Charles, 197
Bordeaux, 30
Bostocks, 186
Boulton, 149, 159, 170, 171, 173, 174, 175, 176

Bowden, P. J., 98
Bowring, 152
Bradford, 3, 164
Brassey, 187
Brazil, 24, 151
brewery, brewing, 15, 122, 174, 198
Brewster, 55, 56, 57, 60, 77
Bridgewater, Duke of, 170, 174
Bristol, 4, 30, 79, 86, 90, 92, 101, 157
British South Africa Company, 194
Brown, John, 169
Browne, Sir Thomas, 92
Brunton, 3
Buckle, 215
bullion, 50, 51, 52, 53, 54, 55, 58, 59, 60, 64, 76, 83, 89, 90
Burke, 140, 176
Burne, Colonel, 5, 6, 7, 8, 9
Butterfield, Herbert, 92, 208

Cadbury, 173, 190, 194
Calico Act, the, 171
Calvinism, 4, 26, 129
capital, 1, 14, 16, 17, 32, 33, 34, 35, 38, 39, 42, 43, 45, 46, 49, 54, 55, 59, 113, 121, 122, 135, 158, 159, 169, 170, 174, 187, 189, 190, 198, 199
capitalism, 2, 3, 35, 88, 92, 128, 131, 133, 135, 136, 158, 169, 172, 173
capital goods, 168, 192, 193, 199
Caribbean, the, 107
Carr, E. H., 115, 131, 172, 208, 215
Carron ironworks, the, 118
Cary, John, 17, 79, 83, 86, 90
charity, 16, 17, 77, 78, 79, 81, 84, 85, 86, 87, 91, 131, 132
Charles I, 3, 4, 6, 7, 8, 9, 10, 18
Charles II, 15, 53, 55, 155
Chamberlen, Peter, 81, 82, 91
Chamier, Anthony, 45, 46
Cheriton, 7
Chester, 4
Child, Josiah, 14, 15, 17, 76, 77, 78, 79, 82, 83, 86, 90, 91, 154
children, child welfare, 43, 78, 81, 173, 174
Civil War, the, chap. I, 74, 96, 115; resources, 5, 6, 10; strategy, 6, 7, 8, 9
Clapham, Sir John, 128, 161, 203, 205, 212
Clarendon, 13, 107
Clark, G. N., 49
Cliffords, 36, 38, 148
Clive, Robert, 149
Clow, 166
coal, 182, 184, 191, 192
Cobbett, 59
Cockayne crisis, the, 12, 71, 103, 105, 145, 147
Colchester, 97, 101
Colbert, 29, 80
Cole, Professor, 158, 162
colonies, colonial trade, 27, 28, 29, 30, 39, 41, 45, 50, 52, 74, 115; 'Old Colonial System', 29
Comenius, 9, 89, 91
commission trade, 35, 43, 44
Como, 99
Congreve, 92
Constantinople, 100
Co-op movement, 188
Coppock, D. J., 179, 180, 182, 183, 189
Corn Laws, 66, 140, 151, 152
costs, 26, 42, 44, 109, 110, 111, 113, 123, 192
Coulton, 129
Court, de la, 107, 124
Courtauld, 194
Coventry, 190, 194
Crawshaw, Richard, 168
Creighton, 201
Cromwell, Oliver, 10, 12, 13, 18, 52, 142, 155
Cromwell, Thomas, 142
Crossley, Mrs, 131, 172, 173
Crossleys, 167
Crystal Palace Exhibition, the, 182, 188, 195
Culliford, 53
Culpepper, 76, 91

Cunningham, William, 69, 73, 79, 137, 140, 202, 205
customs, 15, 27, 42, 53, 68, 77, 95, 121, 122, 124, 147

Danzig, 36, 51
Darwin, 203
Davenant, C., 79, 82
Davis, Ralph, 147
Deane, Phyllis, 119
defence costs, 44, 52, 54, 55, 57, 58, 63, 65, 113, 120, 124
Defoe, Daniel, 20, 78, 83, 88, 89, 91, 112, 149, 158
Delft, 99, 100
Deloney, Thomas, 158
Demant, Canon, chap. 8
Denmark, 36, 52, 53
depression, 28, 38, 46, 81, 104, 108, 122, 178, 179, 180, 183, 186, 188, 189, 190, 192, 197, 200
Derby, 166
devaluation, 42, 114
Devonshire, 97, 163
Dickens, Charles, 88
Digby, Lord, 6, 8, 10
Dill, Samuel, 114
Dillen, Dr van, 28, 116, 117
Dobb, M., 11
Dorman Long, 198
Dowlais ironworks, 174
Downing, Sir George, 14, 15, 55, 107, 110, 113, 118, 146, 154, 155
Dutch Wars, the, 12, 13, 26, 29, 39, 51, 52, 80, 104, 108

East Anglia, 25, 80, 97, 101, 160, 163
East India, 15, 24, 34, 38, 50, 51, 54
East India Company, 15, 29, 27, 38, 79, 149
Eastland Company, 13, 29, 50, 97, 146
economic change, 1, 3, 12, 40, 42, 44, 132, 134
economic interest, 11, 17, 67, 71, 91, 142
economic nationalism, x, 16, 23, 28, 37, 116, 123, 124, 154
economic policy, 12, 13, 14, 17, 48, 62, 63, 66, 68, 69, 70, 71, 72, 75, 76, 90, 91, 108, 113, 118, 124, 133, 134, chap. 9, 142, 149, 150, 154
Edgehill, 7, 8
education, 87, 88, 89, 91, 131, 133, 173, 182, 194, 210
Egypt, 167
Ehrman, J., 149, 150
Elliot, J. H., 116
Elton, Dr, 142
Elwill, Sir John, 163
Employment, 23, 33, 43, 46, 48, 55, 71, 76, 82, 89, 92, 117, 118, 131, 133, 147, 179, 183; statute of, 59
English Channel, the, 26
entrepôt system, the, 25, 30, 32, 34, 35, 37, 41, 44, 111
entrepreneurs, 27, 31, 86, 113, 133, chap. 10, 180, 189, 193, 194, 195, 197, 198, 200
Escott, T. H. S., 187
Essex, 97, 160
Essex, Earl of, 7, 8
Exeter, 4, 30, 98, 122, 163
excise, 15, 95, 117, 119, 121
expenditure, government foreign, 57, 58, 120
exports, x, 12, 25, 26, 30, 31, 32, 41, 42, 46, 50, 78, 80, 96, 97, 98, 99, 103, 104, 108, 110, 111, 144, 146, 147, 162, 163, 166, 171, 180, 181, 182, 183, 187, 193, 198, 199, 200

Fabians, the, 133, 135, 173, 176
factories, 43, 44, 58, 83, 156, 164, 167, 173, 174, 186, 189, 193
Fairbairn, William, 175
Fairfax, 3, 10
Fay, C. R., 191
finance, 14, 15, 27, 34, 35, 36, 38, 39, 46, 59, chap. 7, 148, 149, 158, 162, 174, 178, 198
Finer, Professor, 142
Finisterre, battle of, 90

Firmin, 17, 75, 79, 82, 89
fish, 23, 24, 25, 33, 43, 46, 50, 55, 56, 71, 122, 123
Fisher, Professor, F. J. 98, 141
fleet, 4, 14, 28, 29, 31, 44, 52, 53, 54, 68, 124
Fletcher, T. W., 192, 200
Florence, 99, 159
food, 24, 25, 28, 33, 42, 80, 81, 84, 111, 117, 123, 124, 132, 133, 156, 189, 192
Forster's Education Act, 194
Foster, Serjeant, 4, 5
Foster, William, 164, 165
France, 22, 23, 24, 28, 29, 30, 31, 32, 33, 35, 36, 39, 41, 52, 74, 76, 80, 81, 89, 90, 91, 94, 106, 111, 115, 116, 120, 126, 127, 153, 154, 206
Frederick the Great, 68
Freeman Hardy and Willis, 188
free trade, 47, 89, 151, 152, 154, 171
Fuller, Thomas, 96, 97

Gardiner, 1
Gasquet, 129
Gay, E. F., 67
Geer, de, 35, 36
Genovesi, 90
George III, 149, 174
Germany, 22, 25, 30, 32, 36, 41, 45, 62, 66, 67, 69, 73, 90, 94, 118, 141, 189, 190, 199, 202, 205
Geyl, Professor, 114
Giffen, Sir R., 181, 182, 184, 187, 193
Gilbert's Act, 84, 85
gilds, rôle of, 160, 161, 171
Gladstone, 150, 151, 155, 203
Glasgow, 30
Glass, Professor, 119
Gloucester, 7
Goffe, William, 81, 82
Goldie, George Taubman, 194
Goring, 10
Gott, Benjamin, 156, 164
Gouda, 100
Gournay, de, 90
government, 11, 12, 14, 15, 20, 44, 49, 74, 75, 91, 136, 141, 142, 146, 147, 149; policy chap. 9
grain, 23, 24, 25, 28, 50, 51, 191, 192
Guinness, 194, 197

Haarlem, 25, 30, 32, 45, 100
Hague, the, 107, 118
Hale, Matthew, 82
Halifax, 97, 131, 164, 167
Hamilton, Professor, 115
Handfield-Jones, S. J., 179
Hanover, 37
Hanway, Jonas, 84, 87, 89
'Hard Currency' areas, 55, 56, 58
Harford, Robert, 82
Hargreaves, 159
Harley, 89
Harmsworth, Alfred, 194
Harper, A., 147
Harrington, 18
Harrods, 187
Hart, Dr Simon, 125
Hartlib, Samuel, 81, 82, 89, 91
Heathcote, 14
Heaton, Professor, 164
Heckscher, Professor, 49, 63, 70, 71, 141
Hepworths, 188
Heukelom, van, 43, 47
Hewins, W. A. S., 66, 69, 73
Heyking, von, 66
Hill, Christopher, chap. 1, 141
Hill, Sam, 97, 164
Hinton, R. W. K., 13, 146, 147, 148
Hobson, C. K., 46
Hoffman, W., 182, 183, 184, 185, 186
Hofstadter, Richard, 214
Holroyd, Joseph, 97
Home and Colonial Stores, 188
Hopes, 45
Hopton, Lord, 4, 7, 9
Horrockses, 162, 167
Hotham, 4
Hounslow, 4
House of Commons, 1, 13, 18, 149, 164, 178

Houtman, 24
Houtzager, D., 121
Hudson River, 195
Huguenots, the, 32
Hull, 4, 7
Hume, David, 154
Hume, Deacon, 151, 152, 155
Huskisson, 150, 155

ICI, 194
Iliffe's Publications, 194
immigrants, 31, 32, 65, 91, 101, 102, 103, 133, 156, 189
imperialism, 55, 60, 66
India, 166, 171
industrialists, 2, 14, 15, 27, 40, 42, 66, 155, 163, 166, 170, 199
Industrial Revolution, the, x, 1, 84, 122, 126, 132, 138, chap. 10, 180, 188, 195, 196
industry, 12, 14, 17, 26, 27, 31, 32, 33, 34, 37, 39, 40, 42, 43, 44, 46, 47, 55, 64, 65, 66, 68, 75, 80, 89, 90, 94, 95, 101, 102, 103, 104, 106, 107, 108, 109, 110, 111, 112, 117, 120, 121, 122, 123, 126, 129, 133, 136, 137, 142, 150, 152, 153, 156, 157, 161, 162, 163, 164, 165, 166, 167, 168, 169, 174, 178, 179, 180, 181, 182, 183, 185, 186, 187, 189, 191, 192, 193, 195, 196, 197, 198, 200
interest, 32, 35, 48, 57, 76, 121, 144, 148
inventions, 44, 157, 159, 164, 165, 167, 169, 170, 175, 176
investment, 14, 33, 34, 35, 36, 37, 38, 39, 40, 44, 45, 46, 48, 59, 71, 117, 126, 152, 158, 171, 179, 180, 182, 190, 191, 193
Ireland, 33, 53, 54, 133, 156
iron, 156, 168, 169, 170, 174, 180, 182, 184, 191, 192, 198
Italy, 25, 41, 50, 54, 76, 94, 95, 99, 106, 110, 153, 154

James I, 12, 14, 18, 145, 147
James, Margaret, 74
Janssen, 14
Japan, 186
Java, 24
Jeffreys, J. B., 188, 193
Johnson, Dr, 92, 158, 172, 203
Jones, A. H. M., 127
Jordan, Professor, 16, 17

Kent, 85
Keynes, John Maynard, ix, x, 48, 49, 60, 71, 72, 82, 154, 155, 179, 191, 210, 212
King Gregory, 119
King's Lynn, 7

labour, 17, 25, 33, 42, 64, 74, 77, 80, 83, 89, 92, 109, 110, 122, 123, 124, 125, 151, 159, 167, 174, 175, 172, 182, 186, 187, 189, 190, 191, 193
laissez-faire, 2, 11, 68, 70, 74, 79, 131, 155, 172
Lancashire, 165, 166, 190
Land tax, 13, 121
Lavenham, 97
Leeds, 156, 164, 171, 175, 197
Leeuw, David, 45
Legge, Will, 9
Leicester, 159
Leiden, 25, 31, 32, 43, 101, 102, 103, 104, 105, 106, 107, 109, 110, 111, 112, 116, 117, 118, 122, 123, 160
Letwin, W., 11
Levant, the, 23, 28, 41, 100, 107, 110
Levant Company, 28, 79
Lever, William, 168, 170, 173, 187, 192, 193, 194, 196
Lewis, John, 187, 188, 192
Lilienthal, David, 135
Lincolnshire, 198
Liptons, 188, 190, 194
List, Frederick, 68
Liverpool, 30, 189, 197
loans, 35, 36, 37, 38, 39, 57, 60, 76, 113, 120, 124, 128, 129, 132, 170
Locke, 14, 79, 82, 155

London, 4, 5, 7, 8, 11, 30, 35, 36, 38, 39, 47, 59, 75, 81, 85, 86, 90, 105, 148, 166, 175, 189
Long Parliament, the, 3
Lostwithiel, 7
Luddites, the, 175
Luzac, E., 125
luxury goods, 17, 55, 65, 172
Lynch, Judge, 93
Lyons, 31, 116
Lyons, Joseph, 188

Macaulay, 130, 133, 176, 195
Machiavelli, 114
Mackworth, Humphrey, 19, 83
'Majolica, English', 167
Malthus, 133, 134
Manchester, 66, 151, 171, 175, 181, 192
Mandeville, 79, 81, 89, 91, 172
Maitland, 202
Manfields, 186
Mann, 165
Marshall, Alfred, 154, 178, 197
Marston Moor, 8, 10
Martineau, Harriet, 173
Mantoux, 158, 159, 164, 170
Marxism, 1, 2, 11, 16, 17, 19, 20, 138, 141, 142, 196, 203, 205
Mason, Josiah, 167
mass-market, 182, 189, 190, 191, 199
materialism, 74, 76, 196
mechanization, 131, 156, 159, 160, 166, 171, 175, 176, 179, 180, 195, 196
Mediterranean, the, 23, 24, 34, 41, 60, 98, 99, 100, 103, 107
mercantilism, ix, x, 12, 23, 25, 33, chap. 3, chap. 4, chap. 5, 141, 147, 149, 150, 151, 152, 153, 155, 171, 172
merchants, 11, 14, 15, 16, 17, 23, 26, 27, 30, 34, 35, 38, 39, 40, 43, 45, 54, 59, 64, 65, 66, 69, 74, 75, 77, 79, 84, 86, 87, 90, 124, 142, 146, 149, 150, 158, 162, 163, 164, 169, 170
Mexico, 195
McCulloch, J. R., 94
McGregor, 151, 155
Middle Ages, 128, 129, 130, 134, 160, 171
middle class, 1, 4, 11, 17, 112, 163, 196
Milan, 99
Mill, John Stuart, 196, 207
Milton, John, 81, 89
Minton, Herbert, 167
Mond, Ludwig, 194, 198
monopoly, 2, 13, 66, 100, 145, 152, 171, 176
More, Hannah, 92
Morris, William, 136, 196
Mousnier, R., 127
Mun, Thomas, 23, 49, 50, 51, 52, 54, 55, 64, 76. 80, 90, 113, 154
munitions, 168, 169
Musson, A. E., 180, 182

Nantes, 30
Napier, 197
Naples, 90
Naseby, 8, 9
national debt, 57, 58, 60, 121, 125, 148, 149
Napoleonic Wars, the, 29
naval stores, 28, 51, 57; *see also*, fleet
Navigation Acts, 14, 15, 29, 53, 65, 68, 71, 108, 116, 145, 147
Neck, Joshua van, 36, 149
Nelson, 17, 79
Netherlands, the, x, 13, chap. 2, 50, 51, 52, 55, 57, 59, 60, 64, 74, 77, 80, 91, 94, 95, 99, 100, 101, 102, 103, 104, 105, 106, 107, 108, 109, 110, 111, 112, 113, chap. 7, 129, 144, 145, 146, 147, 153, 163, 205, 206, 209
Newbury, 4, 5, 7, 8,
Newcastle, 4, 8
'New Draperies', the, 96, 98, 100, 101, 102, 161
Newfoundland, 30
Newnes, George, 194

Newton, 14, 155
Nicolson, Sir Harold, 203
North, Dudley, 83, 94
Northampton, 186
Northcliffe, Lord, 194
North Sea, 50
Norway, 51, 52, 53
Norwich, 86, 97, 98, 101, 111, 122, 163, 164

'Old Draperies', the, 12, 103
Oldham, 131
Oldknow, Samuel, 166
Ostend, 43
Oxenford, 53, 54, 55, 57, 58
Oxford, 8, 9

pacifism, 26
Paris, 115
Parliament, 1, 3, 4, 6, 9, 10, 13, 14, 52, 64, 77, 81, 89, 141, 142, 152
Parsons, Charles, 194, 195
Paycocke, 160, 162
payments balance of, ix, 46, 48, 53, 54, 55, 56, 57, 58, 64, 66, 71, 72, 75, 76, 77, 83, 89, 90, 107, 137, 147, 148
Pennington, 3
Papillon, 15
Pearson, W. D., 195
Peel, Robert, 150, 151, 152, 155, 173
Pepys, Samuel, 14, 52, 148, 149
Percy, Lord, 9
Peterloo, 175
Phelps Brown, E. H., 179
Pilkington, 197
plantations, 29, 54
Platt, John, 131
Plockhoy, Cornelius, 82, 91
Poland, 36, 91, 94
poor, the, 17, 76, 77, 78, 80, 81, 82, 83, 84, 88, 89, 91, 92, 117, 118, 126, 131, 172, 189
Pope, 155, 172
population, 12, 24, 30, 31, 33, 34, 39, 40, 44, 46, 78, 80, 85, 86, 101, 120, 125, 133, 161, 162, 181, 185, 190
Porter, 152
Port Sunlight, 192
Portugal, 36, 41, 209
precious metals, ix, 24, 34, 48, 49, 50, 54, 58, 115
pressure groups, 14, 15, 142, 143, 144, 145, 146, 148, 149, 150, 153, 155, 206
Preston, 167
Price, Dr Jacob, 145
prices, 13, 16, 26, 42, 82, 111, 117, 144, 178, 179, 186, 191, 192, 198, 199
Price, J. M., 11
private enterprise, 68, 69, 84, 181
private interest, chap. 9
Privy Council, the, 12, 14, 59, 74, 147, 153
Production, 1907 Census of, 193
profit, 25, 27, 29, 30, 34, 39, 45, 60, 74, 123, 147, 170, 178, 179
protection, x, 26, 28, 32, 41, 42, 47, 64, 66, 104, 113, 144, 146, 152, 171, 179
Prussia, 23, 36, 37, 68, 69, 126
public enterprise, 170, 171
publishing, 194

Quakers, 75, 79
Queensbury, 164

Ramsay, G. D., 99
Randalls, 186
raw materials, 17, 25, 28, 33, 42, 46, 95, 100, 102, 103, 105, 108, 109, 110, 111, 113, 142, 144, 147, 171, 184, 191, 192
Ray, John, 119
rentiers, 27, 45
Restoration, the, 14, 20, 29, 74, 75, 80, 83, 85, 86, 91, 92, 103, 108, 113
retail trade, 185, 187, 188, 189, 193
Rhodes, Cecil, 194
Ricardo, 152
Rice Bush, 81
Richmond, Duke of, 9

Robbins Report, the, x, xi, 213, 214
Robinson, Joan, 154
Roebuck, 168
Rogers, Thorold, 16
Rostow, W. W., 179, 182, 188
Rotherham, 170
Rotterdam, 31, 91, 99
Rouen, 167
Roundheads, 2, 3, 5, 7
Rous, 149
Rousseau, 140, 155
Rowton Heath, 6
Royal Niger Company, the, 194
Royalists, 2, 3, 4, 6, 8, 9, 10, 16
Rupert, Prince, 4, 7, 8, 9, 10
Ruskin, 196
Russia, 28, 36, 38, 53, 59, 84, 97
Ruthven, 7, 8

salt, 23, 24, 50, 122
Scandinavia, 22, 36, 50
Schmoller, 67, 68, 69, 70, 77
Schroeder, von, 90
Scotland, 24, 25, 104, 166
Seeley, Sir John, 73, 141
'service trades', 182
Settlement Laws, 88
Seven Years War, the, 31, 37, 80
Shaw, G. B., 135
Sheffield, 169, 198
Shell, 186
shipbuilding, 25, 33, 42, 46, 116, 117, 123, 146, 191
shipping, 23, 26, 27, 29, 30, 43, 53, 121, 124, 142, 144, 145, 147, 152
Shropshire, 7
Smiles, Samuel, 159, 195
Smith, Adam, 62, 63, 64, 65, 68, 70, 71, 74, 75, 88, 94, 95, 130, 131, 145, 153, 154, 155, 172, 204
Smith, W. H., 188
socialism, 64, 65, 135
social standards, 16, 83, 84, 118, 125, 189, 192, 195, 196
Sonnenfels, 90
South Africa, 194
South Sea Company, 37
Spain, 4, 20, 23, 24, 25, 28, 29, 30, 31, 32, 36, 41, 50, 98, 99, 100, 102, 103, 104, 106, 107, 108, 113, 115, 116, 118, 123, 126, 153, 205
Spencer, Herbert, 196
Spiegel, van de, 124
Stafford, 198
state intervention, 66, 68, 69, 70, 71, 73, 74, 113, 171
steel, 169, 179, 182, 191, 192, 198
St John, Oliver, 146
Stoke-on-Trent, 167
Strafford, 4
Strutt, 166
Stubbs, 202
Suffolk, 86, 96, 97
sugar, 17, 30, 33, 41, 53, 122, 186
Supple, Dr, 12
Sutherland, L., 148, 149
Sweden, 35, 51, 53, 141, 153
Switzerland, 118
Sydenham, Lord, 151

tariffs, x, 27, 32, 42, 106, 107, 111, 113, 116, 152, 199
Tawney, R. H., ix, 70, 74, 76, 84, 87, 128, 141
taxation, x, 15, 18, 26, 27, 31, 42, 44, 95, 111, chap. 7, 141
technology, 22, 23, 33, 42, 91, 94, 96, 99, 103, 111, 116, 118, 132, 156, 162, 164, 165, 166, 167, 174, 175, 180, 184, 188, 191, 194, 198, 199
Temple, Sir William, 119, 121
Tennessee Valley Authority, the, 135
textiles, 24, 25, 30, 31, 32, 33, 41, 42, 45, 46, 50, 56, 64, 68, 80, 89, chap. 6, 116, 117, 118, 122, 142, 144, 145, 152, 156, 159, 160, 161, 162, 163, 164, 165, 166, 167, 168, 169, 171, 185, 186, 189, 193
Thirty Years War, the, 98
Thomson, Poulett, 151, 155
timber, 24, 25, 28, 50, 51, 52
Tiverton, 30

tobacco, 17, 24, 30, 33, 52, 53, 122, 144, 145, 189
Topsham, 4
Toynbee, Arnold, 114
trade, 2, 12, 13, 14, 17, 22, 23, 24, 25, 26, 27, 28, 29, 30, 31, 32, 34, 35, 37, 38, 39, 40, 41, 42, 44, 45, 46, 48, 49, 50, 51, 52, 53, 54, 56, 58, 59, 60, 61, 63, 64, 66, 68, 71, 77, 78, 81, 90, 94, 95, 98, 112, 116, 120, 121, 122, 123, 124, 126, 150, 153, 158, 169, 171, 178, 182, 186, 189, 195, 196
Trade, Board of, 15, 53, 77, 144, 151, 152
Trade, Commission, on, 12
tradesmen, 5, 64, 79, 142, 148, 155
trading corporation, 2, 13, 29, 65, 145
transport, 25, 29, 32, 36, 41, 42, 43, 53, 58, 122, 123, 124, 161, 162, 169, 170, 179, 182
Trevelyan, G. M., 5, 209
Trevor Roper, Professor, 11
Turkey, 15, 25, 54, 100, 106, 108, 113
Turnham Green, 4, 7

unions, 16, 136, 142, 175, 180
Unwin, George, 66, 69, 73, 86, 87, 141
Ure, Dr, 174
Utrecht, 32, 33, 44, 86, 100

Vaughan, 198
Venice, 99, 100, 121
vested interests, ix, 19, 141, 146, 148, 150
Victorian, x, 16, 88, 132, 134, 173, 176, chap. 11, 202, 204, 205
Viner, Professor, 63, 66, 70, 72
Vries, Dr de, 116, 117, 122, 124

Wadsworth, 165
wages, ix, 16, 26, 32, 42, 44, 74, 75, 77, 78, 109, 110, 113, 117, 118, 123, 125, 131, 171, 175, 179, 180, 185, 186, 187, 189, 190, 192, 193, 199
Walker, Samuel, 170
Walpole, 148, 155
war, 25, 29, 31, 35, 37, 46, 51, 58, 60, 81, 114, 121, 124
Warburton, 8, 9
Warrington, 192
Warwick, 4
Watt, James, 134, 159, 170, 171, 176
Webb, Beatrice, 197
Wedgwood, C. E., 2, 8
Wedgwood, Josiah, 149, 156, 159, 167, 173, 176
welfare, ix, 16, 17, 42, 43, 46, 55, 71, 74, 75, 76, 77, 78, 79, 81, 82, 83, 85, 86, 87, 88, 90, 91, 92, 115, 125, 126, 137, 152, 172, 173, 197
West Indies, the, 24, 25, 29, 35, 38
Westphalia, Peace of, 14
Whiteleys, 187
Whitbread, Samuel, 173, 174
Whitworth, 187
Wilkinson, John, 159, 169
Wilmot, Lord, 9
Wilson, Carus, Professor, 159
Wilson, John, 166
Wiltshire, 98, 99, 105, 106
Wine, 23, 24, 55
Winstanley, 81
Witt, De, 126
Woude, A. M. van der, 125
Wycherley, 92

Yarranton, 82
York, 8; Yorkshire, 3, 80, 85, 86, 97, 106, 111, 163
Young, Colonel, 5, 6, ,7, 9
Young, G. M., 187